AMERICAN FIGHTER AIRCRAFT OF WORLD WAR II

AMERICAN FIGHTER AIRCRAFT OF WORLD WAR II
1941–45

EDWARD WARD

First published in 2023

Reprinted in 2025

Copyright © 2023 Amber Books Ltd

All rights reserved. No part of this publication may be reproduced, stored in a retrieval system, or transmitted in any form or by any means, electronic, mechanical, photocopying, recording, or otherwise, without prior written permission of the copyright holder.

Published by Amber Books Ltd
United House
London N7 9DP
United Kingdom
www.amberbooks.co.uk
Facebook: amberbooks
Instagram: amberbooksltd
Twitter: @amberbooks
Pinterest: amberbooksltd

ISBN: 978-1-83886-326-5

Editor: Michael Spilling
Designer: Mark Batley
Picture research: Terry Forshaw

Printed in China

Contents

Introduction	6
Early-war Fighters	8
Late-war Fighters	34
Heavy Fighters	74
Naval Types	94
Jet Aircraft	118
INDEX	124
PICTURE CREDITS	128

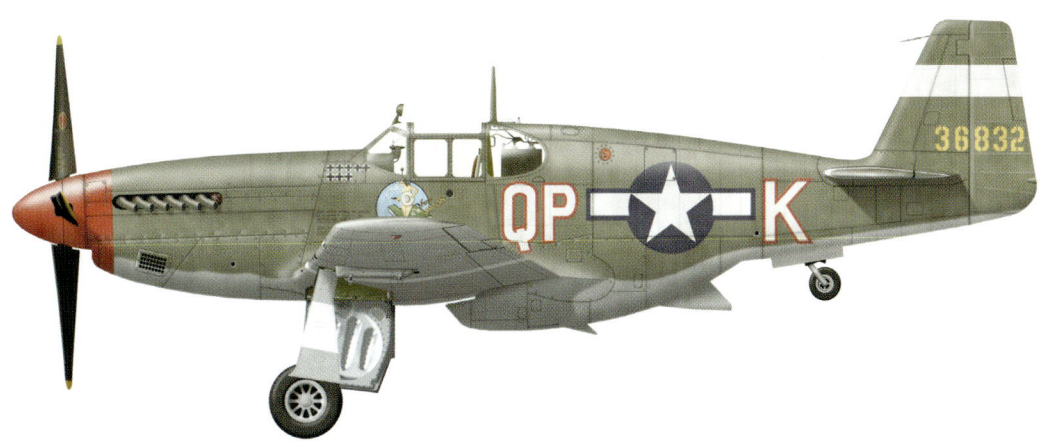

Introduction

At the outbreak of World War II, American fighter design was lagging behind the rest of the world. It is a measure of both the incredible lengths that US designers were willing to go to and the unrivalled industrial might of the United States that by 1945, less than four years after the US was drawn into the fighting, American fighters were demonstrably among the world's best and available in vast numbers. US aircraft equipped not just American units, but a large proportion of Allied air forces as well.

The development of fighter aircraft in the USA was pursued completely separately by the aviation branches of the Army and Navy, though both were subject to budgetary constraints following the end of World War I, which became stricter still as a result of the Great Depression. On land, these coupled with the fact that the Air Corps was subject to the whims of the Army's commanding officers, many of whom had little interest in, or were overtly hostile to, the novel realm of military aviation. Furthermore, by the 1930s the US Army Air Corps (USAAC) had fully adopted a doctrine based overwhelmingly on strategic bombing and the idea that 'the bomber will always get through', which further lessened the perceived usefulness of the fighter aircraft.

'Pursuit' aircraft, as they were referred to by the Army, were seen as primarily useful for tactical operations in support of ground forces and as such, high-altitude performance and long range were seen as largely irrelevant for these types. Just before the USA entered the war the first steps were taken to redress the balance, with such excellent aircraft as the P-47 and P-38 in development. However, the P-40 and P-39 that the United States Army Air Forces (as the US Army

Vought F4U-1 Corsairs from the US Navy's VF-12 (Fighter Squadron 12) on manoeuvres, March 1943.

INTRODUCTION

Republic P-47N-5 Thunderbolts in a three-ship formation (S/N 44-88576, 88589, 88577), 1945.

Air Corps were renamed in June 1941) entered the war with were not capable of matching enemy aircraft at the altitudes in which combat was routinely taking place (though both were excellent performers at lower levels), forcing the Army Air Force into the embarrassing situation of having to obtain the British Supermarine Spitfire in order to adequately perform the tasks required of it.

Naval fighters

By contrast, the Navy was in many ways far more willing to pursue new developments in aviation but was, like its equivalents overseas, highly suspicious that the new-fangled cantilever monoplane could successfully operate from an aircraft carrier. As a result, the F4F, which was virtually the sole US carrier fighter for the first two years of war, was a distinctly conservative design and while probably the best naval fighter available to the Allies until the Corsair appeared, it was painfully slow for a fighter type by 1941. The highly successful F4U Corsair and F6F Hellcat were already in development by the outbreak of war and once introduced, utterly dominated aerial combat at sea.

A similar situation pertained in the USAAF with the introduction of the three outstanding land-based US fighters of the war, the P-38 Lightning, P-47 Thunderbolt and iconic P-51 Mustang. The latter machine, boasting great range in its Merlin-powered form, was able to take the fight to the enemy and proved utterly dominant over its Axis foes. More than 15,000 had been built by the war's end, yet it had formed no part in USAAF planning in 1941, its development occurring instead due to happenstance and the enthusiasm of a few individuals in the face of USAAF indifference. By 1945, this trio of exceptional aircraft were themselves on the brink of being superseded by the first jet fighters, the war ending just as the first entered operational service – and the P-80 Shooting Star, arguably the best of the first generation of Allied jet fighters, formed the vanguard of the post-war USAAF, by now the most powerful air force in the world.

EARLY-WAR FIGHTERS

The fighter types with which the USAAF went to war were dominated by the P-39 Airacobra and P-40 Warhawk. The first was a highly radical machine and the other utterly conventional, yet both shared the same problems of lack of altitude performance – though both were effective at lower levels, proving manoeuvrable, easy to fly and highly reliable. This chapter also features a selection of other US-built types, most of which saw the majority of their active service in the air arms of other nations.

- Curtiss Hawk III
- Curtiss-Wright CW-21 Demon
- Boeing P-26 Peashooter
- Seversky P-35
- Curtiss P-36 & Hawk Model 75
- Republic P-43 Lancer
- Bell P-39 Airacobra
- Curtiss P-40 Warhawk

The P-39Q represented the final attempt to mould the Airacobra into a world-class fighter. This is a P-39Q-20, most of which were built for the Soviet Union and delivered without guns in the underwing pods, although this example was destined for the USAAF and retained its armament.

EARLY-WAR FIGHTERS

Curtiss Hawk III

One of the oldest American designs to see combat during World War II, the Hawk III had been a formidable fighter in its day, but was obsolete by the outbreak of war.

The culmination of a line of Curtiss biplanes that had dominated the fighter scene throughout the interwar period, the Hawk III was destined never to see operational service with its nation of origin, instead being used intensively by the Chinese Air Force against the Japanese over several years.

The Hawk III derived from the US Navy's F-11C Goshawk, which saw limited service in the US (although 52 were sold to the Chinese as the Hawk II) and in the Second Sino-Japanese War. Twenty-seven examples of the developed BF2C-1 Goshawk saw brief service with the US Navy, the type being the last Curtiss fighter accepted into the USN. However, the export version, the Hawk III, was destined for a long and active career overseas.

Reliable in combat

China received 102 examples of the Hawk III, and these were in action during 1937 over Nanking. Despite being somewhat inferior to the Mitsubishi A5M, the Hawk III scored several kills against the Japanese monoplane. In Chinese service, the Hawk's reliability and immensely strong structure, a legacy of its carrier origins, rendered the aircraft popular with its crews.

Although superseded as an air superiority asset by the Soviet Polikarpov I-15 and I-16, the Hawk III achieved its last known air-to-air kill on 26 May 1940. When a Japanese bomber was destroyed with two I-15s, the Hawk III continued as a ground-attack aircraft before being relegated to the training role, a task it performed in China until at least 1944.

As well as China, the Hawk III was supplied to Thailand, which obtained a production licence and built 50 examples. These aircraft were active in the Franco-Thai war and the Japanese invasion before being relegated to the training role, persisting in Thai service until at least 1949. A Thai Hawk III was shot down by an RAF Bristol Beaufighter in April 1944. This represented the last known combat involving the Curtiss biplane, with the pilot escaping by parachute.

Curtiss Hawk III
Weight (maximum take-off): 2065kg (4552lb)
Dimensions: Length: 7.42m (24ft 4in), Wingspan: 9.6m (31ft 6in), Height: 3.04m (10ft)
Powerplant: One 570kw (770hp) Wright R-1820-04 Cyclone 9-cylinder air-cooled radial piston engine
Maximum Speed: 410km/h (255mph)
Range: 1167km (725 miles)
Ceiling: 8200m (26,900ft)
Crew: 1
Armament: One 7.62mm (0.3in) M1919 Browning machine gun fixed forward firing in right wing, one 12.7mm (0.5in) M2 Browning machine gun fixed forward firing in left wing; one 215kg (475lb) bomb on under-fuselage shackle or one 53kg (117lb) bombs under each wing

Curtiss Hawk III

Curtiss Hawk III of the Chinese Nationalist Air Force, Autumn 1937, at the outbreak of the Second Sino-Japanese War. It is from the 24th Pursuit Squadron, assigned to the 5th Pursuit Group, based at Yangchow (Yangzhou).

Curtiss-Wright CW-21 Demon

As a creditable attempt to produce a lightweight fighter with an emphasis on climb performance, the CW-21s of the Royal Netherlands East Indies Air Force saw brief but intense combat against the invading Japanese.

Curtiss-Wright CW-21B Demon
This aircraft is from the Military Aviation of the Royal Netherlands East Indies Army (ML-KNIL) Air Group IV, No. 2 Squadron (2-VLG IV), Andir, Java, Spring 1941.

Curtiss-Wright CW-21B Demon
Weight (maximum take-off): 2041kg (4500lb)
Dimensions: Length: 8.03m (26ft 4in), Wingspan: 10.66m (35ft), Height: 2.6m (8ft 8in)
Powerplant: One 630kW (850hp) Wright R-1820-G5 Cyclone piston engine
Maximum Speed: 536km/h (333mph)
Range: 1010km (628 miles)
Ceiling: 10,455m (34,300ft)
Crew: 1
Armament: Four 7.62mm (0.3in) M1919 Browning machine guns fixed forward firing in forward fuselage

In the 1930s, Curtiss-Wright was an industrial giant, and the company's St Louis Division produced several designs independently of the main company, most famously the C-46 Commando transport aircraft. In 1935, Director of Engineering George Page initiated the design of an advanced high-speed cabin monoplane designated the CW-19L. No market existed for such an aircraft, so the aircraft was re-engined and marketed as a trainer: the A-19R. This featured somewhat unpleasant handling characteristics but possessed an outstanding rate of climb, leading Page to scheme an interceptor variant of the aircraft.

The CW-21 was the result, boasting a rocket-like 1463m (4800ft) per minute climb rate. To put that in context, the later Curtiss P-40C could manage only 820m (2690ft) per minute. This remarkable vertical performance was possible only because the aircraft was extremely lightly built, featuring no armour protection nor self-sealing fuel tanks. As such, it was not intended to engage enemy fighters, rather to intercept and destroy bombers – the reasoning being that if attacked by enemy single-seaters, it could simply climb away to safety.

Flying Tigers

China was interested in the CW-21, and while demonstrating the prototype in China, company test pilot Robert Fausel used it to successfully intercept a Japanese Fiat BR.20 bomber in April 1939. Three CW-21s were purchased for use by the AVG (the 'Flying Tigers').

However, all three crashed during a delivery flight due to contaminated fuel. Meanwhile, Curtiss-Wright had improved the basic design. An intended Allison-powered CW-21A was not built, but the CW-21B featured inward-retracting undercarriage. This replaced the cumbersome bathtub fairings of the CW-21. Twenty-four examples were obtained by the Netherlands East Indies and were embroiled in action during the Japanese invasion of Java in February 1942. Dutch pilots claimed four Japanese aircraft destroyed, but all bar one of the CW-21Bs were destroyed in a month of fierce fighting, the lightly built aircraft proving horrifically vulnerable to the A6M Zero and its 20mm (0.79in) cannon armament.

EARLY-WAR FIGHTERS

Boeing P-26 Peashooter

A groundbreaking design, the P-26 was both the first all-metal fighter aircraft produced in America and the first monoplane fighter for the USAAC. By 1941, however, it was obsolete.

First flown in 1932, the P-26, with its art-deco spats and flamboyant colour schemes, epitomized the Army Air Corps in the last years of peace. Yet this somewhat rotund little fighter, despite apparently hailing from an earlier age, did see brief combat service in World War II. Initial deliveries to the Army began in December 1933, and the P-26 was unusual among military aircraft in that it was cheaper than the aircraft it replaced: Boeing's own P-12 biplane fighter.

Despite representing a clear advance over the biplane fighters it replaced, the P-26 marked a transitional moment in fighter design, with its fixed undercarriage, open cockpit, and wire-braced wings. By the end of 1936, when the frontline US inventory peaked, with six squadrons operating the type, the Boeing fighter was no longer in the vanguard of international design, and US usage began to wind down. The following year, the type saw action for the first time in Chinese hands over Nanking, with clashes between the P-26 and Japanese Mitsubishi A5Ms representing the first instance of all-metal monoplane fighters meeting in combat.

Waning usage

By December 1941, the only P-26s in operational US service on the American continent were nine examples based at Albrook Field in the Panama Canal zone. However, 31 P-26s had been sold to the Philippines Army Air Corps in the late 1930s, and in May 1941, this force was absorbed into the USAAF.

Throughout December 1941, the P-26s fought an overwhelming force of more-modern Japanese aircraft and were credited with shooting down one Mitsubishi G3M bomber and three A6M Zero fighters before the surviving Boeings were burned to prevent their capture. Remarkably, examples of the P-26 in Guatemalan service would see action as late as 1954 during that nation's coup d'état.

Boeing P-26 Peashooter

This Peashooter is in the blue/yellow colour scheme that was standard prior to the introduction of the familiar olive drab/neutral grey wartime camouflage. It is aircraft 33-125 from the 34th Pursuit Squadron of 1st Pursuit Group, based at Selfridge Field, Michigan, in 1936.

Boeing P-26A

Weight (maximum take-off): 1524kg (3360lb)
Dimensions: Length: 7.19m (23ft 7in), Wingspan: 8.5m (28ft), Height: 3m (10ft)
Powerplant: One 450kW (600hp) Pratt & Whitney R-1340-27 Wasp 9-cylinder air-cooled radial piston engine
Maximum Speed: 377km/h (234mph)
Range: 580km (360 miles)
Ceiling: 8400m (27,400ft)
Crew: 1
Armament: Two 7.62mm (0.3in) M1919 Browning machine guns or one 7.62mm (0.3in) M1919 machine gun and one 12.7mm (0.5in) M2 Browning machine gun

Seversky P-35

The P-35 – the US Army's first cantilever monoplane with retractable undercarriage – was quickly surpassed as a fighter design. Those that saw combat proved too slow and unwieldy to survive against newer Japanese fighters.

Designed by Georgian émigré Alexander Kartveli and derived, rather unexpectedly, from a three-seat amphibian, the P-35 flew for the first time in August 1935. Following a fly-off of various fighter prototypes, the P-35 was judged the winner despite suffering from engine problems, and a production contract was issued. The first of 77 P-35s were delivered to the USAAC in July 1937, and although none of this initial production run of fighters would remain in frontline service by the time the US entered the war, they provided invaluable experience to Kartveli and his design team as well as to service personnel experiencing the switch to large, high performance all-metal monoplane fighters in the years leading up to Pearl Harbor.

Swedish delivery

Meanwhile, the P-35 had caught the eye of Sweden, who contracted with Seversky Aircraft, in the same month that the company name was changed to Republic Aviation, for the supply of 120 examples of an export version designated the EP-1. In February 1941, after the delivery of 60 EP-1s, the US government requisitioned the balance of 60 aircraft and supplied them to the Air Corps as the P-35A. Forty-eight of these aircraft were despatched to the Philippines to bolster air defences, arriving still bearing their Swedish markings. Thrown into action in December 1941 to oppose the Japanese invasion, the P-35A's most spectacular success came when 1st Lt. Samuel H. Marrett managed to destroy the minesweeper W-10 with repeated strafing attacks. Some sources claim the P-35As managed to down one Japanese aircraft, while others say it did not down any aircraft. Either way, the P-35A had proved a dismal failure in air combat, not only proving too slow and lacking the manoeuvrability necessary to engage Japanese fighters, but also proving highly vulnerable, as it was not fitted with armour or self-sealing fuel tanks. The sole surviving Philippines-based P-35A made the type's last combat mission on 3 May 1942, strafing Japanese positions. The P-35As retained in the US were subsequently transferred to Ecuador.

Seversky P-35A

Weight (maximum take-off): 3050kg (6724lb)
Dimensions: Length: 8.18m (26ft 10in), Wingspan: 10.97m (36ft), Height: 2.97m (9ft 9in)
Powerplant: One 780kW (1050hp) Pratt & Whitney R-1830-45 Twin Wasp air-cooled radial piston engine
Maximum Speed: 470km/h (292mph)
Range: 1530km (950 miles)
Ceiling: 9600m (31,500ft)
Crew: 1
Armament: Two 7.62mm (0.3in) M1919 Browning machine guns fixed forward firing in upper cowling and two 12.7mm (0.50in) Browning M2/AN machine guns fixed forward firing in wings; up to 160kg (350lb) of bombs

Seversky P-35A

A P-35A flown by L. Boyd Wagner, CO of 17th Pursuit Squadron, stationed at Nichols Field, Luzon, Philippines, 1941.

EARLY-WAR FIGHTERS

Curtiss P-36 & Hawk Model 75

Although it scored the first USAAF air-to-air victories of World War II, the P-36 would see very little frontline use in US service, but the aircraft proved hugely successful in French and Finnish hands, fighting both for and against the Allies.

The first US fighter to favourably compare to the latest European designs in the late 1930s, the Curtiss Model 75 was designed to compete for an Army Air Corps specification issued in 1934 for an all-metal low-wing monoplane design with a top speed of at least 482km/h (300mph). The fact that Boeing had already supplied the USAAC's first 'modern' monoplane fighter, the P-26, had concerned Curtiss company management, who feared that Curtiss might fail to retain its position as the pre-eminent US fighter manufacturer.

To that end, the company hired designer Donovan R. Berlin, who had gained extensive experience with stressed-skin monoplane construction while working at Northrop. Berlin joined Curtiss in October 1934, just seven months before the Army's deadline for its new fighter competition. The Curtiss monoplane that Berlin designed, inexplicably designated 'Design 75' (Curtiss had never previously used design numbers), was typical of contemporary international fighter design.

Fighter competition
Flown for the first time in April 1935, the Model 75 was powered by a new Wright XR-1670 14-cylinder radial, this choice of engine no doubt being influenced by the fact that Wright was part of the same parent company as Curtiss. Unfortunately, the XR-1670, an unhappy outgrowth of Wright's highly successful Whirlwind, proved unable to generate the promised 662kW (900hp). As it turned out, none of the entries for the Army's fighter competition were ready in time, and the Air Corps postponed the deadline to August 1935, allowing Curtiss to substitute a Pratt & Whitney R-1535 Twin Wasp Junior. This, too, gave trouble, but the contest was once again delayed, allowing the Model 75 to receive its third engine within a year, this time a 699kW (950hp) Wright XR-1820-39 Cyclone (redesignated, in this form, as the Model 75B).

Curtiss P-36A Hawk

This example (38-92) is from the 47th Pursuit Squadron, 15th Pursuit Group, based at Haleiwa Field, Hawaii, in December 1941, from where Lt Harry Winston Brown flew against the Pearl Harbor attackers. Wearing 'pajama tops, tuxedo trousers, house-shoes, flight helmet and goggles', he claimed two victories, for which he was awarded the Silver Star. He ended the war with seven kills.

EARLY-WAR FIGHTERS

Curtiss P-36A Hawk
This P-36A was part of the 79th Pursuit Squadron, 20th Pursuit Group, based at Moffett Field, California, November 1939. The tail designator indicates it is the 21st aircraft.

The fighter contest was finally held in April 1936, and although the Curtiss was still dogged by engine problems, so was its principal competitor, the Seversky SEV-1XP. The Seversky aircraft was judged the winner and received a production contract as the P-35, but the Model 75B was deemed to have sufficient potential for the Air Corps to order a development contract for three test examples designated Y1P-36 to be powered by the Pratt & Whitney R-1830 Twin Wasp.

Fitted with a decent engine at last, the Y1P-36s proved around 16km/h (10mph) faster than the prototype, and during evaluations at Wright Field, test pilots were highly enthusiastic about the excellent flying characteristics and handling of the Curtiss fighter. Based on this evaluation, the USAAC placed a contract for 210 aircraft in July 1937, the biggest single order the Air Corps had placed since World War I. Deliveries of the P-36A (little different to the Y1P-36) began in April 1938, with the 20th Pursuit Group being the first to receive the aircraft. Most P-36As were completed with the higher compression R-1830-17 engine, resulting in a maximum speed increase to 504km/h (313mph), though the P-36C, which introduced a more powerful armament, was slightly slower. The P-36B was a one-off conversion with an R-1830-25 engine, which did not enter production.

Hawk 75

While the P-36 was entering service with the USAAC, Curtiss was engaged in an active marketing campaign for a simplified export version with fixed landing gear and a Wright Cyclone engine. It was dubbed the Hawk 75 to capitalize on the excellent reputation of Curtiss's earlier Hawk biplane fighters. Thirty fixed-gear Hawk 75-Ms were acquired by China as well as a production licence for the Hawk 75A-5, broadly equivalent to the P-36A with retractable undercarriage, though only a few examples were actually completed.

In addition, the Hawk 75-H demonstrator was personally purchased by Madame Chiang Kai-Shek as a gift for General Claire Chennault, commander of the American Volunteer Group. Sadly, the Hawk 75-Ms achieved little success, due largely to poor serviceability and inadequate pilot training. Argentina acquired 29 examples of the fixed-gear Hawk 75-O and built a further 20 under licence, retaining them in service until 1953. Thailand operated 12 examples of the Hawk 75-N armed with a 23mm (0.9in) Danish Madsen cannon in a fairing under each wing. Thai Hawks saw action during the brief Franco-Thai war of 1941, with two Hawk pilots each claiming a Morane-Saulnier MS 406 shot down, although these claims were refuted by the French.

As soon as Curtiss was permitted to do so by the US Government, it marketed an export version of the standard P-36, and France was to become the first export customer for the

---

Curtiss P-36A
Weight (maximum take-off): 2726kg (6010lb)
Dimensions: Length: 8.69m (28ft 6in), Wingspan: 11.38m (37ft 4in), Height: 2.57m (8ft 5in)
Powerplant: one kW (hp) Pratt & Whitney R-1830-17 Twin Wasp 14-cylinder air-cooled radial piston engine
Maximum Speed: 504km/h (313mph)
Range: 1006km (625 miles)
Ceiling: 10,000m (32,800ft)
Crew: 1
Armament: One 7.62mm (0.3in) M1919 machine gun and one 12.7mm (0.5in) M2 Browning machine gun fixed firing forward in upper front fuselage decking; some later aircraft fitted with an optional hardpoint under each wing capable of carrying up to 69kg (152lb) each

---

15

EARLY-WAR FIGHTERS

French Air Force Curtiss 75A Hawk fighters patrol French airspace, 1939–40.

Hawk 75A. Despite the fact that the unit price of each Curtiss fighter was around double that of the Morane-Saulnier MS 406 or Bloch MB-150 of generally similar performance, French interest was maintained by the glowing report of the highly respected French test pilot Marcel Detroyat, who flew a Y1P-36 in March 1938, coupled with ongoing delays to domestic fighter designs.

Ultimately, France would receive 454 H75As (the Hawk name was not used by the Armee de l'Air) in four production batches, the H75A-1, A-2 and A-3 all utilizing various models of the R-1830 Twin Wasp. The final version, the H75-C1 (designated Hawk 75A-4 by Curtiss), was fitted with the R-1820-G205A Cyclone, an engine that would be plagued with oil circulation problems in both Armee de l'Air and RAF service.

The first French unit to equip with the Curtiss fighter was Groupe de Chasse II/5 La Fayette, which began to receive its aircraft in March 1939. On 20 September 1939, an H75A-1 piloted by Sergeant André-Armand Legrand shot down a Messerschmitt Bf 109E, this being the first Allied air-to-air victory in the West.

The Curtiss H75 proved to be the most successful fighter flown by France until the capitulation of June 1940, shooting down 311 aircraft, making up a third of all French victories, despite forming considerably less than a third of the fighter force. Seven French pilots would achieve 'ace' status with the Curtiss fighter.

From France to Britain

French aircraft on order when France fell were diverted to the RAF, which named the aircraft the 'Mohawk'. British tests revealed that the Mohawk was 'more manoeuvrable at high speed than the Hurricane or Spitfire', eliciting considerable interest in official circles, but the comparatively modest performance of the Mohawk saw its operational use with the RAF limited to India and Burma, where the Curtiss fighter would see much use, flying combat sorties until the end of 1944.

Norway had also ordered the fighter, but only 12 had been delivered by the time Norway fell to the invading Germans in May 1940, most still in their crates.

As well as continuing in Vichy service, with some H75s used in combat against the Operation Torch landings in North Africa, 44 captured French and Norwegian H75As were refurbished by the Germans and sold to Finland, proving highly effective against Soviet aircraft. Nicknamed Sussu ('Sweetheart'), the Finnish Hawks were credited with 190 victories between 1941 and 1944, with the most successful P-36/Hawk 75 pilot of any nation, Altto Kalevi Tervo, personally

EARLY-WAR FIGHTERS

shooting 15 Soviet aircraft down. The Finnish Curtiss aircraft remained in frontline service until 1948.

Pearl Harbor and Dutch East Indies
Of all the nations that flew the various derivatives of the Model 75 in combat, its country of origin made the least use of the Curtiss fighter. Nonetheless, its victories in US service were of undeniable historic significance, as the P-36 was the first US aircraft to attain an air-to-air victory during World War II. The P-36s of the 15th Pursuit Group at Wheeler Field, Hawaii, were in the process of being replaced by the P-40 when the Japanese attacked Pearl Harbor. Despite many of the aircraft being destroyed on the ground, Lts. Gordon Sterling and Phillip Rasmussen managed to destroy one Nakajima B5N each, with a further three P-36 victory claims being made later in the day. The Pearl Harbor action would prove to be the only instance in which the US would fly the P-36 in combat.

However, the P-36 did see further action in the Pacific theatre with the air force of the Netherlands East Indies (now Indonesia), who had ordered 20 Cyclone-powered Hawk 75A-7s in October 1939. These saw short but vicious action during the Japanese invasion, the last two Dutch Hawks being shot down on 5 February 1942.

Curtiss Model 75A-8

Weight (maximum take-off): 2667kg (5880lb)
Dimensions: Length: 8.6m (28ft 6in), Wingspan: 8.5m (28ft), Height: 3m (10ft)
Powerplant: One 895kW (1200hp) Wright R-1820-G205A cyclone radial piston engine
Maximum Speed: 518km/h (322mph)
Range: 580km (360 miles)
Ceiling: 9860m (32,300ft)
Crew: 1
Armament: Four wing-mounted 7.62mm (0.3in) M1919 Browning machine guns and two fuselage-mounted 12.7mm (0.5in) M2 Browning machine guns

---

Curtiss Hawk Model 75
A P-36C in olive drab and neutral grey, early 1942. The tail designator is restricted to the aircraft number (22) and last four digits of the serial number (38-191).

Curtiss Hawk Model 75
This Hawk 75A-5 flew with Chinese Nationalist forces from Kunming in 1942.

EARLY-WAR FIGHTERS

Republic P-43 Lancer

As a stepping stone after the outdated P-35 and the superlative P-47, the P-43 introduced the rear fuselage-mounted turbo-supercharger and boasted a prodigious range, but was lacking in manoeuvrability and proved vulnerable in combat.

During 1940, two improved P-35 developments, the AP-4 and XP-41, were submitted for evaluation in a USAAC fighter contest. Both featured an aerodynamically improved fuselage, inward-retracting undercarriage and the same semi-elliptical wing as the P-35. However, the AP-4 also featured a turbo-supercharger in the rear fuselage. The Curtiss P-40 ultimately won the contest, but the AP-4 demonstrated excellent high-altitude performance, and the Air Corps opted to order a test batch of 13 aircraft to be designated the YP-43. These aircraft were delivered by April 1941, by which time reports coming from the fighting in Europe suggested that the YP-43 was already outdated. By this time, Alexander Kartveli had schemed an improved AP-4 derivative with the 1400hp R-1280 engine, but this too was superseded even before prototype construction had begun by the XP-47 Thunderbolt, which promised still better performance. The Air Corps, meanwhile, ordered more P-43s to keep Republic's factory busy, increase production capacity and safeguard its workforce until P-47 production could begin.

Republic P-43A

This Republic P-43A Lancer served with the 55th Pursuit Group, based at Hamilton Field in early 1941. It carries the double fuselage command stripes of a squadron commander and the corresponding coloured cowling.

Wet wing

The P-43 saw only limited use in US hands. Difficulties experienced with the turbo-superchargers curtailed their use as fighters, and all USAAC production P-43 and P-43As were converted to reconnaissance aircraft with cameras in the rear fuselage. Further production occurred primarily for lend-lease supply to China. In Chinese service, the P-43 proved unpopular with its 'wet wing', where the wing structure was sealed to form one large fuel tank. Although this conferred great range, it also leaked constantly, particularly around rivets and joints. This propensity to leak caused in-flight fires and led to the loss of several aircraft and pilots. The unprotected wet wing was also highly vulnerable to combat damage, and Japanese pilots noted the P-43's propensity to catch fire when hit.

Republic P-43A

Weight (maximum take-off): 3846kg (8479lb)
Dimensions: Length: 8.69m (28ft 6in), Wingspan: 10.97m (36ft), Height: 4.27m (14ft)
Powerplant: One 890kW (1200hp) Pratt & Whitney R-1830-49 Twin Wasp air-cooled 14-cylinder radial piston engine
Maximum Speed: 573km/h (356mph)
Range: 1050km (650 miles)
Ceiling: 11,000m (36,000ft)
Crew: 1
Armament: Two 12.7mm (0.5in) M2 Browning machine guns fixed forward firing in upper nose cowling and two 12.7mm (0.5in) M2 Browning machine guns in wings

Despite this, due to the shortage of modern aircraft in China, the Republic fighter was utilized by both Chinese and American forces until it was removed from frontline service in December 1943. The excellent range and good high-altitude performance had seen the P-43 regularly function as a reconnaissance aircraft in Chinese service, and it would perform this role with considerable success in both US and Australian hands (eight P-43s being supplied to the RAAF in August 1942) until its replacement by the faster and longer-ranged F-5 Lightning.

Bell P-39 Airacobra

The P-39 demonstrated Bell's willingness to break with convention but proved largely unpopular in American service. By contrast, the aircraft delivered outstanding service in the Soviet Union, where it was rated more highly than any other lend-lease fighter.

The aircraft was conceived in 1936 in response to the Air Corps' Circular Proposal X-609 for a heavily armed single-engine, high-altitude 'interceptor' powered by a turbo-supercharged V-12 engine. The P-39's unusual design was dictated by its primary armament, the Oldsmobile 37mm (1.46in) cannon. In order for the weapon to be located in the nose and on the aircraft's centreline – thereby maximising accuracy and ease of access – the idea was formulated to mount the engine amidships and utilize an extension shaft to drive the propeller, with the nose-mounted cannon firing straight through the centre of the propeller spinner. With the concentration of weight of the mid-mounted engine on the aircraft's centre of gravity, the new fighter was expected to possess excellent manoeuvrability, while the removal of the engine from the nose freed up room for further gun armament and a nosewheel undercarriage (another unconventional feature for a fighter in this era). The Bell proposal won the approval of the Army Air Corps, and a single prototype designated the XP-39 was ordered, flying for the first time on 6 April 1938.

Short-lived prototype

Fitted with an Allison V-1710-17 engine rated at 846kW (1150hp) with a General Electric B-5 turbo supercharger mounted on the port side of the fuselage, the lightweight, unarmed prototype demonstrated excellent performance, achieving a top speed of 628km/h (390mph) at 6100m (20,000ft), an altitude it could reach in five minutes – an outstanding rate of climb for the late 1930s. Unfortunately for the P-39's future career, the complexity and dubious reliability of the turbo supercharger installation, along with the Army Air Corps' fixation on low-level close support operations, saw the requirement for turbo supercharging dropped, and the P-39's high altitude performance was badly compromised. The prototype was modified to initial production standard with the turbo supercharger removed, decreased wingspan and lengthened fuselage. In this form, as the XP-39B, the aircraft now took two and half minutes longer to reach 6000m (20,000ft), and maximum speed dropped to 603km/h (375mph). However, manoeuvrability at low level was improved, and the Air Corps were satisfied with the changes. The first batch of 13 YP-39 service test aircraft was duly completed without turbo superchargers. The addition of some armour protection further increased

---

Bell P-39D Airacobra
Weight (maximum take-off): 4018kg (8858lb)
Dimensions: Length: 9.21m (30ft 2in), Wingspan: 10.37m (34ft), Height: 3.6m (11ft 10in)
Powerplant: One 858kW (1150hp) Allison V-1710-35 V-12 liquid-cooled piston engine
Maximum Speed: 579km/h (360mph)
Range (with drop tank): 1770km (1100 miles)
Ceiling: 9784m (32,100ft)
Crew: 1
Armament: One 37mm (1.46in) M4 Cannon fixed firing through propeller spinner; two 12.7mm (0.5in) Colt-Browning M2 machine guns fixed forward firing in fuselage nose; two 7.62mm (0.3in) Browning M1919 machine guns fixed forward firing in wings; up to 227kg (500lb) bomb under fuselage

---

Bell P-39D Airacobra
A P-39D with the 39th Pursuit Squadron, 31st Pursuit Group, during the Louisiana Maneuvers, September 1941.

EARLY-WAR FIGHTERS

weight and eroded performance, but the aircraft were deemed satisfactory, and further production was authorised as the P-39C. Only 20 examples of this variant were produced before its substitution with the P-39D, which had four wing guns instead of two and the provision to carry a 227kg (500lb) bomb or 289L (75 US gal) drop tank. This was the first P-39 to be ordered in quantity, and an eventual total of 923 would be delivered.

RAF Airacobra I

Before any of the P-39Ds were received by the USAAF, however, Bell had begun to supply the RAF with the Airacobra I, a model similar to the P-39D but equipped with a Hispano 20mm (0.79in) cannon in place of the Oldsmobile 37mm (1.46in) weapon. Unfortunately for the British, Bell had been somewhat disingenuous concerning the aircraft's performance, stating that the aircraft was capable of 644km/h (400mph) and operating at 11,000m (36,000ft), figures that had been achieved by a specially prepared prototype that weighed a tonne less than production Airacobras. Delivered to 601 Squadron in September 1941, the Airacobras proved pleasant to fly, but their rate of climb and ceiling were inferior to both the Hurricane and Spitfire, armament accessibility was poor and firing the guns led to a potentially lethal concentration of carbon monoxide to accrue inside the cockpit and caused the compass to stop working. Four missions were flown over French ports, during which invasion barges were strafed, but the modifications required to bring the Airacobra to an acceptable state, coupled with a spate of unexplained crashes, led to the withdrawal of the Airacobra from RAF service by December. The balance of the RAF order was then split between the Soviet Union and, following Pearl Harbor, the USAAF, where the aircraft was designated the P-400.

Following America's entry into the war, 100 P-400s and 90 P-39Ds were despatched to Australia to reinforce Army Air Force units already operating in the Pacific area. In action against the Japanese, the Bell fighter proved disappointing, the 37mm (1.46in) cannon gave trouble and the poor rate of climb meant Japanese raids were often unable to be intercepted. On the other hand, some pilots achieved considerable success with the P-39, and, when it was working, the 37mm (1.46in) cannon could prove devastating – on more than one occasion A6M Zeros disintegrated completely when hit head-on by fire from it. The situation in the Pacific improved once the P-38 Lightning arrived in the theatre with its superior high-altitude performance, releasing the Airacobras to operate at low level, where their performance and handling were at their best.

Airacobra Mk IA

Airacobra Mk 1A of 601 (City of London) Squadron at Duxford during the short RAF service of the type, between October and December 1941. It belongs to Squadron Leader Edward John Gracie DFC, who died in February 1944, piloting a Mosquito night-fighter as a wing commander.

Airacobra Mk IA

Weight (maximum take-off): 4014kg (8850lb)
Dimensions: Length 9.19m (30ft 2in), Wingspan 10.36m (34ft), Height 3.61m (11ft 10in)
Powerplant: One 858kW (1150hp) Allison V-1710-E4 V-12 liquid-cooled piston engine
Maximum Speed: 571km/h (355mph)
Range: 580km (360 miles)
Ceiling: 7315m (24,000ft)
Crew: 1
Armament: One 20mm (0.79in) Hispano cannon firing through propeller hub, two 12.7mm (0.5in) Browning machine guns in nose, four 7.7mm (0.303in) Browning machine guns in wings

---

Eastern Front service

US P-39s also saw action in the close support role during Operation Torch and its aftermath in North Africa, subsequently escorting shipping in the Mediterranean and supporting the Allied invasion of Sicily and mainland Italy. P-39 units in this theatre saw considerable action until the last were replaced by the P-47 in 1944.

By this time, the primary recipient of the P-39 was the Soviet Union, where the Bell aircraft would see most of its service and prove almost perfectly suited to the conditions prevailing on the Eastern Front. The first Airacobras to arrive in December 1941 were 212 aircraft intended for the RAF, with the 20mm (0.79in) centreline cannon, two 12.7mm (0.5in) machine guns on the nose and a further four 7.7mm (0.303in) machine guns in the wings. Making its Soviet combat debut in May 1942, the Airacobra was immediately successful, one unit claiming 64 aircraft shot down, of which 45 were fighters, for the loss of eight Airacobras in just two months of operations. By June 1942, new P-39Ds were beginning to be delivered directly from the US via Iran, and ultimately almost half of all P-39 production would arrive in the USSR.

Bell P-39N Airacobra

Weight (maximum take-off): 3995kg (8807lb)
Dimensions: Length: 9.21m (30ft 2in), Wingspan: 10.37m (34ft), Height: 3.6m (11ft 10in)
Powerplant: One 895kW (1200hp) Allison V-1710-85 V-12 liquid-cooled piston engine
Maximum Speed: 605km/h (376mph)
Range: 1570km (976 miles)
Ceiling: 11,665m (38,271ft)
Crew: 1
Armament: One 37mm (1.46in) M4 Cannon fixed firing through propeller spinner; two 12.7mm (0.5in) Colt-Browning M2 machine guns fixed forward firing in fuselage nose; two 7.62mm (0.3in) Browning M1919 machine guns fixed forward firing in wings; up to 227kg (500lb) bomb under fuselage

Following the P-39D, the P-39E was intended to have a 1600kW (2100hp) Continental I-1430-1 engine. However, this was never fitted, and the three P-39Es built were retained on experimental work. The P-39F was identical to the D model, except that it was fitted with a different propeller, and the P-39G, L, M, and N differed little except in the model of V-1710 engine fitted. The final and most numerous model was the P-39Q, of which 4905 were built, almost all of which were supplied to the Soviet Union. This featured two 12.7mm (0.5in) Brownings in pods under the wings, though these were usually discarded in service to improve rate of roll.

Assigned to units covering ground forces from enemy air attack, the poor altitude performance of the Airacobra was irrelevant. It was well armed, manoeuvrable, handled well, was fast at low altitude, and Soviet pilots rated it equal, or superior, to contemporary models of Bf 109 and Fw 190. The P-39 was also sturdy, its tricycle landing gear was well-suited to rough fields, and in contrast to other Soviet fighters, the radio was reliable. Perhaps most importantly for the average VVS pilot, the Airacobra was easy to fly, and it was the combination of pleasant flying characteristics and combat effectiveness that led to its diminutive nickname of *Kobrushka* ('little Cobra'). In the hands of a good pilot, the Airacobra was highly effective: Grigory Rechkalov shot down 48 of his 54 confirmed 'kills' in the P-39, the most scored by any pilot flying a US-built aircraft during the war. The final Soviet aerial victory against a German aircraft occurred on 9 May 1945, when a P-39 shot down an Fw 189 over Prague.

France and Italy also utilized the P-39 in combat. A total of 165 P-39N and P-39Qs were supplied to the Free French Air Force in North Africa from May 1943, eventually equipping six *groupes de chasses* engaged in supporting the Allied push northwards through Italy. One-hundred-and-forty-nine P-39N and Qs were operated by the Italian Co-Belligerent Air Force following the armistice of 8 September 1943. Operations by the Italian P-39s in the close support and ground attack role began during September 1944 over the Albanian front, and both French and Italian units flew the P-39 until the end of the conflict.

P-39N Airacobra

The RAF's hasty rejection of the Airacobra is in stark contrast to the Soviet Air Force's effective use of it, having received not only the unwanted RAF aircraft but many more under the Lend-Lease programme. Featured is a P-39N of the 100th Guards Fighter Aviation Regiment on the Ukrainian Front in Spring 1944. Its pilot was Petr Guchek, who gained at least 20 kills.

EARLY-WAR FIGHTERS

Curtiss P-40 Warhawk

The most important American fighter of the early war years, the Curtiss P-40 did not possess outstanding performance but was agile, tough and dependable. Built in large numbers, it served with distinction in the air forces of many nations.

While Don Berlin's Hawk 75 was proving a great success both domestically and on the export market, Curtiss-Wright were quick to look at ways in which the design could be further improved to maintain the company's position at the forefront of fighter development. Concentrating on an aircraft that married the proven airframe of the Hawk 75 with a V-12 liquid-cooled engine, Curtiss schemed two parallel developments: the Model 75-I, which utilized an Allison V-1720 engine with turbo supercharger intended to deliver good altitude performance, and the Model 75-P, which featured a V-1710 engine with a conventional gear-driven supercharger. The former aircraft also featured a cockpit moved towards the tail, resulting in an extremely long nose and almost non-existent forward view when on the ground. Despite this impediment, the Army were sufficiently interested to order 13 service test examples of this aircraft as the YP-37. But the poor view, suspect reliability of the turbo-supercharger and general lack of interest within the USAAC for high-altitude fighter operations saw attention shift to the less radical Hawk 75-P. Although the Allison V-1710 was rated only for altitudes up to 4575m (15,000ft), the Air Corps saw coastal defence and ground attack as the principal tasks for its fighter force. As such, it was unworried by the comparatively poor service ceiling of the new aircraft. This attitude would severely hamper US fighter operations once committed to combat.

First flight

The V-1710-33-powered XP-40 flew for the first time on 14 October 1938. Initially, it proved to be capable of only a 481km/h (299mph) top speed. This was markedly improved once the radiator was moved to its definitive position under the nose, resulting in a speed increase of nearly 70km/h (45mph) and bestowing the P-40 with

Bearing the well-known 'sharkmouth' marking of No. 112 Squadron, these RAF Tomahawk Mk IIBs were based in Egypt during 1941, flying fighter sweeps over the Western Desert.

EARLY-WAR FIGHTERS

Curtiss P-40C Warhawk
This P-40 Warhawk flew with the 36th Squadron, 8th Pursuit Group.

Curtiss P-40C
Weight (maximum take-off): 3655kg (8058lb)
Dimensions: Length: 9.66m (31ft 9in), Wingspan: 11.37m (37ft 4in), Height: 3.22m (10ft 7in)
Powerplant: One 813kW (1090hp) Allison V-1710-33 V-12 liquid-cooled piston engine
Maximum Speed: 555km/h (345mph)
Range: 1287km (800 miles)
Ceiling: 8990m (29,500ft)
Crew: 1
Armament: Two 12.7mm (0.5in) Colt Browning M2 machine guns fixed forward firing in fuselage nose; four 7.62mm (0.3in) Browning M1919 machine guns fixed forward firing in wings

its instantly recognizable sharklike profile. Entered in a January 1939 fighter competition that also included the Lockheed XP-38 Lightning and Bell XP-39 Airacobra, the XP-40 was judged the clear winner by the Army Air Corps, and a large production contract was placed for 524 P-40s. Assigned the Curtiss designation of Hawk 81A, the first production P-40 flew in April 1940, and deliveries to the Air Corps began in September, the three squadrons of the 8th Pursuit Group at Langley Field, Virginia being the first to convert to the type.

Modifications
By this time, however, reports of aerial combat over Europe suggested that the P-40 was deficient in several crucial areas when compared to contemporary European fighters. A series of modifications was undertaken by Curtiss, who sought to improve the P-40's combat capability. As such, the P-40B saw the meagre original armament of just two 12.7mm (0.5in) machine guns in the fuselage nose augmented by the addition of a 7.62mm (0.3in) Colt-Browning machine gun in each wing. Protection for the fuel and pilot was added in the form of self-sealing fuel tanks, a bulletproof windscreen and armour both in front of and behind the cockpit. The engine remained unchanged and the extra weight of the armour and armament, though it resulted in only a slight drop in top speed, increased wing loading and caused a marked deterioration in manoeuvrability.

The P-40B was the first variant to be deployed beyond the continental United States, with 55 and 31 examples of the Curtiss fighter deployed to Hawaii and the Philippines respectively by the end of April 1941. One-hundred and thirty-one P-40Bs would be constructed before production switched to the P-40C, which saw the wing armament doubled to four 7.62mm (0.3in) machine guns and featured a new fuel system

EARLY-WAR FIGHTERS

and improved radio. Though the new features were welcome, the engine remained unchanged, weight increased once again and performance and manoeuvrability were further eroded. Deliveries of the P-40C began in April 1941, and a total of 324 would be built, completing the initial Army contract for 524 P-40s.

By this time, the P-40 was being produced in export form as the Hawk 81A, and the first nation to place an order with Curtiss was France, who were already operating the Hawk 75. Unfortunately for the French, although an order for 230 Hawk 81A-1s was placed in October 1939, approval for export of the new Curtiss fighter was withheld until March 1940.

Although 57 examples were crated and ready for delivery by the end of May 1940, no Hawk 81A would be delivered to France before the capitulation to Germany in June, and the entire contract was taken over by the British Purchasing Commission. It would be the RAF that first took the Curtiss into action.

Tomahawk IIA

The initial 140 aircraft were stripped of their French radios, gunsights and FN-Browning 7.5mm (0.29in) machine guns and fitted with the minimum amount of British equipment to allow them to enter RAF service as the Tomahawk I. Four 7.7mm (0.303in) Browning machine guns were fitted in the wing, but in most respects the aircraft was equivalent to the initial P-40 production standard and as such lacked self-sealing fuel tanks and armour, both regarded as essential requisites for a fighter operating over Western Europe. As a result, the Tomahawk I was judged unsuitable for use by Fighter Command and was instead issued to Army Cooperation units for tactical reconnaissance and used as a conversion trainer for aircrew destined to fly more capable Tomahawk models.

The balance of the French order was delivered to Hawk 81A-2 standard, known as the Tomahawk IIA to the RAF, featuring self-sealing fuel tanks, armour protection for the pilot and American 7.62mm (0.3in) Colt-Browning machine guns in the wings and a US radio.

A follow-on British order for a further 950 Tomahawks was placed, all but the initial 20 of which were completed to Tomahawk IIB standard, with British 7.7mm (0.303in) wing guns. The Tomahawk would see most of its

---

Model H-81A-2

Weight (maximum take-off): 3655kg (8058lb)
Dimensions: Length: 9.66m (31ft 9in), Wingspan: 11.37m (37ft 4in), Height: 3.22m (10ft 7in)
Powerplant: One 858kW (1150hp) Allison V-1710-33 V-12 liquid cooled piston engine
Maximum Speed: 571km/h (355mph)
Range: 1450km (900 miles)
Ceiling: 8800m (29,000ft)
Crew: 1
Armament: Two 12.7mm (0.5in) Colt Browning M2 machine guns fixed forward firing in fuselage nose; four 7.62mm (0.3in) Browning M1919 machine guns fixed forward firing in wings

Curtiss Hawk Model H-81A-2
This H-81 Tomahawk was piloted by R.T. Smith, 3rd Pursuit Squadron, American Volunteer Group "Flying Tigers", December 1941.

EARLY-WAR FIGHTERS

Curtiss P-40C Tomahawk
This P-40C Tomahawk served with the 39th Pursuit Squadron, 31st Pursuit Group.

Curtiss P-40E Warhawk
This P-40E Warhawk from the 11th Squadron, 343rd Fighter Group, was stationed in the Aleutian Islands in 1942.

service with British Commonwealth forces in Africa, and it was here that the aircraft would first be adorned with the shark mouth markings that were to become iconic and forever associated with the type. Over the Western Desert, the Tomahawk proved superior to the Hawker Hurricane but was not in the same league as the Spitfire. Furthermore, its poor performance at altitude limited it to low- and medium-level operations.

Considered broadly equivalent in combat performance to its primary opponents (the Messerschmitt Bf 109E and Macchi MC.202 Folgore), the Tomahawk became the primary fighter type available in the African theatre. Its excellent reliability, great strength and easy flying characteristics endeared it to pilots, and some individuals achieved considerable success with the type – for example, the Australian Clive Caldwell, the highest scoring P-40 ace of any nation, who achieved 22 of his eventual 28.5 victories with the Tomahawk.

China adopts the shark mouth
Throughout 1941, with the threat of a German invasion receding, limited stocks of RAF Tomahawks were made available to other nations. The first recipient of these aircraft was China, which bought 100 examples for supply to the American Volunteer Group (AVG), better known as the 'Flying Tigers'. Although always referred to simply as 'P-40's' by the AVG itself, the aircraft were in fact Hawk 81A-2s released from British contracts and finished in the RAF temperate fighter camouflage

Curtiss P-40C
Weight (maximum take-off): 3655kg (8058lb)
Dimensions: Length: 9.66m (31ft 9in), Wingspan: 11.37m (37ft 4in), Height: 3.22m (10ft 7in)
Powerplant: One 813kW (1090hp) Allison V-1710-33 V-12 liquid cooled piston engine
Maximum Speed: 555km/h (345mph)
Range: 1287km (800 miles)
Ceiling: 8990m (29,500ft)
Crew: 1
Armament: Two 12.7mm (0.5in) Colt Browning M2 machine guns fixed forward firing in fuselage nose; four 7.62mm (0.3in) Browning M1919 machine guns fixed forward firing in wings

EARLY-WAR FIGHTERS

Curtiss P-40E Warhawk

This P-40E, named 'Holdin' My Own', was the personal mount of First Lieutenant Dallas A. Clinger. Not one of the original 'Flying Tigers' pilots of the American Volunteer Group (AVG) who flew against the Japanese in China from late 1941, Clinger scored five aerial victories against the Japanese while flying with the 23rd Fighter Group. The distinctive 'shark's mouth' marking was copied from illustrations of RAF Tomahawks in the Western Desert.

Redesign
The P-40D and P-40E featured a slightly narrower fuselage, redesigned canopy and improved cockpit.

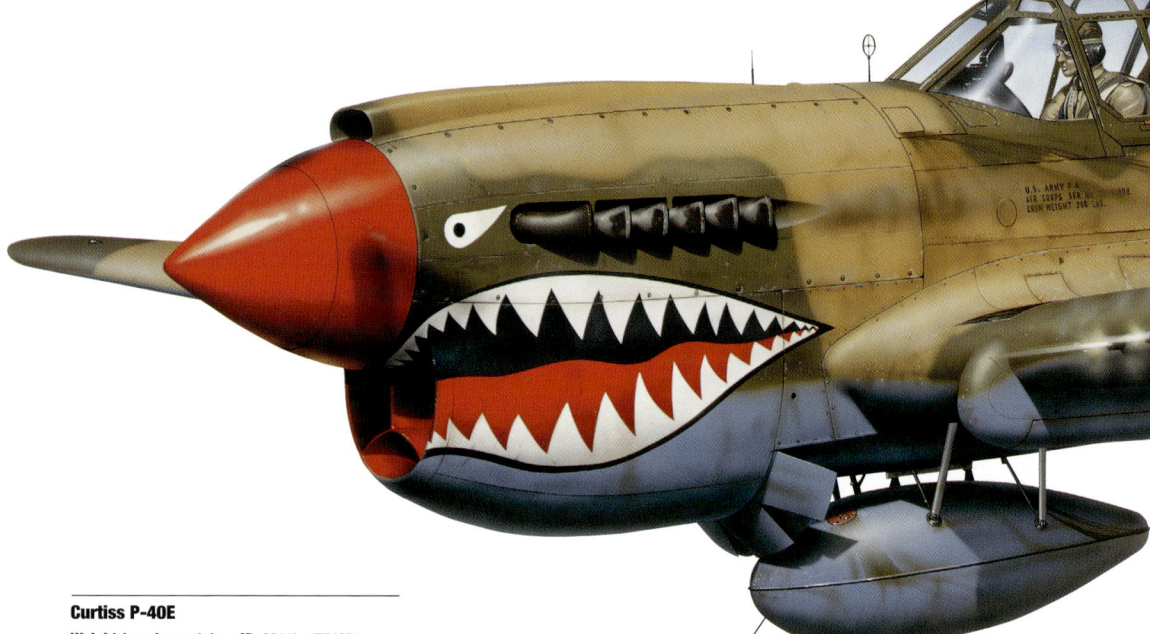

Drop tank
A 52 gallon drop tank was introduced on the P-40C, and all subsequent models included this feature, which extended the aircraft's combat radius significantly.

Curtiss P-40E

Weight (maximum take-off): 3511kg (7740lb)
Dimensions: Length: 10.16m (33ft 4in), Wingspan: 11.37m (37ft 4in), Height: 3.76m (12ft 4in)
Powerplant: One 895kW (1200hp) Allison V-1710-33 V-12 liquid cooled piston engine
Maximum Speed: 563km/h (350mph)
Range: 1287km (800 miles)
Ceiling: 9450m (31,000ft)
Crew: 1
Armament: Four 12.7mm (0.5in) Colt Browning M2 machine guns fixed forward firing in wings; 227kg (500lb) bomb under fuselage

EARLY-WAR FIGHTERS

Tail art
The tail art on Dallas Clinger's P-40 shows a cowboy urinating on the Rising Sun.

scheme. Delivered direct from Curtiss to Rangoon, the aircraft arrived in June 1941, but would not see combat until after the Pearl Harbor attack.

Adopting the shark's mouth nose art as used on RAF Tomahawks in the Western Desert, the unit subsequently claimed 286 Japanese aircraft destroyed by the time it was absorbed into the USAAF as the 23rd Pursuit Group in July 1942.

Soviet Tomahawks
As well as small numbers supplied to Egypt and Turkey, a further major recipient of ex-RAF Tomahawks was the Soviet Union, with 195 Tomahawk IIBs sent from British stocks as military aid and a further 20 obtained direct from Curtiss.

As this predated the passing of the Lend-Lease Act, the latter aircraft were paid for in gold. Soviet Tomahawks were rushed into service, beginning combat operations in October 1941 over Moscow, and 17 kills were scored in the aircraft's first month of service. Soviet pilots generally rated the P-40 as superior to the Hurricane but inferior to the P-39 and Yak-1, though the easy flying characteristics and good manoeuvrability of the Curtiss fighter were appreciated. The immense strength of the Curtiss airframe was

EARLY-WAR FIGHTERS

particularly noteworthy and useful: during a single mission, Aleksei Khlobystov managed to destroy two German aircraft by ramming them – a unique achievement. In Soviet service, early P-40 use was hampered by the relative scarcity of spares and the poor quality of Russian lubricants, which led directly to many engine failures.

Far East baptism of fire

Following its baptism of fire in British service, the first US P-40s to see action were the P-40B and P-40Cs based on Hawaii when the Japanese launched their attack on Pearl Harbor. Although at least 62 P-40s were destroyed on the ground at Wheeler Field, a handful managed to get airborne and were credited with the destruction of five Japanese aircraft. By the end of the day, only two P-40Cs and 25 P-40Bs remained airworthy in Hawaii.

In the Philippines, the P-40s did not fare much better. Twenty-six P-40s were lost on the first day of fighting, almost all on the ground at Clark Field, though the first aerial victory in the Philippines theatre fell to the guns of a P-40B.

Over the course of the next few weeks, the P-40 force was effectively wiped out in the Philippines, although the campaign did result in the first US 'ace' of the war: Lt Col. Boyd Wagner achieved five of his eventual eight victories with the P-40. Wagner's aircraft was a P-40E, the first model of a significantly altered version of the Curtiss fighter.

Kittyhawk

By 1940, with production of the P-40 in full swing, Curtiss sought to improve the basic design of the aircraft by fitting it with a more powerful engine. The Allison V-1710-39(F3R) offered 858kW (1150hp) at take-off and introduced a war emergency rating of 1096kW (1470hp) that could be maintained for five minutes. With a different airscrew reduction gear to the V1710-33 of the earlier P-40s, the new engine was shorter and offered a raised thrust line. As a result, the nose contours of the aircraft were markedly changed, the radiator was enlarged and moved forward, the fuselage cross section reduced and the undercarriage shorter. The fuselage guns were omitted, and wing armament was increased to four 12.7mm (0.5in) machine guns to compensate. Designated the Hawk 87 by Curtiss, the changes in basic structure were sufficiently minimal that production could be phased in rapidly and the British Purchasing Commission placed an order for 560 aircraft, named 'Kittyhawk' for RAF service, in May 1940. The USAAC followed in June, after the relatively poor showing of the Curtiss P-46, intended as a replacement for their own P-40 but which could only deliver performance as good as or inferior to the new P-40 model, which also promised to be in production sooner.

The P-40D was basically the same as the British aircraft, but only 22

Curtiss P-40F

Weight (maximum take-off): 4540kg (10,000lb)
Dimensions: Length: 10.17m (33ft 4in), Wingspan: 11.37m (37ft 4in), Height: 3.76m (12ft 4in)
Powerplant: One 969kW (1300hp) Packard V-1650-1 Merlin V-12 liquid cooled piston engine
Maximum Speed: 586km/h (364mph)
Range: 965km (600 miles)
Ceiling: 10,485m (34,400ft)
Crew: 1
Armament: Six 12.7mm (0.5in) Browning machine guns; up to 317kg (700lb) bomb load

---

Curtiss P-40F Warhawk
This Curtiss P-40F-15 (41-19746) from the 87th Fighter Squadron/79th Fighter Group was flown by Charles 'Jazz' Jaslow and based at Causeway LG, Tunisia, in 1943.

EARLY-WAR FIGHTERS

Curtiss P-40K Warhawk
This P-40K Warhawk was piloted by Colonel Bruce K. Holloway, the commanding officer of the 23rd Fighter Group, based in China, August 1943.

Curtiss P-40K
Weight (Maximum take-off): 4536kg (10000lb)
Dimensions: Length 10.17m (33ft 4in), Wingspan 9.67m (31ft 9in), Height 3.76m (12ft 4in)
Powerplant: One 988kW (1325hp) Allison V-1710-73 V-12 liquid cooled piston engine
Maximum speed: 595km/h (370mph)
Range: 1127km (700 miles)
Ceiling: 8534m (28,000ft)
Crew: One
Armament: Six 12.7mm (0.5in) Browning machine guns; up to 317kg (700lb) bomb load

would be delivered before production switched to the P-40E, which was identical except for its upgraded armament of six machine guns. The RAF received both four- and six-gun armed Kittyhawks but all were designated as Kittyhawk Is, and nearly all were shipped direct to Africa for operations in the Western Desert.

None of the newer P-40s had arrived in Hawaii by the time of Pearl Harbor. However, 74 P-40Es had been shipped to the Philippines by December 1941. In near-constant action against the Japanese invaders, only 18 P-40s were left by 26 December, and the last five airworthy examples were destroyed by their crews on 6 May 1942. A similar situation prevailed in Java, where a mere 38 examples of the P-40 were ever received and were rapidly overwhelmed.

In China, after the AVG became the 23rd FG, P-40Es began to be supplied but were always in short supply. Reinforced later by the 16th Fighter Squadron, these units flew the P-40E to the end of the war, supplemented later by the P-40K.

Western Desert

While these desperate actions were being taken in the Far East, the Kittyhawk was introduced to the Western Desert by 3 Squadron RAAF in December 1941, replacing the Tomahawk, the first RAF squadron to fly the type being 112 Squadron, which took the Kittyhawk into action in January 1942 and were also the first unit to utilize the aircraft as a fighter-bomber by fitting bomb shackles for a single 144kg (250lb) bomb. Unofficially dubbed 'Kittybombers', ground attack suited the Curtiss fighter's low-altitude engine and the Kittyhawk proved highly effective in this role, the Kittyhawk following Allied armies throughout the campaign in Italy.

US P-40s began to form part of the Desert Air Force in July 1942, and the type would prove highly effective in American hands, with 23 pilots eventually achieving 'ace' status with the P-40 in the Mediterranean theatre. The high point of the USAAF P-40's career was likely the 'Palm Sunday Massacre' of 18 April 1943, when 47 P-40s with 12 Spitfires flying top cover

Displaying the short-lived red-bordered 'star-and-bar' insignia of July–September 1943, this Warhawk was photographed flying from Randolph Field. The serial number identifies it as a P-40E-1, a repossessed Kittyhawk Mk IA built for Lend-Lease to Britain; a P-40K-type fin has been fitted.

shot down 24 Ju 52s, nine Bf 109s and one Bf 110, as well as forcing another 35 Ju 52s to crash land along the Sicilian shoreline.

Merlin-powered P-40Fs

Concerns regarding the inadequate performance of the P-40 at height resulted in the trial fitting of a Rolls-Royce Merlin in a P-40D, designated the XP-40F. Following successful flight trials, a Merlin-powered variant entered production as the P-40F, powered by a Packard-built V-1650-1 Merlin rated at 969kW (1300hp) for take-off and with a two-speed supercharger, which allowed for much improved power output at higher altitudes. In total, 1311 P-40Fs would be constructed, 330 of them going to the RAF as the Kittyhawk II. Later P-40Fs featured a lengthened rear fuselage to improve directional stability, the vertical tail surfaces moving 48cm (19in) further aft relative to the horizontal tail, which remained in the same position. The lengthened fuselage was subsequently utilized on all further P-40 models. The parallel development of the P-40K employed the Allison V1710-73(F4R) engine of increased power but was otherwise essentially unchanged from the P-40E.

Increasingly outperformed by contemporary aircraft, Curtiss introduced the lightened P-40L, which dropped two of the machine guns and reduced fuel and ammunition capacity. Dubbed the 'Gypsy Rose Lee' after the famed contemporary striptease artiste, the stripped-down P-40L was Merlin-powered. However, shortages of this engine saw many P-40F and P-40Ls modified with Allison engines in which guise they were designated the P-40R-1 and R-2 respectively. The P-40M was produced primarily for lend-lease requirements, with all but five of the 600 built being assigned to the RAF, where they were known as the Kittyhawk III. Powered by the Allison V-1710-81 engine delivering 895kW (1200hp) at take-off, the P-40M was otherwise identical to the P-40K, but its performance was usefully improved particularly in rate of climb.

P-40K and P-40N

By the time the P-40N was first produced in February 1943, it was clear that the P-40 was becoming

outmoded, and production of this variant was undertaken largely because the switch to another aircraft type on the Curtiss assembly line, or significant modification to the basic design, would cause unacceptable delays in the delivery of aircraft to Allied nations. A further weight reduction programme was undertaken resulting in an aircraft 310kg (683lb) lighter in combat trim than the preceding P-40M. As such, the P-40N (or 'Kittyhawk IV' in British Commonwealth service) was the fastest P-40 variant to be produced, at 608km/h (378mph), and would become the most produced variant of all, with 5215 completed.

Comparatively little use was made of the P-40N by the USAAF, with major use of the type occurring in the New Guinea campaign of 1943. In the Mediterranean, however, the P-40N formed the initial equipment of the 99th Fighter Squadron, manned by the famed African American 'Tuskegee Airmen' for the first eight months of their combat deployment.

Other major users of the later P-40s were the Soviet Union in both Air Force and Naval units, which received 2178 P-40E, K, L and N models. Soviet Naval squadrons were unusual among P-40 operators in that as well as using the aircraft as a regular fighter, they employed the aircraft for the anti-shipping role, in which it achieved considerable success with skip-bombing techniques.

The Kittyhawk was the most numerous fighter ever operated by the Royal Australian Air Force, ultimately replaced by the Spitfire in frontline units. New Zealand also flew Kittyhawks in the Pacific until they were superseded by the Vought Corsair, and other wartime users to take the P-40 into combat included Canada and France.

The final P-40 variant, the P-40Q, introduced a bubble canopy, a revised nose, clipped wings and a water injection-equipped Allison V-1710-121 engine. Although it achieved the impressive speed of 679km/h (422mph) in trials during 1944, sufficient availability of P-51s and P-47s rendered this final P-40 variant superfluous and production did not ensue.

Curtiss P-40N
Weight (maximum take-off): 4018kg (8850lb)
Dimensions: Length: 10.17m (33ft 4in), Wingspan: 11.37m (37ft 4in), Height: 3.76m (12ft 4in)
Powerplant: One 895kW (1200hp) Allison V-1710-81 V-12 liquid-cooled piston engine
Maximum Speed: 560km/h (348mph))
Range (max with external fuel tank): 2010km (1250 miles)
Ceiling: 9449m (31,000ft)
Crew: 1
Armament: Six 12.7mm (0.5in) Browning machine guns; up to 317kg (700lb) bomb load

Curtiss P-40N Warhawk
Flown by First Lt. D.W. Meuten, this P-40N-5 (42-105834) 'Yellow 51' was part of the 8th Fighter Squadron/49th Fighter Group, based in Gusap, New Guinea, in 1944.

EARLY-WAR FIGHTERS

P-40E Warhawk

CUTAWAY KEY

1 Rudder aerodynamic balance
2 Rudder upper hinge (port external)
3 Radio aerial bracket/ insulator
4 Rear navigation light (port and starboard)
5 Tailfin structure
6 Rudder post/support tube
7 Rudder structure
8 Rudder trim tab
9 Rudder trim tab push-rod (starboard external)
10 Elevator tab
11 Elevator structure
12 Elevator aerodynamic balance
13 Tailplane structure
14 Rudder lower hinge
15 Rudder control horn
16 Tab actuator flexible drive shafts
17 Tailplane attachment lugs
18 Elevator control horn
19 Tab control rear sprocket housing/ chain drive
20 Tailwheel retraction mechanism
21 Access panel
22 Tailwheel door
23 Retractable tailwheel
24 Tailwheel leg
25 Lifting point
26 Tailwheel lower attachment
27 Trim control cable turnbuckles
28 Elevator control cables
29 Tailwheel upper attachment
30 Access panel
31 Port tailplane
32 Port elevator
33 Radio aerials
34 Monocoque fuselage structure
35 Hydraulic reserve tank
36 Automatic recognition device
37 Aerial lead-in
38 Radio aerial mast
39 Hand starter crank stowage
40 Radio bay access door (port)
41 Radio receiver/ transmitter
42 Support frame
43 Battery stowage
44 Ventral aerial (optional)
45 Hydraulic system vent and drain
46 Rudder control cable turnbuckle
47 Oxygen bottles
48 Radio equipment installation (optional)
49 Hydraulic tank
50 Hydraulic pump
51 Wingroot fillet
52 Streamline ventral cowl
53 Wing centreline splice
54 Fuselage fuel tank, capacity 51.5 Imp gal (234 litres)
55 Canopy track
56 Fuel lines
57 Rear-vision panels
58 Pilot's headrest
59 Rearward-sliding cockpit canopy
60 Rear view mirror (external)
61 Bulletproof windshield
62 Instrument panel coaming
63 Electric gunsight
64 Throttle control quadrant
65 Trim tab control wheels
66 Flap control lever
67 Pilot's seat
68 Elevator control cable horn
69 Seat support (wing upper surface)
70 Hydraulic pump handle
71 Control column
72 Rudder pedal/brake cylinder assembly
73 Bulkhead
74 Oil tank, capacity 108 Imp gal (491 litres)
75 Ring sight
76 Flap control push rod rollers
77 Aileron control cables
78 Aileron cable drum
79 Aileron trim tab drive motor
80 Aileron trim tab
81 Port aileron
82 Port navigation light
83 Pitot head
84 Wing skinning
85 Ammunition loading panels
86 Bead sight
87 Coolant expansion tank, capacity 132 litres (29 Imp gal)
88 Carburettor intake
89 Engine bearer support attachment
90 Air vapour eliminator
91 Hydraulic emergency reserve tank
92 Junction box
93 Engine support tubes
94 Engine mounting vibration absorbers
95 Exhaust stacks
96 Cowling panel lines
97 Allison V-1710-39 engine
98 Carburettor Intake fairing
99 Propeller reduction gear casing
100 Coolant thermometer
101 Propeller hub shaft
102 Spinner
103 Curtiss Electric propeller
104 Radiator (divided) intakes
105 Intake trunking
106 Oil cooler radiator (centreline)
107 Glycol radiators (port and starboard)
108 Radiator mounting brackets
109 Glycol radiator intake pipe
110 Port mainwheel
111 Controllable cooling gills
112 Access panel (oil drain)
113 Engine bearer support truss
114 Fresh air intake
115 Wingroot fairing
116 Fuselage frame/wing attachment
117 Walkway
118 Wing/fuselage splice plate
119 Split flap structure
120 Aileron fixed tab
121 Starboard aileron
122 Starboard wingtip construction
123 Starboard navigation light
124 Wing rib
125 Multi (7)-spar wing structure
126 Inboard gun ammunition box (235 rounds)
127 Centre gun ammunition box (235 rounds)
128 Outboard gun ammunition box (235 rounds)
129 Three 12.7mm (0.50in) M-2 Browning machine-guns
130 Ammunition feed chute
131 Starboard wheel well
132 Wing centre section main fuel tank
133 Undercarriage attachment
134 Wing centre section reserve fuel tank, capacity 133 litres (29.2 Imp gal)
135 Retraction cylinder
136 Retraction arm/links
137 Machine-gun barrel forward support collars
138 Blast tubes
139 Bevel gear
140 Undercarriage side support strut
141 Gun warm air
142 227kg (500lb) bomb (ventral stores)
143 Undercarriage oleo leg fairing
144 Undercarriage fairing door
145 Machine/gun ports
146 Hydraulic brake line
147 One (or two) underwing 18kg (40lb) bomb(s)
148 Oleo leg
149 Torque links
150 Axle
151 762mm (30in) diameter smooth contour mainwheel tyre
152 Tow ring/jack point 153 Ventral auxiliary tank
154 Vent line
155 Sway brace pads
156 External fuel line
157 Shackle assembly
158 Filler neck
159 Alternative ventral 114 kg (250 lb) bomb with:
160 Extended percussion fuse

EARLY-WAR FIGHTERS

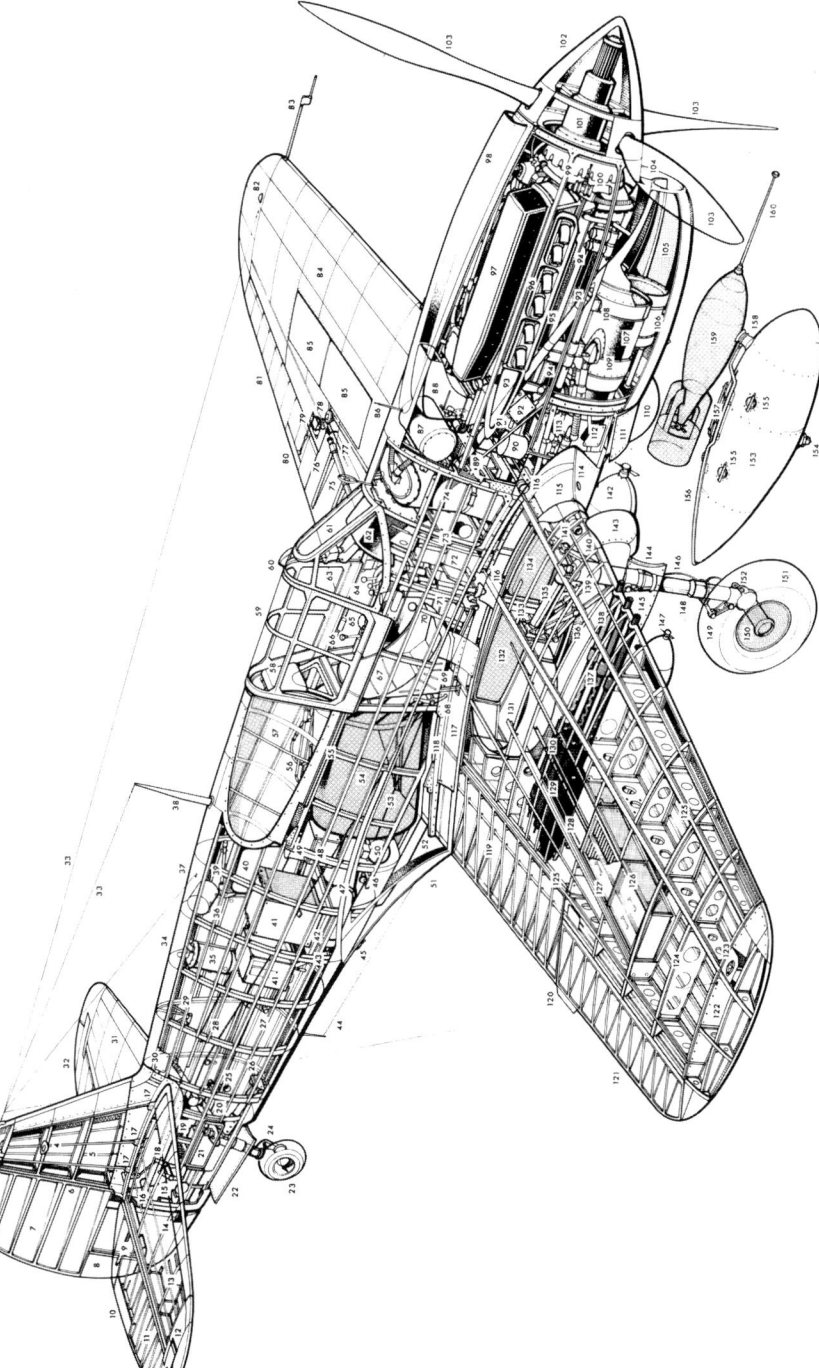

This cutaway view of a P-40E Warhawk shows the aircraft's simple, rugged design.

P-40E WARHAWK

Weight (maximum take-off): 3511kg (7740lb)
Dimensions: Length: 10.16m (33ft 4in), Wingspan: 11.37m (37ft 4in), Height: 3.76m (12ft 4in)
Powerplant: One 895kW (1200hp) Allison V-1710-33 V-12 liquid cooled piston engine
Maximum Speed: 563km/h (350mph)
Range: 1287km (800 miles)
Ceiling: 9450m (31,000ft)
Crew: 1
Armament: Four 12.7mm (0.5in) Colt Browning M2 machine guns fixed forward firing in wings; 227kg (500lb) bomb under fuselage

LATE-WAR FIGHTERS

After the outbreak of war the USAAF was dominated by two outstanding single engine types – the P-47 Thunderbolt, and P-51 Mustang – both of which proved staggeringly successful and were built in large numbers. The Thunderbolt became the most-produced US fighter of all time. Also featured in this chapter is the P-66 Vanguard, a promising design that was little used, and the Supermarine Spitfire, which the USAAF was compelled to acquire when its own fighter types proved inadequate in the opening phase of the war.

- Vultee P-66 Vanguard
- North American P-51 Mustang
- Republic P-47 Thunderbolt
- Supermarine Spitfire
- Bell P-63 Kingcobra

A flight of North American P-51D and P-51B Mustangs from the 375th Fighter Squadron, 361st Fighter Group, fly above England, July 1944.

LATE-WAR FIGHTERS

Vultee P-66 Vanguard

Although extremely obscure today and barely used by the US, the P-66 was, for a time, the most numerous fighter in the Chinese Air Force and saw combat against the Japanese in 1942 and 1943.

The P-66 resulted from Vultee's plan to produce several different aircraft, utilizing the same wings, tailplane and rear fuselage to drive down development and tooling costs. As it transpired, this intriguing approach resulted in only two designs that would enter production: the highly successful BT-13 Valiant trainer, of which nearly 10,000 examples were built, and the rather less successful P-66 Vanguard.

Flown for the first time in 1939, the Vanguard performed adequately for its era and was noted for its excellent handling. In a bid to reduce drag, the prototype was initially fitted with an extension shaft for the propeller and close-fitting engine cowling tapering to a pointed propeller spinner.

This led to cooling difficulties that were never satisfactorily overcome, and the substitution of conventional cowling resulted in only an insignificant increase in drag. As a result, all production Vanguards flew with an orthodox cowling.

Chinese service

One-hundred-and-forty-four were ordered by Sweden, to be designated the J-10, and production was in full swing when, in September 1941, the US government placed an embargo on military exports to all countries except the United Kingdom. After the Pearl Harbor attack, the USAAF issued around 50 of the embargoed aircraft to the 14th Pursuit Group for the defence of airfields in the continental United States. The RAF evaluated the aircraft as a possible advanced trainer, but the decision was made to supply the P-66 to China instead. In Chinese service, the P-66 proved lacklustre, as much due to the poor levels of maintenance and training prevalent in the Chinese Air Force during 1942 as any significant fault in the aircraft itself.

Nonetheless, the P-66 was capable of the occasional victory, such as on 8 June 1943, when Capt. Chow Chi-Kai took off in a Vanguard during a Japanese air raid and single-handedly shot down three of the attacking bombers. Twelve P-66s intended for China but abandoned at Karachi were also taken on strength by the US 74th Fighter Squadron, though it is unclear if these were ever used in combat. After 1943, the P-66 served as a trainer in Chinese service, some reportedly surviving into 1947.

Vultee P-66

Weight (maximum take-off): 3352kg (7384lb)
Dimensions: Length: 8.66m (28ft 5in), Wingspan: 10.97m (36ft), Height: 2.87m (9ft 5in)
Powerplant: One 890kW (1200hp) Pratt & Whitney R-1830-33 Twin Wasp air-cooled 14-cylinder radial piston engine
Maximum Speed: 547km/h (340mph)
Range: 1370km (850 miles)
Ceiling: 8595m (28,200ft)
Crew: 1
Armament: Two 12.7mm (0.50in) fixed forward firing machine guns in upper nose cowling and four 7.7mm (0.303in) in wings

---

Vultee P-66 Vanguard

This is 42-6902, serving with the 49th Pursuit Squadron, 14th Pursuit Group at March Air Base in California during 1942. Along with 103 others, incuding many former RAF examples, this aircraft was delivered to the Chinese Nationalist Air Force, where they briefly saw combat against the Japanese.

North American P-51 Mustang

Somewhat ironically, the most famous American fighter of World War II was designed by a German, originally developed for British requirements and at first treated with indifference by the USAAF. Ultimately, it would achieve more aerial victories than any other US type.

Arguably the finest fighter of World War II and one of the greatest military aircraft of all time, the P-51 Mustang owed its existence more to chance than to any official policy or plan. North American Aviation Inc had produced very few military aircraft by 1939, and the P-51 would be its first fighter design. Contact between the company and the British Purchasing Commission, an organization founded to obtain war materials from American companies, first occurred in late 1939. At this time, the RAF were desperate for fighters and had placed a sizable order for Curtiss P-40s. The suggestion was made that North American might use their production facilities to build this aircraft under licence. Unimpressed by the prospect of building Curtiss aircraft, North American General Manager James 'Dutch' Kindelberger proposed that they design a new and better fighter for British needs.

North American's first fighter

Plans for just such a fighter had in fact already been prepared by North American under the supervision of Chief Designer Edgar Schmued, a Bavarian aircraft engineer who had emigrated to the US in 1931 after a few years working for General Motors in Brazil. The plans featured highly innovative features such as a laminar flow aerofoil section (based on NACA research) and the placement of engine and oil cooling radiators in a ventral duct behind the wing for maximum efficiency. Impressed by North American's plans, despite the fact the company had never designed a fighter aircraft, the British gave the project the go-ahead in April 1940, following up with a formal contract in May 1941. The contract stipulated a delivery date of January 1941, and the design and production team worked 16-hour shifts seven days a week to finish the prototype in a mere 102 days, though a further 20 would elapse before the engine was delivered and fitted.

Designated the NA-73X by North American, the aircraft was flown for the first time on 26 October 1940 but was badly damaged in a crash landing following engine

North American A-36A

The A-36A was an attack aircraft variant of the famed P-51 Mustang fighter, but was actually in service before the P-51. The A-36A shared the Mustang's airframe but never had the upgrade to the Rolls-Royce Merlin engine.

North American A-36A

Weight (maximum take-off): 4535kg (10,000lb)
Dimensions: Length: 9.83m (32ft 3in), Wingspan: 11.28m (37ft 0.25in), Height: 3.71m (12ft 2in)
Powerplant: One 988kW (1325hp) Allison V-1710-87 liquid-cooled piston V12 engine
Maximum Speed: 590km/h (365mph)
Range: 885km (550 miles)
Ceiling: 7650m (25,100ft)
Crew: 1
Armament: Six 12.7mm (0.50in) AN/M2 Browning machine guns; up to 454kg (1000lb) of bombs on two underwing hardpoints

failure due to fuel starvation less than a month later. Although the aircraft was subsequently repaired, flight testing had to be completed with the first of the 320 production aircraft on order for the British, and by the end of the year,

LATE-WAR FIGHTERS

North American P-51B
A P-51B Mustang (43-12173) nicknamed 'Peg O' My Heart' of the 355th Fighter Squadron, 354th Fighter Group.

North American P-51B
Assigned to 334th Fighter Squadron, 4th Fighter Group, Eighth Air Force, this aircraft (43-6832) 'Miss Dallas' was named by pilot Victor France, from Dallas, Texas.

North American P-51B
This P-51B (42-106616) was piloted by 2nd Lt. Thomas F. Miller of the 356th Fighter Squadron, 354th Fighter Group, Eighth Air Force, based at Lasheneden, Kent, England, in May 1944.

LATE-WAR FIGHTERS

North American P-51B
Weight (maximum take-off): 5352kg (11,800lb)
Dimensions: Length: 9.83m (32ft 3in), Wingspan: 11.28m (37ft), Height: 4.16m (13ft 8in)
Powerplant: One 1200kW (1620hp) Packard V-1650-3 Merlin V-12 liquid-cooled piston engine
Maximum Speed: 708km/h (440mph)
Range (with external fuel tanks): 2655km (1650 miles)
Ceiling: 12,800m (42,000ft)
Crew: 1
Armament: Four 12.7mm (0.5in) Browning M2 machine guns fixed forward firing in wings; up to 908kg (2000lb) bomb load; modification in field to permit carriage of three rocket launch tubes under each wing

---

the name 'Mustang' had been officially adopted by the RAF.

First victory
The first Mustang Mk I was tested by the Aircraft and Armament Experimental Establishment (A&AEE) in the UK during the summer of 1941 and was extremely warmly received, being described as the best fighter aircraft so far received from the USA. Speed, handling and manoeuvrability were all considered excellent, though the aircraft suffered the same issue as other aircraft powered by the Allison V-1710 engine, such as the P-40, in that its performance rapidly diminished at altitudes above around 3965m (13,000ft) due to its lack of a two-stage supercharger. As most aerial combat over Western Europe took place above that altitude, it was decided that the aircraft would be ideal for the tactical reconnaissance role with the RAF's Army Cooperation squadrons.

Fitted with a single F-24 camera mounted at an oblique angle directly behind the cockpit, the Mustang retained its armament of four 12.7mm (0.5in) and four 7.62mm (0.3in) Browning machine guns and was well able to give a good account of itself in combat should the opportunity occur.

The first missions were flown on May 1942, and Mustang squadrons participated in supporting the Dieppe landings three months later. The first air-to-air victory was achieved during this operation when Pilot Officer Hollis H. Hills, a Canadian pilot flying with the RAF, claimed a Focke Wulf Fw 190 on 19 August 1942. Subsequently, Mustang units were employed on 'Ranger' and 'Rhubarb' sorties, performing reconnaissance and attacking targets of opportunity across Europe. The aircraft's long-range capability was already in evidence as the Mustang became the first UK-based single-engine aircraft to operate over Germany when a mission was flown to reconnoitre the Dortmund-Ems Canal. During these low-level missions, it was discovered that the Mustang I could outrun all enemy aircraft – the Allison-powered Mustang was faster than most later Merlin variants at sea level – and during the initial 18 months of operations, Mustangs were responsible for destroying or heavily damaging over 200 locomotives, 200 canal barges and many aircraft on the ground.

A further batch of 150 aircraft was ordered by the RAF, with four 20mm (0.79in) cannon replacing the machine guns, and designated the Mustang IA. So effective were the Mustang I and IA in their low-level role that the RAF retained the aircraft in service until the conclusion of hostilities.

North American P-51B
A P-51B (42-106950), nicknamed 'The Iowa Beaut', of the 354th Fighter Squadron, 355th Fighter Group, Eighth Air Force.

LATE-WAR FIGHTERS

P-51B Mustang

CUTAWAY KEY

1. Plastic (Phenol fibre) rudder trim tab
2. Rudder frame (fabric covered)
3. Rudder balance
4. Fin front spar
5. Fin structure
6. Access panel
7. Rudder trim-tab actuating drum
8. Rudder trim-tab control link
9. Rear navigation light
10. Rudder metal bottom section
11. Elevator plywood trim tab
12. Starboard elevator frame
13. Elevator balance weight
14. Starboard tailplane structure
15. Reinforced bracket (rear steering stresses)
16. Rudder operating horn forging
17. Elevator operating horns
18. Tab control turnbuckles
19. Fin front spar/ fuselage attachment
20. Port elevator tab
21. Fabric-covered elevator
22. Elevator balance weight
23. Port tailplane
24. Tab control drum
25. Fin root fairing
26. Elevator cables
27. Tab control access panels
28. Tailwheel steering mechanism
29. Tailwheel mount
30. Tailwheel leg assembly
31. Forward-retracting steerable tailwheel
32. Tailwheel doors
33. Lifting tube
34. Fuselage aft bulkhead/break point
35. Fuselage break point
36. Control cable pulley brackets
37. Fuselage frames
38. Oxygen bottles
39. Cooling-air exit flap actuating mechanism
40. Rudder cables
41. Fuselage lower longeron
42. Rear tunnel
43. Cooling-air exit flap
44. Coolant radiator assembly
45. Radio and equipment shelf
46. Power supply pack
47. Fuselage upper longeron
48. Radio bay aft bulkhead (plywood)
49. Fuselage stringers
50. SCR-695 radio transmitter-receiver (on upper sliding shelf)
51. Whip aerial
52. Junction box
53. Cockpit aft glazing
54. Canopy track
55. SCR-552 radio transmitter-receiver
56. Battery installation
57. Radiator/ supercharger coolant pipes
58. Radiator forward air duct
59. Coolant header tank/radiator pipe
60. Coolant radiator ventral access cover
61. Oil-cooler air inlet door
62. Oil radiator
63. Oil pipes
64. Flap control linkage
65. Wing rear spar/ fuselage attachment bracket
66. Crash pylon structure
67. Aileron control linkage
68. Hydraulic hand pump
69. Radio control boxes
70. Pilot's seat
71. Seat suspension frame
72. Pilot's head/back armour
73. Rearward-sliding clear-vision canopy
74. External rear-view mirror
75. Ring and bead gunsight
76. Bullet-proof windshield
77. Gyro gunsight
78. Engine controls
79. Signal-pistol discharge tube
80. Circuit-breaker panel
81. Oxygen regulator
82. Pilot's footrest and seat mounting bracket
83. Control linkage
84. Rudder pedal
85. Tailwheel lock control
86. Wing centre-section
87. Hydraulic reservoir
88. Port wing fuel tank filler point
89. Port Browning guns
90. Ammunition feed chutes
91. Gun-bay access door (raised)
92. Ammunition box troughs
93. Aileron control cables
94. Flap lower skin (Alclad)
95. Aileron profile (internal aerodynamic balance diaphragm)
96. Aileron control drum and mounting bracket
97. Aileron trim-tab control drum
98. Aileron plastic (Phenol fibre) trim tab
99. Port aileron assembly
100. Wing skinning
101. Outer section sub-assembly
102. Port navigation light
103. Port wingtip
104. Leading-edge skin
105. Landing lamp
106. Weapons/stores pylon
107. 227kg (500lb) bomb
108. Gun ports
109. Gun barrels
110. Detachable cowling panels
111. Firewall/integral armour
112. Oil tank
113. Oil pipes
114. Upper longeron/ engine mount attachment
115. Oil-tank metal retaining straps
116. Carburettor
117. Engine bearer assembly
118. Cowling panel frames
119. Engine aftercooler
120. Engine leads
121. Packard V-1650 (R-R Merlin) 12-cylinder liquid-cooled engine
122. Exhaust fairing panel
123. Stub exhausts
124. Magneto
125. Coolant pipes
126. Cowling forward frame
127. Coolant header tank
128. Armour plate
129. Propeller hub
130. Spinner
131. Hamilton Standard Hydromatic propeller
132. Carburettor air intake, integral with (133)
133. Engine-mount front-frame assembly
134. Intake trunk
135. Engine-mount reinforcing tie
136. Hand-crank starter
137. Carburettor trunk vibration-absorbing connection
138. Wing centre-section front bulkhead
139. Wing centre-section end rib
140. Starboard mainwheel well
141. Wing front spar/fuselage attachment bracket
142. Ventral air intake (radiator and oil cooler)
143. Starboard wing fuel tank
144. Fuel filler point
145. Mainwheel leg mount/pivot
146. Mainwheel leg rib cut-outs
147. Main gear fairing doors
148. Auxiliary fuel tank (plastic/pressed-paper composition, 108 US gal/409 litres)
149. Auxiliary fuel tank (metal 75 US gal/ 284 litres)
150. 0.69m (27in) smooth-contour mainwheel
151. Axle fork
152. Towing lugs
153. Landing-gear fairing
154. Main-gear shock strut
155. Blast tubes
156. Wing front spar
157. Gun bay
158. Ammunition feed chutes
159. Ammunition boxes
160. Wing rear spar
161. Flap structure
162. Starboard aileron tab
163. Starboard aileron
164. Starboard aileron tab adjustment mechanism (ground setting)
165. Wing rib strengthening
166. Outboard section structure
167. Outer section single spar
168. Wingtip sub-assembly
169. Starboard navigation light
170. Detachable wingtip

LATE-WAR FIGHTERS

In performance tests, the P-51B reached a speed of 710 km/h (441mph) at 9100m (30,000ft); with drop tanks, it could achieve a combat radius of 1210km (750 mi) and so act as a bomber escort.

P-51B MUSTANG

Weight (maximum take-off): 5352kg (11,800lb)
Dimensions: Length: 9.83m (32ft 3in), Wingspan: 11.28m (37ft), Height: 4.16m (13ft 8in)
Powerplant: One 1200kW (1620hp) Packard V-1650-3 Merlin V-12 liquid-cooled piston engine
Maximum Speed: 708km/h (440mph)
Range (with external fuel tanks): 2655km (1650 miles)
Ceiling: 12,800m (42,000ft)
Crew: 1
Armament: Four 12.7mm (0.5in) Browning M2 machine guns fixed forward firing in wings; up to 908kg (2000lb) bomb load; modification in field to permit carriage of three rocket launch tubes under each wing

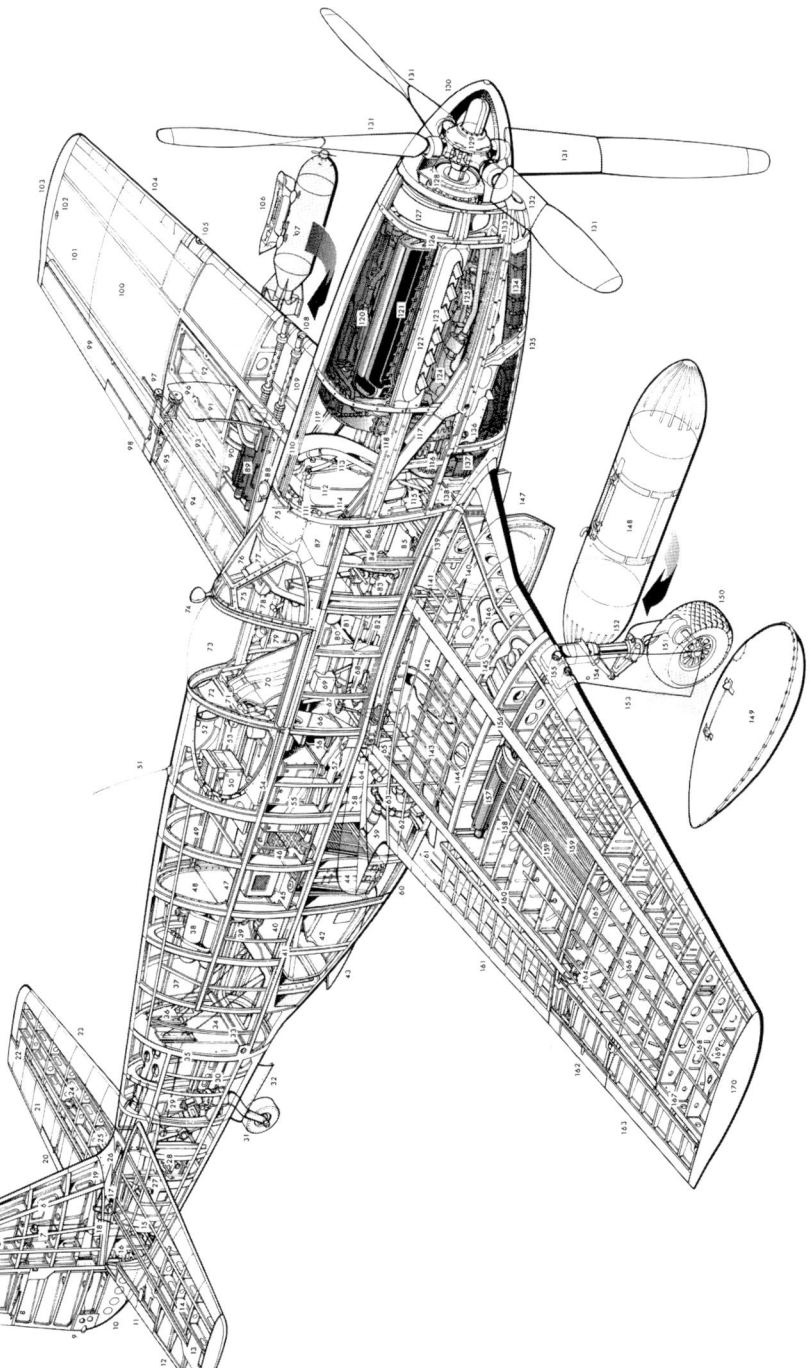

LATE-WAR FIGHTERS

Rapidly assembled variant

A condition of the export agreement for the Mustang stated that North American had to hand over two examples of the aircraft to the USAAC, free of charge, for official testing. These two aircraft were designated the XP-51 by the Air Corps and speculatively named 'Apache' by North American, though the Army would never adopt this name once it eventually ordered P-51s in quantity. Surprisingly, given the enormous success of the aircraft later in USAAF hands, the XP-51s languished unflown for several months at Wright Field.

After Pearl Harbor, interest in the XP-51 increased somewhat, especially with flight testing revealing the latent qualities of the aircraft. However, with immediate fighter requirements covered by aircraft already in production, North American discovered an unfilled contract for 500 dive bombers and quickly developed a Mustang variant optimized for dive bombing and ground attack. This variant featured a bomb shackle capable of carrying bombs up to 227kg (500lb) under each wing, along with dive brakes, fitted in the upper and lower wing skin, which kept the aircraft stable in a 402km/h (250mph) oblique dive.

This new Mustang was duly ordered by the USAAF in April 1942 and was designated A-36A by the time deliveries began in September. Enthusiastic reports filtering back from RAF Mustang pilots coupled with excellent flight test reports meant the P-51 could no longer be ignored, and the USAAF placed an order for 310 P-51As in June 1942.

Mediterranean action

Neither the P-51A nor the A-36 would be the first Mustang to see operational service with US forces, however, as the USAAF requisitioned 57 Mustang IAs ordered by the RAF and assigned them to the 12th Air Force in North Africa for tactical reconnaissance use. The IAs were fitted with two F-24 obliquely mounted cameras and officially designated F-6A – but usually referred to simply as the P-51. The first operational American P-51 sortie occurred on 9 April 1943, when Lt Alfred Schwab flew from Tunisia to perform an armed reconnaissance mission over the Mediterranean. The P-51s proved just as successful in this role as their RAF counterparts and continued in use as the Allied armies pushed into Italy in 1944.

Following the F-6A/P-51 into service was the A-36, again issued to the 12th Air Force. Too late to see action in Africa, the A-36s were operational from June 1943 and saw intensive action in the invasion of Sicily, subsequently covering the Salerno landings and supporting the Allied effort on the Italian mainland before re-equipping in mid-1944.

P-51A

Further development resulted in the P-51A, with gun armament reduced to four 12.7mm (0.5in) machine guns in the wings – although the wing could carry the same bomb load as the A-36A and was also plumbed to allow the use of external fuel tanks. Of the 310 produced, 50 went to the RAF as the Mustang Mk II (as part replacement for the 57 Mustang IAs requisitioned by the USAAF) and a further 35 were converted to F-6B standard with two oblique cameras. The F-6B was used in Europe to photograph the French coastline in preparation for the D-Day landings and would remain operational with the 9th Air Force until just before the end of the war.

The P-51A, however, was principally employed against Japanese forces, operating in concert with A-36As over the India-Burma border from the summer of 1943 onwards. In November, P-51As utilized drop tanks to provide long range escort to B-24s and B-25s performing raids in the Rangoon area, preceding the P-51's more famous long-range escort duties over Western Europe by two weeks. Meanwhile, the RAF used their Mustang IIs to supplement their earlier Mustangs in tactical reconnaissance work with the 2nd Tactical Air Force, remaining in service until VE day.

P-51B and P-51C

The Rolls-Royce built aircraft was the first to appear, designated the Mustang X. Performance was a mere 2km/h (1.5mph) less than forecast and a full 100km/h (61mph) faster than the best speed attainable by a standard Mustang I. Rate of climb was also nearly double that of the Allison-powered aircraft. Six weeks after the first flight of the Mustang X, the first XP-51B was completed by North American. This aircraft featured the supercharger intercooler and radiator in a deepened ventral scoop; a much more aerodynamically efficient solution than the nose mounting of the Rolls-Royce machine, and as a result, it was faster still, the production P-51B demonstrating a speed of 729km/h (453mph) at 8778m (28,800ft).

Although conversion of Mustang Is to Mustang Xs by Rolls-Royce was considered for a time, the adoption of large-scale production of the P-51B in the US obviated the need for such a scheme. Existing USAAF P-51 contracts were switched to cover P-51Bs, and such was the enthusiasm for the new Mustang that North American were instructed to establish a second production line at Dallas, Texas. Dallas-built aircraft were designated

LATE-WAR FIGHTERS

P-51B MUSTANG

Weight (maximum take-off): 5352kg (11,800lb)
Dimensions: Length: 9.83m (32ft 3in), Wingspan: 11.28m (37ft), Height: 4.16m (13ft 8in)
Powerplant: One 1200kW (1620hp) Packard V-1650-3 Merlin V-12 liquid-cooled piston engine
Maximum Speed: 708km/h (440mph)
Range (with external fuel tanks): 2655km (1650 miles)
Ceiling: 12,800m (42,000ft)
Crew: 1
Armament: Four 12.7mm (0.5in) Browning M2 machine guns fixed forward firing in wings; up to 908kg (2000lb) bomb load; modification in field to permit carriage of three rocket launch tubes under each wing

In performance tests, the P-51B reached a speed of 710 km/h (441mph) at 9100m (30,000ft); with drop tanks, it could achieve a combat radius of 1210km (750 mi) and so act as a bomber escort.

LATE-WAR FIGHTERS

Rapidly assembled variant

A condition of the export agreement for the Mustang stated that North American had to hand over two examples of the aircraft to the USAAC, free of charge, for official testing. These two aircraft were designated the XP-51 by the Air Corps and speculatively named 'Apache' by North American, though the Army would never adopt this name once it eventually ordered P-51s in quantity. Surprisingly, given the enormous success of the aircraft later in USAAF hands, the XP-51s languished unflown for several months at Wright Field.

After Pearl Harbor, interest in the XP-51 increased somewhat, especially with flight testing revealing the latent qualities of the aircraft. However, with immediate fighter requirements covered by aircraft already in production, North American discovered an unfilled contract for 500 dive bombers and quickly developed a Mustang variant optimized for dive bombing and ground attack. This variant featured a bomb shackle capable of carrying bombs up to 227kg (500lb) under each wing, along with dive brakes, fitted in the upper and lower wing skin, which kept the aircraft stable in a 402km/h (250mph) oblique dive.

This new Mustang was duly ordered by the USAAF in April 1942 and was designated A-36A by the time deliveries began in September. Enthusiastic reports filtering back from RAF Mustang pilots coupled with excellent flight test reports meant the P-51 could no longer be ignored, and the USAAF placed an order for 310 P-51As in June 1942.

Mediterranean action

Neither the P-51A nor the A-36 would be the first Mustang to see operational service with US forces, however, as the USAAF requisitioned 57 Mustang IAs ordered by the RAF and assigned them to the 12th Air Force in North Africa for tactical reconnaissance use. The IAs were fitted with two F-24 obliquely mounted cameras and officially designated F-6A – but usually referred to simply as the P-51. The first operational American P-51 sortie occurred on 9 April 1943, when Lt Alfred Schwab flew from Tunisia to perform an armed reconnaissance mission over the Mediterranean. The P-51s proved just as successful in this role as their RAF counterparts and continued in use as the Allied armies pushed into Italy in 1944.

Following the F-6A/P-51 into service was the A-36, again issued to the 12th Air Force. Too late to see action in Africa, the A-36s were operational from June 1943 and saw intensive action in the invasion of Sicily, subsequently covering the Salerno landings and supporting the Allied effort on the Italian mainland before re-equipping in mid-1944.

P-51A

Further development resulted in the P-51A, with gun armament reduced to four 12.7mm (0.5in) machine guns in the wings – although the wing could carry the same bomb load as the A-36A and was also plumbed to allow the use of external fuel tanks. Of the 310 produced, 50 went to the RAF as the Mustang Mk II (as part replacement for the 57 Mustang IAs requisitioned by the USAAF) and a further 35 were converted to F-6B standard with two oblique cameras. The F-6B was used in Europe to photograph the French coastline in preparation for the D-Day landings and would remain operational with the 9th Air Force until just before the end of the war.

The P-51A, however, was principally employed against Japanese forces, operating in concert with A-36As over the India-Burma border from the summer of 1943 onwards. In November, P-51As utilized drop tanks to provide long range escort to B-24s and B-25s performing raids in the Rangoon area, preceding the P-51's more famous long-range escort duties over Western Europe by two weeks. Meanwhile, the RAF used their Mustang IIs to supplement their earlier Mustangs in tactical reconnaissance work with the 2nd Tactical Air Force, remaining in service until VE day.

P-51B and P-51C

The Rolls-Royce built aircraft was the first to appear, designated the Mustang X. Performance was a mere 2km/h (1.5mph) less than forecast and a full 100km/h (61mph) faster than the best speed attainable by a standard Mustang I. Rate of climb was also nearly double that of the Allison-powered aircraft. Six weeks after the first flight of the Mustang X, the first XP-51B was completed by North American. This aircraft featured the supercharger intercooler and radiator in a deepened ventral scoop; a much more aerodynamically efficient solution than the nose mounting of the Rolls-Royce machine, and as a result, it was faster still, the production P-51B demonstrating a speed of 729km/h (453mph) at 8778m (28,800ft).

Although conversion of Mustang Is to Mustang Xs by Rolls-Royce was considered for a time, the adoption of large-scale production of the P-51B in the US obviated the need for such a scheme. Existing USAAF P-51 contracts were switched to cover P-51Bs, and such was the enthusiasm for the new Mustang that North American were instructed to establish a second production line at Dallas, Texas. Dallas-built aircraft were designated

LATE-WAR FIGHTERS

North American P-51C-10NT
Weight (maximum take-off): 5352kg (11,800lb)
Dimensions: Length: 9.83m (32ft 3in), Wingspan: 11.28m (37ft), Height: 4.16m (13ft 8in)
Powerplant: One 1200kW (1620hp) Packard V-1650-3 Merlin V-12 liquid-cooled piston engine
Maximum Speed: 708km/h (440mph)
Range (with external fuel tanks): 2655km (1650 miles)
Ceiling: 12,800m (42,000ft)
Crew: 1
Armament: Four 12.7mm (0.5in) Browning M2 machine guns fixed forward firing in wings; up to 908kg (2000lb) bomb load

North American P-51C
P-51C-10NT (42-103831) 'Ina the Macon Belle' was flown by Lt. Col. Lee Archer on bomber escort duty over Europe.

LATE-WAR FIGHTERS

North American P-51C
This P-51C (2103579) was piloted by Lt. Robert Curtis as part of the 2nd Fighter Squadron, 52nd Fighter Group, 15th Air Force.

North American P-51C
Lt. John E. Davenport's 'Lucky Leaky II' P-51C (42-103363) was assigned to the 504th Fighter Squadron, 339th Fighter Group, Eighth Air Force.

North American P-51C
Thsi P-51C (43-24981) was part of the 26th Fighter Squadron, 51st Fighter Group, Fourteenth Air Force, flying out of Kunming, China, December 1944.

LATE-WAR FIGHTERS

GLOWING CALCULATIONS

While the Allison-powered Mustang would prove to be an excellent low-level combat aircraft, the elevation of the P-51 to iconic levels of fame required a change of both engine and primary role. The first step in this process occurred in April 1942, just before the Mustang entered service with the RAF, when Ronnie Harker, a test pilot for Rolls-Royce, was offered the chance to fly a Mustang I at Duxford in Cambridgeshire. A 30-minute flight convinced Harker that the new aircraft was potentially outstanding and would obviously benefit from the installation of the Rolls-Royce Merlin – specifically the new Merlin 60-series, with its two-stage two-speed supercharger, which delivered high performance at altitudes unattainable by the Allison V-1710. Based on Harker's enthusiastic report, engineers at Rolls-Royce calculated a top speed of 695km/h (435mph) could be achieved at 7772m (25,500ft).

Such figures generated considerable enthusiasm for a Merlin Mustang, and Rolls-Royce were contracted to convert three Mustang Is to Merlin power. While Rolls-Royce were working on the conversions, the company took steps to interest the USAAF in such an aircraft. Thanks largely to the enthusiasm of the assistant military attaché in London, Lt. Col. Tommy Hitchcock, who had personal experience of the P-51 and its specific altitude shortcoming, the USAAF contracted with North American to re-engine two P-51s with Merlins.

While it is unlikely the Army Air Force would have accepted an aircraft powered by a British-built engine, as luck would have it, a Merlin production line had already been established at the Packard car company in Detroit to provide a local engine source for Canadian production of the Lancaster bomber. Consequently, the USAAF stood to obtain a new fighter of potentially outstanding performance without interfering in engine production for existing types.

North American P-51C

Weight (maximum take-off): 5352kg (11,800lb)
Dimensions: Length: 9.83m (32ft 3in), Wingspan: 11.28m (37ft), Height: 4.16m (13ft 8in)
Powerplant: One 1200kW (1620hp) Packard V-1650-3 Merlin V-12 liquid-cooled piston engine
Maximum Speed: 708km/h (440mph)
Range: 1900km (1180 miles)
Ceiling: 12,800m (42,000ft)
Crew: 1
Armament: Four 12.7mm (0.5in) Browning M2 machine guns fixed forward firing in wings; up to 908kg (2000lb) bomb load; modification in field to permit carriage of three rocket launch tubes under each wing

North American P-51C

This P-51C Mustang (42-103867), named 'Shimmy III', was flown by Lt. Col. Chester L. Sluder, the CO of the 325th Fighter Group at Lesina, Italy, June 1944.

P-51C despite differing in only minor details. Both types could carry a 454kg (1000lb) bomb under each wing or external fuel tanks, their fuel capacity being improved by the addition of a 322 litre (85 US gallon) fuselage tank on later production aircraft, with kits made available to retrofit the tank to existing aircraft. With drop tanks fitted, the Mustang offered a range comfortably in excess of that achievable by either the P-47 Thunderbolt or P-38 Lightning and was a more manoeuvrable aircraft than either of them.

Given the pressing need for escort fighters to support the Eighth Air Force's daylight bombing raids, it is somewhat surprising that the first deliveries of the P-51B were assigned instead to the 9th Air Force – a tactical force intended to provide direct support to ground forces in the upcoming invasion of France. This allocation demonstrates just how entrenched the perception of the P-51 as a low-level tactical combat aircraft had become. Despite this, the first P-51B squadrons of the 9th Air Force were used to support 8th Air Force operations pending delivery of their own Mustangs, with the first mission flown on 1 December 1943, when the 354th Fighter Group conducted a fighter sweep over the Belgian coast.

Bomber escort
Deliveries of new P-51Bs, meanwhile, continued to be made to the 9th Air Force, eventually resulting in the 8th AF releasing a P-47 fighter group to the 9th AF in January 1944 in exchange for a fighter group of the desperately needed Mustangs. Early 1944 saw Mustang deliveries greatly increase, and by late spring, nine P-47 and P-38 fighter groups, 21 squadrons, of the 8th Air Force had re-equipped with the P-51. A further five fighter groups would subsequently be formed on later Mustang models.

The early months of 1944 saw the first use of the P-51 as a bomber escort over Europe, though initially these operations were sporadic due to teething mechanical troubles. By 4 March, however, P-51s of the 354th and 4th Fighter Groups became the first Allied single-engine fighters to fly over Berlin. On this occasion, Mustangs claimed eight Luftwaffe fighters destroyed but 23 P-51s, P-47s and P-38s were lost in return. Despite continued mechanical problems leading to a relatively large proportion of P-51s aborting their missions, the tables swiftly turned on the German defenders. For example, the next raid on Berlin saw 81 Luftwaffe aircraft lost in exchange for 11 US fighters, and the P-51 formed the spearhead of the 8th Air Force's campaign to draw Luftwaffe fighters into combat and destroy them.

German fighter opposition declined as a direct result of the Mustang's service entry, allowing the P-51 units to roam away from the bomber formations to attack enemy ground targets of opportunity. At around the same time, four fighter groups re-equipped or were formed on the P-51 in Italy as part of the 15th Air Force, engaged in similar escort work as the 8th AF Mustangs and performing ground attack work as German aerial resistance lessened.

P-51D: teardrop canopy
Although immediately effective, the P-51 was not perfect. A major flaw was the limited visibility from the heavily framed cockpit canopy as originally fitted. As a result, a bulged clear-view Perspex canopy similar to that fitted to the Spitfire was developed by the British company Malcolm and fitted to hundreds of Mustangs in the UK. A better solution was introduced

---

North American P-51D
Weight (maximum take-off): 5493kg (12,100lb)
Dimensions: Length: 9.83m (32ft 3in), Wingspan: 11.28m (37ft), Height: 4.16m (13ft 8in)
Powerplant: One 1110kW (1490hp) Packard (Rolls-Royce) V-1650-7 Merlin 12-cylinder liquid-cooled piston engine
Maximum Speed: 703km/h (437mph)
Range (with external fuel tanks): 2655km (1650 miles)
Ceiling: 12,800m (42,000ft)
Crew: 1
Armament: Six 12.7mm (0.5in) Browning M2 machine guns fixed forward firing in wings; up to 908kg (2000lb) bomb load; later production aircraft fitted with provision for three rocket launch tubes under each wing

---

with the P-51D, which introduced a large teardrop-shaped clear canopy and cut down rear fuselage, allowing for 360-degree visibility. The P-51D became the most-produced P-51 variant of all, with 7956 being produced from both factories along with 1337 P-51Ks, which were identical save for being fitted with a different propeller. The P-51D was equipped with the same V-1650-7 Merlin engine as later production B and C models and was marginally slower than either. The loss of side area as a result of cutting down the rear fuselage also resulted in some directional instability, which led to the adoption of a dorsal fin fillet, a feature that could be retrofitted to earlier production P-51Ds and adopted to improve the handling of the P-51B and C.

P-51Ds began to supplement earlier models in Eighth Air Force units from June 1944 and would continue in service to the end of the war and beyond. P-51D variants also included 136 P-51Ds and 163 P-51Ks, modified for the photo reconnaissance duties as the F-6D and F-6K respectively, and 10 examples of the TP-51 trainer with

LATE-WAR FIGHTERS

North American P-51D
Nicknamed 'Passion Wagon', this P-51D Mustang (serial number 44-13691) served with the 364th Fighter Squadron, 357th Fighter Group.

North American P-51D
This P-51D (44-13859), from the 55th Fighter Squadron, 20th Fighter Group, displays 'A Nameless Beauty' nose artwork and was flown by Lt. Walter H. 'Moon' Mullins.

North American P-51D
This aircraft was assigned to 336th Fighter Squadron, 4th Fighter Group, Eighth Air Force and was the personal aircraft of Major Frederick W. Glover, CO of 336 FS.

LATE-WAR FIGHTERS

North American P-51D
This P-51D, named 'Bonnie B III', flew with the 353rd Fighter Squadron, 354th Fighter Group, Eighth Air Force.

tandem controls. Another P-51D was modified with a passenger seat to allow General Eisenhower to be flown over the battlefields after D-Day, but this did not feature dual controls.

Long-range missions

By the summer of 1944, the Mustang was ranging far and wide over Europe. In June 1944, a particularly striking example of its capability occurred when 70 aircraft escorted B-17s to attack a target near Berlin before flying on a distance of 3365km (1470 miles) with the bombers to land at airfields in the Soviet Union. From there, the Mustangs flew to Italy and flew escort missions with the 15th Air Force before returning to the UK two weeks later.

Such were the demands of the Eighth, Ninth and 15th Air Forces that the introduction of the Merlin Mustang in numbers to units fighting the Japanese only took place relatively late in the war, the first P-51Bs and Cs arriving in China in March 1944. P-51Ds were the initial Mustang variants operated from the Philippines in late 1944, and P-51Ds would begin escorting B-29s in the Pacific Operational Area in early 1945, continuing until VJ Day. Two P-51D-equipped fighter groups flew onto Iwo

This P-51 Mustang (44-13410), named 'Lou II', served with the 361st Fighter Group, Eighth Air Force.

LATE-WAR FIGHTERS

North American P-51D
This P-51D served with the 380th Fighter Squadron, 363rd Fighter Group, Ninth Air Force.

North American P-51D
Weight (maximum take-off): 5493kg (12,100lb)
Dimensions: Length: 9.83m (32ft 3in), Wingspan: 11.28m (37ft), Height: 4.16m (13ft 8in)
Powerplant: One 1110kW (1490hp) Packard (Rolls-Royce) V-1650-7 Merlin 12-cylinder liquid-cooled piston engine
Maximum Speed: 703km/h (437mph)
Range (with external fuel tanks): 2655km (1650 miles)
Ceiling: 12,800m (42,000ft)
Crew: 1
Armament: Six 12.7mm (0.5in) Browning M2 machine guns fixed forward firing in wings; up to 908kg (2000lb) bomb load; later production aircraft fitted with provision for three rocket launch tubes under each wing

Jima less than a month after the US invasion of that island and flew their first B-29 escort mission, to Tokyo, on 7 April 1945. Each Mustang carried a 625 litre (165 US gallon) drop tank under each wing, allowing them to make the 2540km (1580 miles) round trip. Escort missions to mainland Japanese targets required a flying time of seven to eight hours, almost entirely over water, and these missions would prove to be the longest regular escort missions undertaken during World War II and the ultimate wartime vindication of the Merlin engine and Mustang airframe combination.

In addition to US forces, the Merlin Mustang variants were also operated in large numbers by the RAF, the Mustang Mk III (designated as both P-51B and C by the British) entering service with 65 Squadron at the end of 1943. A further twelve squadrons were to equip on the type, and though some Mustang IIIs were utilized for tactical reconnaissance (as were the Mustang I and II before them), most were employed – like their US cousins – in escort duties, covering the increasing number of daylight raids being undertaken by RAF Bomber Command during 1944 and 1945. Some units attached to 2nd Tactical Air Force moved to France following D-Day, but those remaining in the UK were employed in the defence against V-1 flying bombs, accounting for 232 shot down. Towards the end of the war, the P-51D and K began to arrive in RAF units as the Mustang Mk IV, supplementing the Mustang IIIs already in service.

The only other wartime users were China, who took delivery of 50 P-51Ds, and Australia, who took 40 on charge – although these were actually operated by the Netherlands East Indies Air Force. Australia itself had selected the P-51D to produce under licence as the Commonwealth CA-17 Mustang Mk XX, the first of which flew in April 1945, although none had been delivered by VJ Day. By war's end, the Mustang had been credited with 6209 victories (in both US and British service), slightly fewer than the Supermarine Spitfire, though it should be noted that the Spitfire was in frontline service for around twice as long as the Mustang. The top-scoring Mustang pilot was Major George Preddy, who was credited with 23 victories in the P-51 and P-47.

XP-51F and G
Development of a higher performance Mustang model saw North American engage in an extensive weight reduction programme combined with aerodynamic improvements to the P-51D airframe. This work resulted in the XP-51F, which possessed a gross weight around one ton lighter than a standard P-51D, and the even lighter XP-51G, which utilized a British-built Rolls-Royce Merlin 145 and five-bladed Rotol propeller. Both demonstrated outstanding performance, but it was the XP-51F that was developed into

LATE-WAR FIGHTERS

North American P-51D Mustang
Li'l Butch was a P-51D of the 47th Fighter Squadron, 15th Fighter Group, Seventh Air Force, based at Iwo Jima in the Pacific in 1945. Prominent wing and fuselage bands, spinner and fin triangle were added to prevent confusion with Japanese aircraft.

Canopy
The pilot sat under an aft-sliding, blown 'bubble' canopy, which provided improved visibility compared to the standard canopy on the high-backed P-51B/C.

Intake
The liquid-cooled engine was provided with a belly-mounted radiator that was fed by this large ventral airscoop. The radiator's location made it vulnerable to ground fire.

LATE-WAR FIGHTERS

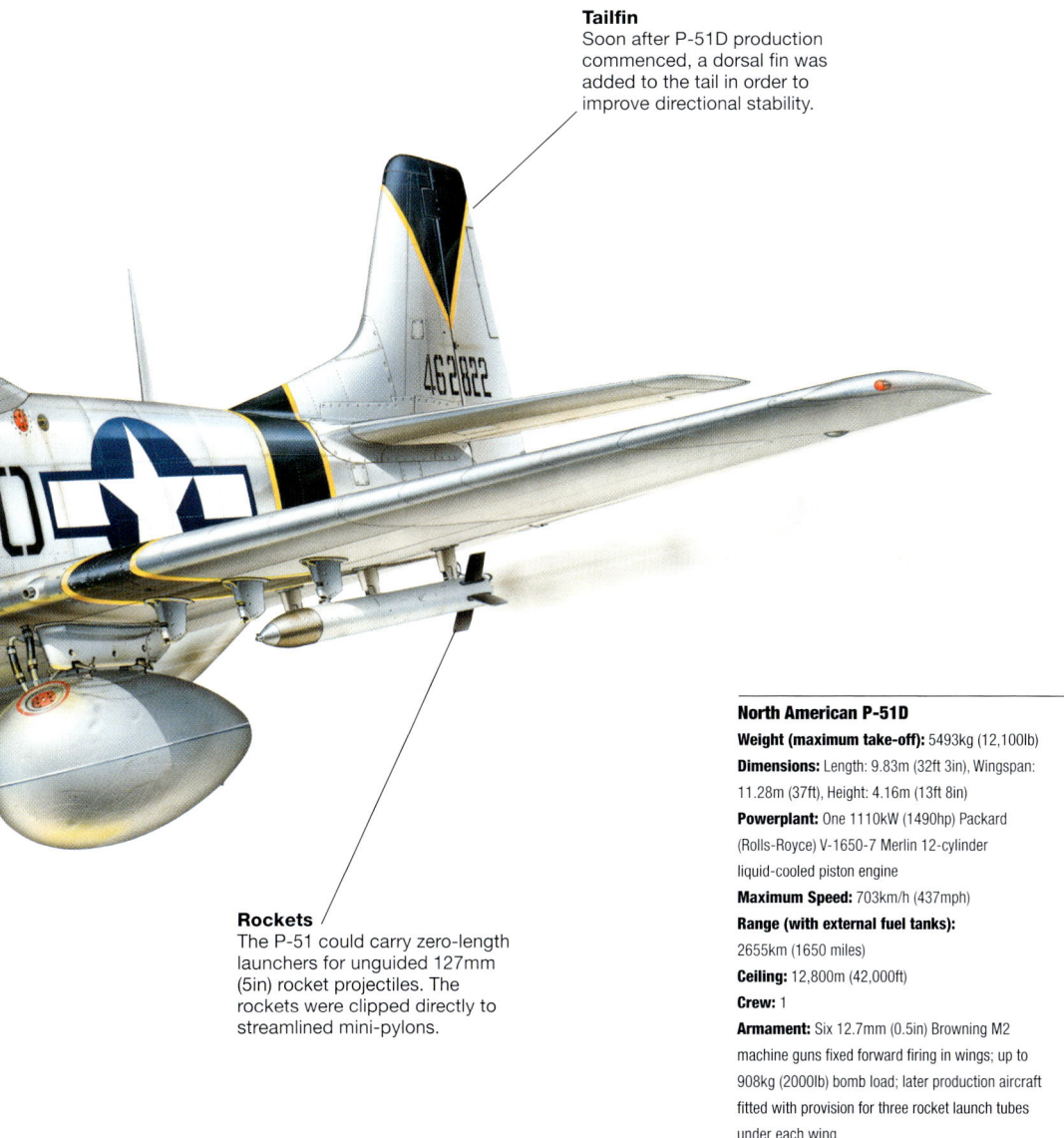

Tailfin
Soon after P-51D production commenced, a dorsal fin was added to the tail in order to improve directional stability.

Rockets
The P-51 could carry zero-length launchers for unguided 127mm (5in) rocket projectiles. The rockets were clipped directly to streamlined mini-pylons.

North American P-51D
Weight (maximum take-off): 5493kg (12,100lb)
Dimensions: Length: 9.83m (32ft 3in), Wingspan: 11.28m (37ft), Height: 4.16m (13ft 8in)
Powerplant: One 1110kW (1490hp) Packard (Rolls-Royce) V-1650-7 Merlin 12-cylinder liquid-cooled piston engine
Maximum Speed: 703km/h (437mph)
Range (with external fuel tanks): 2655km (1650 miles)
Ceiling: 12,800m (42,000ft)
Crew: 1
Armament: Six 12.7mm (0.5in) Browning M2 machine guns fixed forward firing in wings; up to 908kg (2000lb) bomb load; later production aircraft fitted with provision for three rocket launch tubes under each wing

LATE-WAR FIGHTERS

North American P-51D
P-51D-25-NT 'Glamorous Glen III' flew with the 362nd Fighter Squadron, 357th Fighter Group, Eighth Air Force.

the P-51H production model, capable of a blistering 783km/h (487mph) at 7620m (25,000ft). 555 P-51Hs had been delivered by VJ Day but were still being deployed when the war ended, and none saw operational use.

Similarly, the remarkable twin-engine P-82 'Twin Mustang', consisting of two lengthened P-51H fuselages joined by a new wing centre section, was still undergoing flight testing at the end of the conflict, though this aircraft would eventually see service as a night fighter during the Korean War.

Post-war service
The P-51D also saw extensive use in Korea as a ground-attack aircraft, suffering heavy losses, especially to ground fire. Post-war service of the Mustang was extremely widespread, with over 25 nations eventually operating the type, mostly in P-51D guise. The US Air National Guard used the P-51D until 1957, and it was used as a chase plane for test work for at least another 11 years.

The final air-to-air combat involving the Mustang took place during the so-called Football War between Honduras and El Salvador in 1969, when a Honduran F4U-5 Corsair shot down a Salvadorean Mustang. The Dominican Republic only retired their P-51Ds in 1984, a mere 42 years after the aircraft entered service with the RAF.

Today, around 170 Mustangs survive in airworthy condition. Several are used for air-racing – in 2017, the modified P-51D 'Voodoo' achieved the highest speed ever officially recorded by a piston engine aircraft in level flight at 855.41km/h (531.53mph).

North American P-51K
Weight (maximum take-off): 5493kg (12,100lb)
Dimensions: Length: 9.83m (32ft 3in), Wingspan: 11.28m (37ft), Height: 4.16m (13ft 8in)
Powerplant: One 1110kW (1490hp) Packard (Rolls-Royce) V-1650-7 Merlin 12-cylinder liquid-cooled piston engine
Maximum Speed: 703km/h (437mph)
Range (with external fuel tanks): 2655km (1650 miles)
Ceiling: 12,800m (42,000ft)
Crew: 1
Armament: Six 12.7mm (0.5in) Browning M2 machine guns fixed forward firing in wings; up to 908kg (2000lb) bomb load; later production aircraft fitted with provision for three rocket launch tubes under each wing

North American P-51K
Nicknamed 'Prince Jocelyn', this P-51K flew with the 359th Fighter Squadron, 356th Fighter Group, stationed at Martlesham Heath, UK, early 1945.

Republic P-47 Thunderbolt

The largest and heaviest single-engine fighter to see service during World War II, the massive Thunderbolt was somewhat sidelined in the popular imagination by the P-51. However, the P-47 was a more versatile fighter, and later models proved both faster and longer-ranged than the Mustang.

The P-47 ultimately derived from a three-seat amphibian produced by Alexander de Seversky and his designer (and fellow Georgian) Alexander Kartveli in the early 1930s. Developed first into the P-35 and then the P-43 Lancer, Kartveli then sought to design a more combat-worthy fighter than the latter aircraft. A modified P-43 with a more powerful Pratt & Whitney R-2180-1 Twin Hornet engine was ordered into production by the USAAC as the P-44 'Rocket', but reports coming in from Europe suggested that this would be inferior to contemporary European designs. Kartveli also developed a lightweight fighter to be powered by the V-12 Allison V-1710 engine. Confusingly designated the P-47A Thunderbolt, it too was deemed wanting before construction began. Instead, Kartveli reworked the unbuilt P-44 design with the Pratt & Whitney R-2800 Double Wasp, an engine that promised performance in the 1492kW (2000hp) class, and in this form, construction of a prototype went ahead as the XP-47B, a design completely unrelated to the P-47A.

Maiden flight

The XP-47B flew for the first time on 6 May 1941. Superficially resembling the earlier P-43, the new fighter was some 65 per cent heavier, and possessed a span and length around 2m (6ft 6in)

Predecessor to the Thunderbolt, the P-43 Lancer high altitude fighter conducted its final Army tests at Floyd Bennett Field, attaining sub-stratosphere altitudes on test flights.

LATE-WAR FIGHTERS

Republic P-47B
This aircraft (43-25429) was part of the 19th Fighter Squadron, 218th Fighter Group, flying over Saipan in July 1944.

greater than the Lancer. The installed armament of eight 12.7mm (0.5in) machine guns, all in the wings, was considerably heavier than the norm for contemporary USAAC fighters. From the start, the aircraft was protected with self-sealing fuel tanks and armour. The higher-than-expected altitudes at which fighter combat was taking place over Europe had also been noted, and the P-47 utilized a General Electric turbo supercharger in the rear fuselage to help the engine maintain an adequate power output at height.

The earlier P-43 had also featured a turbo supercharger, but Kartveli schemed a far neater installation in the P-47, the complication of long ducting being accepted to allow the unit to be installed in its ideal position, in terms of the centre of gravity, in the rear fuselage, some 6.7m (22ft) from the propeller. To function, exhaust gases from the engine were collected

Unlike the P-51, the P-47 was easily maintained and more forgiving of pilot mistakes, due to its more robust construction.

Republic P-47B
Weight (maximum take-off): 6060kg (13,360lb)
Dimensions: Length: 10.74m (35ft 3in), Wingspan: 12.43m (40ft 9in), Height: 4.31m (14ft 2in)
Powerplant: One 1,500kW (2,000hp) Pratt & Whitney R-2800-21 18-cylinder air-cooled radial piston engine
Speed: 690km/h (429mph)
Range: 885km (550 miles)
Ceiling: 13,000m (42,000ft)
Crew: One
Armament: Eight 12.7mm (0.5in) M2 Browning machine guns in wings

LATE-WAR FIGHTERS

in two rings, one for the left-hand cylinders and the other for the right, then allowed to pass down a duct along each side of the lower fuselage to drive the turbine powering the supercharger. Air for supercharging was taken from an intake in the cowling directly below the engine and blown by the propeller down a duct in the bottom of the fuselage before dividing. Some of the air would then go into the supercharger to be compressed, while the rest passed over an intercooler, which served to cool the compressed air, before it was taken forward along ducts in the fuselage sides to be fed into the carburettor. Exhaust gases, after passing through the turbine, were ejected from a ventral outlet near the tail, and two adjustable doors in the fuselage sides just in front of the unit controlled the flow of cooling air through the intercooler. The system was undoubtedly complicated but worked extremely well and would later prove to be surprisingly resistant to combat damage.

The P-47B was the first American fighter to be fitted with a four-blade propeller and to provide necessary clearance for the propeller, whilst allowing the undercarriage to be contained within the optimum-sized wing, the main undercarriage legs arranged to shorten 23cm (9in) as they retracted. Even though it was fitted with a prototype R-2800 engine that did not develop the designed power, the performance of the XP-47B was impressive, eventually achieving a top speed of 663km/h (412mph) at 7864m (25,800ft) and flight testing proceeded remarkably smoothly.

P-47B and P-47C

The prototype Thunderbolt was lost on 8 August 1942, but by this time, serial production P-47s were rolling off the assembly line, the first being the P-47B, of which 171 were constructed. Differing from the prototype in detail, the most obvious change from the XP-47B was the substitution of its side opening car-type door for a more conventional sliding hood. With production aircraft fitted with R-2800 engines delivering their rated 1491kW (2000hp) at 8473m (27,800ft), the P-47B was capable of 690km/h (429mph), although performance fell off markedly at lower levels, where the turbo supercharger was less effective – the P-47B was only capable of 547km/h (340mph) at 1525m (5000ft). None of the P-47Bs would see operational service, all being retained in the US for training purposes.

However, in September 1942, production of the P-47C began – the first Thunderbolt model to see combat and to be built in reasonably large numbers, with 602 examples rolling off the production line. The P-47C differed from the P-47B primarily in its 20cm (8in) forward fuselage extension, moving the centre of gravity forward and improving flying characteristics.

This modification also allowed for an under-fuselage shackle to be fitted for an external drop tank. Later P-47Cs also received the R-2800-59 engine with water injection, the extra space afforded by the fuselage extension providing room for the 114 litre (30 US gallon) tank

Republic P-47C
Weight (maximum take-off): 6770kg (14,925lb)
Dimensions: Length: 10.99m (36ft 1in), Wingspan: 12.43m (40ft 9in), Height: 3.86m (12ft 8in)
Powerplant: One 1500kW (2000hp) Pratt & Whitney R-2800-21 18-cylinder air-cooled radial piston engine
Speed: 697km/h (433mph)
Range: 1030km (640 miles)
Ceiling: 13,000m (42,000ft)
Crew: One
Armament: Eight 12.7mm (0.5in) M2 Browning machine guns in wings; up to 227kg (500lb)

Republic P-47C
This P-47C was part of the 334th Fighter Squadron, 4th Fighter Group, based in Debden, UK, March 1943.

LATE-WAR FIGHTERS

Republic P-47D
P-47D-25 (42-26459) was part of 352nd Fighter Squadron, 353rd Fighter Group, flying from Raydon, Suffolk, England, in July 1944.

required for the water injection system. The P-47B may be distinguished from later P-47 models by its angled forward radio mast, later aircraft being fitted with a vertical mast.

First deployment

Crated P-47Cs were shipped overseas towards the end of 1942, with the first example arriving in a British port on 20 December 1942. The first Thunderbolt unit, the 4th Fighter Group of the Eighth Air Force, began to receive its new aircraft in January 1943, but teething troubles delayed the first operations of the Thunderbolt until 10 March, when 14 aircraft flew an offensive sweep over France. This debut mission revealed that inadequate electrical suppression rendered the P-47's radio inoperative; another month would elapse before further sorties were undertaken.

Early operations and training saw several aircraft lost to mechanical failure and crashes before contact had ever been made with enemy aircraft, and on 13 April, a P-47 ditching at sea due to engine failure was fired upon by a British Anti-Aircraft battery in the belief it was a Focke-Wulf Fw 190, the only other radial engine fighter operating over Western Europe at the time. Fears that further P-47s might be lost in the same way resulted in the application of recognition markings in the form of white stripes across the tail surfaces and a white ring around the nose cowling. Two days later, P-47s encountered Luftwaffe planes for the first time when aircraft of the 355th Fighter Squadron claimed the destruction of three Fw 190s.

By early May, the P-47C had flown its first bomber escort mission, protecting a B-17 raid on Antwerp, and by the end of the month, the P-47 had accounted for 10 enemy aircraft destroyed, plus seven probables and 18 damaged for the loss of 18 Thunderbolts, five of which were known to be due to engine failure.

P-47D

Early Thunderbolt operations were primarily hampered by the aircraft's lack of range, severely limiting its usefulness as a bomber escort, as most targets were beyond the P-47's combat radius. The P-47C featured provision for an external fuel tank, intended to increase the aircraft's ferry range and not expected to be used for combat operations, and work was undertaken on both sides of the Atlantic to utilize this feature. At the same time, a new P-47 model, the P-47D, was arriving in the UK to supplement the P-47Cs already in service. Initially, the P-47D differed little from its immediate predecessor, with changes centring on small improvements to the turbo supercharger and its associated intakes and vents. An engine change to the R-2800-59 featuring a different electrical system along with water injection improved power output, and therefore speed, at altitude. Increasing orders from the USAAF saw Republic build a new factory at Evansville, Indiana for P-47 construction, and Curtiss was subcontracted to produce P-47s at their factory in Buffalo, New York.

Curtiss-built aircraft were virtually identical to the standard P-47B but were designated P-47G. Two P-47Gs were converted as TP-47G trainers with an extra seat for the pupil in front of the standard cockpit, but no further production was undertaken.

This photograph shows a P-47 loaded with five of the 127mm (5in) HVAR unguided rockets that the type could carry under each wing.

LATE-WAR FIGHTERS

Half-filled British tanks

The first supplies of the 757 litre (200 US Gallon) ferry tank arrived in Britain during June of 1943, and although the tank could not be used at operational altitudes – being made of resin-impregnated paper, which failed at around 7000m (23,000ft) – P-47s utilized a half-filled tank, which the aircraft used to climb to operational altitude before switching to internal fuel. This allowed the P-47s to fly around 48km (30 miles) further than before and led to several instances of Thunderbolts surprising German fighters that believed themselves out of range. On 30 July 1943, for example, the 78th Fighter Group used the tanks to reach the German border and claimed 16 victories in the ensuing clashes with the Luftwaffe. This action saw Captain Charles P. Loudon shoot down two aircraft to become the first Eighth Air Force pilot to achieve 'ace' status with five aerial victories.

From the summer of 1943 onwards, Thunderbolts played an increasingly important role in Eighth Air Force operations, and a further seven P-47D-equipped fighter groups were operational before the end of the year. Efforts to replace the extemporized ferry tank came to fruition during 1943, with two new drop tanks coming into use: a 284 litre (75 US gallon) tank from the US and a larger 409 litre (108 US gallon) British-made tank. Both of these tanks were made of metal, although P-47s used considerable numbers of a similar paper tank, originally developed for the Hawker Hurricane, as an interim measure until enough of the new tanks were available.

Ground attack role

The year 1943 also saw the first usage of the P-47 in the role that would eventually become its primary mission: ground attack. Individual pilots had strafed ground targets of opportunity on an ad hoc basis while returning from escort duty throughout early 1943, but the first coordinated use of the P-47 as a fighter bomber occurred on 25 November, when 16 Thunderbolts of the 351st Fighter Squadron utilized a shallow angle dive bombing technique to attack the airfield at St. Omer, France, each carrying a single 227kg (500lb) bomb on the centreline rack.

An Eighth Air Force P-47 Thunderbolt attacks a water tower somewhere in France, 1944.

LATE-WAR FIGHTERS

Republican P-47D
Here is a USAAF machine with post-Normandy stripes, from 513th Fighter Squadron, 406th Fighter Group, RAF Ashford (Advanced Landing Ground AAF-417), August 1944.

Republican P-47D
This P-47D served with the 336th Fighter Squadron, 358th Fighter Group, flying from Toul, France, in late 1944. It carries the orange tail markings of the 1st Tactical Air Force.

The provision for carrying a bomb instead of the fuel tank was added to mid-production P-47Ds, and later production blocks featured wing racks that allowed one 454kg (1000lb) bomb under each wing or two 568 litre (150 US gallon) drop tanks, these racks subsequently being retrofitted to many earlier P-47Ds and Cs.

Another major change was the adoption of a clear view 'bubble' canopy and cut down rear fuselage, following the example of the British Hawker Typhoon, which was fitted on two trial airframes designated the XP-47K and XP-47L, the latter aircraft also featuring a fuselage fuel tank of greater capacity. When the bubble canopy and larger fuel tank were introduced onto production aircraft, however, there was no designation change; bubble canopy aircraft were P-47Ds, just like the earlier 'razorback' Thunderbolts.

With the P-47 being successfully introduced to service in Europe, Republic engaged in efforts to improve upon the basic aircraft. The XP-47E was fitted with a pressurized cockpit, but the P-47's increasing usage at lower levels saw development of

Republic P-47D
Weight (maximum take-off): 7938kg (17,500lb)
Dimensions: Length: 10.99m (36ft 1in), Wingspan: 12.43m (40ft 9in), Height: 4.44m (14ft 7in)
Powerplant: One 1,500kW (2000hp) Pratt & Whitney R-2800-59 18-cylinder air-cooled radial piston engine
Maximum Speed: 686km/h (426mph)
Range (with external fuel tanks): 1660km (1030 miles)
Ceiling: 13,000m (42,000ft)
Crew: 1
Armament: Eight 12.7mm (0.5in) M2 Browning machine guns; up to 1100kg (2500lb) of bombs or six zero-length rockets under wings with drop tanks or 10 rockets without drop tanks

LATE-WAR FIGHTERS

Republic P-47D Thunderbolt

A P-47D Thunderbolt of the 56th Fighter Group, based at Boxted, England, in 1944. Pilot David C. Schilling flew 132 combat missions with the 56th and scored 22.5 kills.

Engine
The P-47 was powered by the reliable Pratt & Whitney R-2800 series Double Wasp. This was an 18-cylinder radial air-cooled unit. In the P-47D-25 as illustrated this was an R-2800-21 or -59 with a new water-injection system and an improved turbo-supercharger.

Rockets
127mm (5in) M8 unguided rockets were launched from triple-round tube launchers underwing and were capable of knocking out heavily armoured German Tiger and Panther tanks.

LATE-WAR FIGHTERS

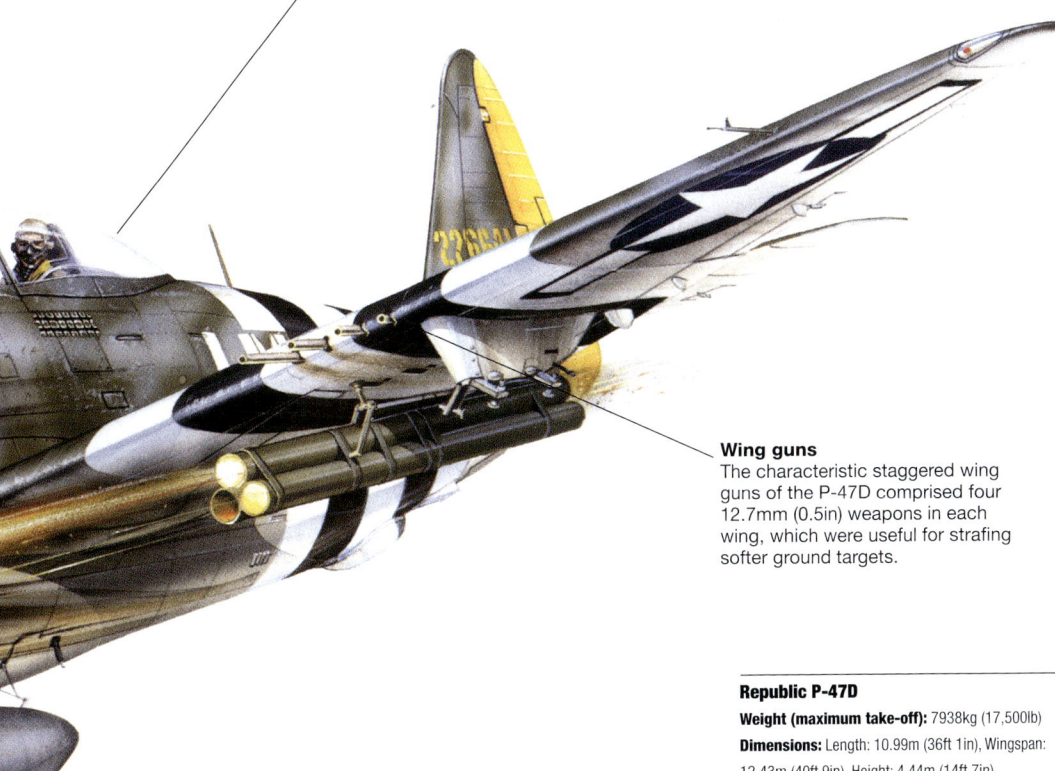

Bubble canopy
The Block 25 P-47D introduced a bubble cockpit canopy as standard. As a result, the pilot's all-round vision was much improved compared to that found on the earlier 'razorback' models.

Wing guns
The characteristic staggered wing guns of the P-47D comprised four 12.7mm (0.5in) weapons in each wing, which were useful for strafing softer ground targets.

Fuel tanks
The main fuel tank in the centre section held 776 litres (205 US gal), and this could be augmented by a drop tank under the centreline carrying a further 284 litres (75 US gal).

Republic P-47D
Weight (maximum take-off): 7938kg (17,500lb)
Dimensions: Length: 10.99m (36ft 1in), Wingspan: 12.43m (40ft 9in), Height: 4.44m (14ft 7in)
Powerplant: One 1500kW (2000hp) Pratt & Whitney R-2800-59 18-cylinder air-cooled radial piston engine
Maximum Speed: 686km/h (426mph)
Range (with external fuel tanks): 1660km (1030 miles)
Ceiling: 13,000m (42,000ft)
Crew: 1
Armament: Eight 12.7mm (0.5in) M2 Browning machine guns; up to 1100kg (2500lb) of bombs or six zero-length rockets under wings with drop tanks or 10 rockets without drop tanks

LATE-WAR FIGHTERS

this variant abandoned. The XP-47F featured a new laminar flow wing, but the single aircraft crashed, and further development was abandoned.

The P-47 was also used to flight test a new inverted V-16 engine designed by Chrysler, the XI-2220, which promised to generate 1864kW (2500hp) but boasted a remarkably small frontal area. The XP-47H, as the XI-2220-engined aircraft was designated, was an astounding looking aircraft with considerable potential, but the airframe modifications required were extensive, and the first flight by an XP-47H only took place in July 1945. By then, the USAAF was utterly fixated on jet power, and the performance of the XP-47H was of largely academic interest, though a second XP-47H was built and briefly tested after the war.

Fighter-bomber

Over the course of 1944, escort duties over Europe were taken over by the P-51 Mustang, and by the end of the year, only one of the Eighth Air Force's fighter groups was still flying the Thunderbolt. Over the same period, the P-47D had become the USAAF's most important fighter-bomber, a task at which the aircraft proved exceptionally well suited due to its impressive load-carrying ability and incredible resistance to battle damage.

By May 1944, the Ninth Air Force could deploy 13 P-47 fighter groups for tactical ground attack missions, ranging across occupied Europe to destroy

Republic P-47D
Weight (maximum take-off): 7938kg (17,500lb)
Dimensions: Length: 10.99m (36ft 1in), Wingspan: 12.43m (40ft 9in), Height: 4.44m (14ft 7in)
Powerplant: One 1500kW (2000hp) Pratt & Whitney R-2800-59 18-cylinder air-cooled radial piston engine
Maximum Speed: 686km/h (426mph)
Range (with external fuel tanks): 1660km (1030 miles)
Ceiling: 13,000m (42,000ft)
Crew: 1
Armament: Eight 12.7mm (0.5in) M2 Browning machine guns; up to 1100kg (2500lb) of bombs or six zero-length rockets under wings with drop tanks or 10 rockets without drop tanks

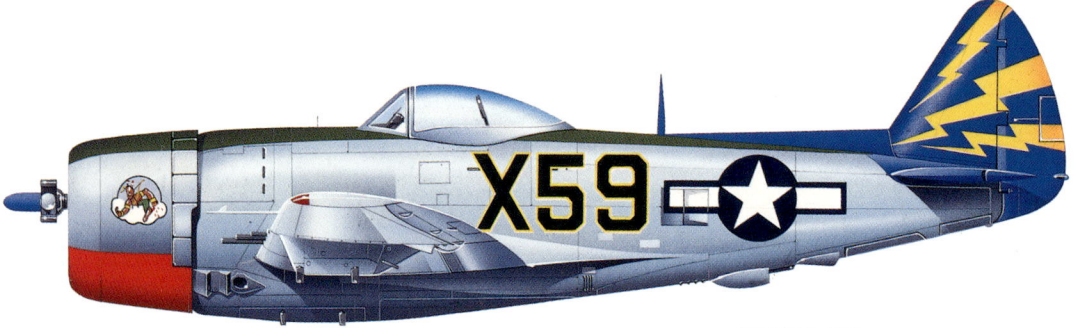

Republic P-47D
This aircraft flew with the 86th Fighter Squadron, 79th Fighter Group, in Fano, Italy, February 1945.

Republic P-47D
P-57M-1 (44-21118) was part of the 63rd Fighter Squadron, 56th Fighter Group, based in Boxted, Essex, England, in early 1945.

LATE-WAR FIGHTERS

Production versions of the optimized P-47N could be distinguished by their underwing rocket launch stubs, clipped wings and dorsal fin fillet with antennae.

trains, airfields, parked aircraft and countless other targets. The lethality of these aircraft was enhanced by the adoption of rocket armament – six or ten of these weapons were carried depending on whether bombs or drop tanks were carried on the underwing racks. The 15th and 12th Air Forces also operated large numbers of P-47s in the Mediterranean theatre, aircraft of the 57th Fighter Group of the Twelfth Air Force, based on Corsica, garnering some fame by featuring in the William Wyler documentary film *Thunderbolt!* depicting ground-attack operations over Italy.

USAAF units in the Pacific also received Thunderbolts, the first being the 348th Fighter Group of the Fifth Air Force in New Guinea, which began operations in July 1943 and was subsequently joined by further P-47 units. The Fifth Air Force managed to obtain a combat radius of 1344km (835 miles) with their P-47Ds by utilizing three drop tanks apiece, and in this way, were able to perform fighter sweeps over Borneo in advance of B-24 raids on the oil refineries at Balikpapan. Like other Thunderbolt units, those attached to the Fifth Air Force saw their role switched primarily to ground attack from January 1945 onwards. In June 1944, in the Central Pacific, P-47Ds of the 318th Fighter Group successfully flew off two aircraft carriers to operate from Saipan a matter of days after US troops landed on the island.

SUPERBOLT

The XP-47J 'Superbolt' was a lightweight version of the P-47 with an improved engine installation. The XP-47J achieved a speed of 805km/h (505mph) on 5 August 1944, the fastest known speed attained by any piston-engined aircraft in level flight during World War II. Though production of this version was briefly considered, the major delay that would be caused by the extensive changes to the P-47 airframe was considered unacceptable. Even better performance estimates for a more powerful Thunderbolt derivative, the 2237kW (3000hp) R-4360-powered XP-72, saw attention switch to the latter aircraft. Two XP-72 prototypes were subsequently built, and though they demonstrated excellent performance, the USAF believed the future lay with jets, and no production occurred.

Thunderbolts also saw action in the China-Burma-India (CBI) theatre, with four P-47 fighter groups based in Burma and one based in China. The CBI theatre was also where all Thunderbolt-equipped RAF squadrons were based. Britain became the second-largest P-47 operator after receiving 240 'razorback' and 590 bubble canopy lend-lease P-47Ds designated Thunderbolt Mk I and Mk II respectively. P-47s eventually

LATE-WAR FIGHTERS

equipped 11 RAF squadrons, replacing Hawker Hurricane Mk IIs, and operated primarily as fighter-bombers from May 1944 onwards, seeing intensive action until the end of the war.

Other nations

In addition to Britain, four other nations were to fly the P-47 in combat during the war, France, Brazil, Mexico and the Soviet Union.

France received 446 P-47Ds, with the first unit converting to the type in August 1943 and initially operating under US Twelfth Air Force control. By the time the French Thunderbolts covered the landings in Southern France in August 1944, four Groupes de Chasse were flying the P-47, later forming part of the French-commanded 1st Tactical Air Force (Provisional).

Thunderbolt II

An RAF Thunderbolt II from 261 Squadron, based at Wangjing at the end of 1944, while conducting missions in support of the Burma campaign. It wears the two-tone blue roundels of South East Asia Command, along with blue identification stripes on the fin, wings and tailplanes. It also features a repetition of its serial on its fin, which was not uncommon for these aircraft.

and being joined by a further two Thunderbolt groups. These were very active in the last few months of the war, performing ground attack missions in support of the advancing Allied armies, and the P-47 would persist in French service after the war long enough to fight against insurgents in Algeria.

As with the French, Brazilian Thunderbolts would also operate as part of the Twelfth Air Force, contributing one squadron to the fighting in Italy which saw considerable action. Brazil received 88 P-47Ds through lend-lease channels.

Two-hundred-and-three P-47s were allocated to the USSR, 196 of which were received, and all but one of which were bubble-canopy P-47Ds.

By contrast, Mexico contributed to the Allied war effort in the Pacific: a single squadron fought as part of the 58th Fighter Group in the Philippines with the Fifth Air Force. On the Eastern Front, the Soviets initially made little use of the Thunderbolt, regarding it as little better than the MiG-3 with disappointing manoeuvrability and poor acceleration at low and medium altitude. The Soviet Navy, however, utilized the P-47 from the winter of 1944 as an anti-shipping

aircraft, employing dive-bombing and masthead altitude attacks.

Final models

Some of the primary targets of P-47 fighter-bombers in the latter half of 1944 were V-1 launching sites, and it was the V-1 that inspired one of the final two P-47 models to see action. The P-47M utilized some of the developmental work that had gone into the XP-47J to produce high speed at low altitude to combat the flying bombs, which typically flew at around 550 km/h (340 mph) and at an altitude of 1000m (3300ft) – 1200m (3900ft).

Thunderbolt II

Weight (maximum take-off): 7938kg (17,500lb)
Dimensions: Length: 10.99m (36ft 1in), Wingspan: 12.43m (40ft 9in), Height: 4.44m (14ft 7in)
Powerplant: One 1,500kW (2000hp) Pratt & Whitney R-2800-59 18-cylinder air-cooled radial piston engine
Maximum Speed: 686km/h (426mph)
Range (with external fuel tanks): 1660km (1030 miles)
Ceiling: 13,000m (42,000ft)
Crew: 1
Armament: Eight 12.7mm (0.5in) M2 Browning machine guns; up to 1100kg (2500lb) of bombs or six zero-length rockets under wings with drop tanks or 10 rockets without drop tanks

---

LATE-WAR FIGHTERS

Republic P-47D

Weight (maximum take-off): 7938kg (17,500lb)
Dimensions: Length: 10.99m (36ft 1in), Wingspan: 12.43m (40ft 9in), Height: 4.44m (14ft 7in)
Powerplant: One 1500kW (2000hp) Pratt & Whitney R-2800-59 18-cylinder air-cooled radial piston engine
Maximum Speed: 686km/h (426mph)
Range (with external fuel tanks): 1660km (1030 miles)
Ceiling: 13,000m (42,000ft)
Crew: 1
Armament: Eight 12.7mm (0.5in) M2 Browning machine guns; up to 1100kg (2500lb) of bombs or six zero-length rockets under wings with drop tanks or 10 rockets without drop tanks

Republic P-47D

A Brazilian machine from 1º Grupo de Aviação de Caça subordinated to the USAAF 350th Fighter Group at Liverno, Italy, in late 1944. It was the mount of Captain Newton Lagares da Silva, the squadron's operations officer.

Production P-47Ms, of which only 130 were built, started to arrive in Britain by the end of 1944, by which time the V-1 attacks were largely over, and teething troubles kept the aircraft from effectively mounting operations before the end of the conflict.

P-47N

Rather more successful was the P-47N, which featured an all-new wing of greater area and was intended as an escort fighter for the B-29 in the Pacific, where a much greater range was required. The P-47N, with one under fuselage and two underwing drop tanks, carried the colossal fuel load of 4792 litres (1266 US gallons), giving it a maximum range of some 3781km (2350 miles). Using the same R2800-57 engine as the P-47M, generating a war emergency power output of 2088kW (2800hp), the P-47N could achieve 740km/h (460mph), a superior performance to the much-vaunted P-51D Mustang, and was arguably the finest fighter aircraft to see meaningful service with US forces during the war.

However, the P-47N entered service only in April 1945, by which time US forces had captured the island of Ie Shima, off the coast of Okinawa, merely 523km (325 miles) from the Japanese mainland. As a result, the P-47N saw most operational usage as a fighter-bomber attacking targets across Southern Japan, although a handful of B-29 escort missions were flown before VJ-Day.

During a fighter sweep over Korea, P-47N pilot Lt. Oscar F. Perdomo managed to shoot down five Japanese aircraft to become an 'instant ace', at the same time becoming the last American to achieve ace status during Wolrd War II, just two days before the Japanese surrender. 1816 P-47Ns were built, with orders for a further 5934 aircraft being cancelled after VJ-Day.

A total of 15,636 Thunderbolts of all models was built, making it the most-produced American fighter of all time, and it is credited with 3795 aerial victories – second only to the P-51 among USAAF fighter types. That said, it destroyed considerably more ground targets than the Mustang. For example, around 9000 locomotives and 6000 armoured fighting vehicles were claimed destroyed between D-Day and VE-Day in Europe alone. Arguably, the P-47 became the most versatile single-engined combat aircraft of the war.

LATE-WAR FIGHTERS

P-47D Thunderbolt

CUTAWAY KEY

1. Rudder upper hinge
2. Aerial attachment
3. Fin flanged ribs
4. Rudder post/fin aft spar
5. Fin front spar
6. Rudder trim tab worm and screw actuating mechanism (chain-driven)
7. Rudder centre hinge
8. Rudder trim tab
9. Rudder structure
10. Tail navigation light
11. Elevator fixed tab
12. Canopy track
13. Starboard elevator structure
14. Elevator outboard hinge
15. Elevator torque tube
16. Elevator trim tab worm and screw actuating mechanism
17. Chain drive
18. Starboard tailplane
19. Tail jacking point
20. Rudder control cables
21. Elevator control rod and linkage
22. Fin spar/fuselage attachment points
23. Elevator
24. Aerial
25. Port tailplane structure (two spars and flanged ribs)
26. Tailwheel retraction worm gear
27. Tailwheel anti-shimmy damper
28. Tailwheel oleo
29. Tailwheel doors
30. Retractable and steerable tail wheel
31. Tailwheel fork
32. Tailwheel mount and pivot (port and starboard)
33. Rudder cables
34. Rudder and elevator trim control cables
35. Lifting tube
36. Elevator rod linkage
37. Semi-monocoque all-metal fuselage construction
38. Fuselage dorsal 'razorback' profile
39. Aerial lead-in
40. Fuselage stringers
41. Supercharger air filter
42. Supercharger
43. Turbine casing
44. Turbosupercharger compartment
45. Turbo-supercharger exhaust hood fairing (stainless steel)
46. Outlet louvres
47. Intercooler exhaust doors (port and starboard)
48. Exhaust pipes
49. Cooling air ducts
50. Intercooler unit (cooling and supercharged air)
51. Radio transmitter and receiver packs (Detrola)
52. Canopy track
53. Elevator rod linkage
54. Aerial mast
55. Formation light
56. Rearward-vision frame cut-out and glazing
57. Oxygen bottles
58. Supercharger and cooling air pipe (supercharger to carburettor) port
59. Elevator linkage
60. Supercharger and cooling air pipe (supercharger to carburettor) starboard
61. Central duct (to intercooler unit)
62. Wingroot air louvres
63. Wingroot fillet
64. Auxiliary fuel tank (100 US gal/379 litres)
65. Auxiliary fuel filler point
66. Rudder cable turnbuckle
67. Cockpit floor support
68. Seat adjustment lever
69. Pilot's seat
70. Canopy emergency release
71. Trim tab controls
72. Back and head armour
73. Headrest
74. Rearward-sliding canopy
75. Rear view mirror fairing
76. 'Vee' windshields with central pillar
77. Internal bulletproof glass screen
78. Gunsight
79. Engine control quadrant (cockpit port wall)
80. Control column
81. Rudder pedals
82. Oxygen regulator
83. Underfloor elevator control quadrant
84. Rudder cable linkage
85. Wing rear spar/fuselage attachment (tapered bolts/bushings)
86. Wing-supporting lower bulkhead section
87. Main fuel tank (205 US gal/776 litres)
88. Fuselage forward structure
89. Stainless steel/Alclad firewall bulkhead
90. Cowl flap valve
91. Main fuel filler point
92. Anti-freeze fluid tank
93. Hydraulic reservoir
94. Aileron control rod
95. Aileron trim tab control cables
96. Aileron hinge access panels
97. Aileron and fuel control linkage
98. Aileron trim tab (port wing only)
99. Frise type aileron
100. Wing rear (No. 2) spar
101. Port navigation light
102. Pitot head
103. Wing front (No. 1) spar
104. Wing stressed skin
105. Four gun ammunition troughs (individual bays)
106. Staggered gun barrels
107. Removable panel
108. Inter spar gun bay access panel
109. Forward gunsight bead
110. Oil feed pipes
111. Oil tank (28.6 US gal/108 litres)
112. Hydraulic pressure line
113. Engine upper bearers
114. Engine control correlating cam
115. Eclipse pump (anti-icing)
116. Fuel level transmitter
117. Generator
118. Battery junction box
119. Storage battery
120. Exhaust collector ring
121. Cowl flap actuating
122. Exhaust outlets to collector ring
123. Cowl flaps
124. Supercharged and cooling air ducts to carburettor (port and starboard)
125. Exhaust outer outlets
126. Cowling frame
127. Pratt & Whitney R-2800-59 18-cylinder twin-row engine
128. Cowling nose panel
129. Magnetos
130. Propeller governor
131. Propeller hub
132. Reduction gear casing
133. Spinner
134. Propeller cuffs
135. Four blade Curtiss constant-speed electric propeller
136. Oil cooler intakes (port and starboard)
137. Supercharger intercooler (central) air intake
138. Ducting
139. Oil cooler feed pipes
140. Starboard oil cooler
141. Engine lower bearers
142. Oil cooler exhaust variable shutter (starboard wing only)
143. Fixed deflector
144. Excess exhaust gas gate
145. Belly stores/weapons shackles
146. Metal auxiliary drop tank (75 US gal/284 litres)
147. Inboard mainwheel well door
148. Mainwheel well door actuating cylinder
149. Camera gun port
150. Cabin air-conditioning intake (starboard wing only)
151. Wingroot fairing
152. Wing front spar/fuselage attachment (tapered bolts/bushings)
153. Wing inboard rib mainwheel well recess
154. Wing front (No. 1) spar
155. Undercarriage pivot point
156. Hydraulic retraction cylinder
157. Auxiliary (undercarriage mounting) wing spar
158. Gun bay warm air flexible duct
159. Wing rear (No. 2) spar
160. Landing flap inboard hinge
161. Auxiliary (No. 3) wing spar inboard section (flap mounting)
162. NACA slotted trailing-edge landing flaps
163. Landing flaps centre hinge
164. Landing flap hydraulic cylinder
165. Four 12.7mm (0.5in) Browning machine-guns
166. Inter-spar gun bay inboard rib
167. Ammunition feed chutes
168. Individual ammunition troughs
169. Underwing stores/weapons pylon
170. Landing flap profile
171. Flap door
172. Landing flap profile
173. Aileron fixed tab (starboard wing only)
174. Frise-type aileron structure
175. Aileron hinge/steel forging spar attachments
176. Auxiliary (No. 3) wing spar outboard section (aileron mounting)
177. Multi-cellular wing construction
178. Wing outboard ribs
179. Wingtip structure
180. Starboard navigation light
181. Leading-edge rib sections
182. Bomb shackles
183. 227kg (500lb) M43 demolition bomb
184. Undercarriage leg fairing (overlapping upper section)
185. Mainwheel fairing (lower section)
186. Wheel fork
187. Starboard mainwheel
188. Brake lines
189. Landing gear air-oil shock strut
190. Machine-gun barrel blast tubes
191. Staggered gun barrels
192. Rocket launcher slide bar
193. Centre strap
194. Front mount (attached below front spar between inboard pair of guns)
195. Deflector arms
196. Triple tube 11.5cm (4.5in) rocket launcher (Type M10)
197. Front retaining band
198. 11.5cm (4.5in) M8 rocket projectile

LATE-WAR FIGHTERS

P-47D THUNDERBOLT

The Republic P-47D was the definitive model of the highly-rated Thunderbolt, able to reach a maximum speed of 752km/h (467mph).

Weight (maximum take-off): 7938kg (17,500lb)
Dimensions: Length: 10.99m (36ft 1in), Wingspan: 12.43m (40ft 9in), Height: 4.44m (14ft 7in)
Powerplant: One 1500kW (2000hp) Pratt & Whitney R-2800-59 18-cylinder air-cooled radial piston engine
Maximum Speed: 686km/h (426mph)
Range (with external fuel tanks): 1660km (1030 miles)
Ceiling: 13,000m (42,000ft)
Crew: 1
Armament: Eight 12.7mm (0.5in) M2 Browning machine guns; up to 1100kg (2500lb) of bombs or six zero-length rockets under wings with drop tanks

LATE-WAR FIGHTERS

Supermarine Spitfire

A critical shortage of genuinely combat-worthy fighters saw the USAAF resort to widespread use of the British Supermarine Spitfire. Over 600 Spitfires would ultimately be supplied to American units and proved highly successful.

The Spitfire had been developed as a dedicated interceptor by RJ Mitchell and his team at Supermarine and had first flown in 1936. When the Spitfire Mk I entered service in 1938, it was the fastest operational military aircraft in the world, and when committed to the Battle of Britain, it proved the equal of the Messerschmitt Bf 109, which had hitherto proved superior to all fighters that had opposed it.

Rolls-Royce engine

Introduction of an improved Rolls-Royce Merlin engine saw the establishment of the higher performance Mk II, which was itself superseded by the Mk V, which was destined to be built in greater numbers than any other Spitfire variant. The Mk V was the first Spitfire to be armed as standard with cannon. It was broadly comparable to the contemporary Bf 109F model, though the introduction of the Focke-Wulf Fw 190 came as a rude shock to Spitfire pilots, as the new German aircraft could outperform the Spitfire V in all parameters save turning circle and provoked a flurry of activity aimed at quickly improving the British fighter.

When the Eighth Air Force arrived in England in 1942, its single-engine fighter squadrons were to be equipped with the P-39 Airacobra, but the personnel arrived ahead of their aircraft. To allow training to commence, Spitfire Vs drawn from RAF stocks were supplied to the 31st Fighter Group during July pending arrival of their Airacobras.

Interceptor role

The Spitfire represented a completely different design philosophy to contemporary American fighters in that it placed a priority on rate of climb and performance at high altitude. This emphasis befitted its intended mission of intercepting bombers approaching from continental Europe. Range and low-altitude performance were therefore of secondary importance, and the British aircraft was smaller, lighter and carried a smaller fuel load as standard than its American equivalents.

British reports regarding the high altitudes at which combat was typically taking place over Western Europe

Supermarine Spitfire Vb
This early example served with the 309th Fighter Squadron, 31st Fighter Group in late summer/autumn 1942 at RAF Westhampnett.

Supermarine Spitfire Vb
Weight (maximum take-off): 3071kg (6525lb)
Dimensions: Length: 9.12m (29ft 11in), Wingspan (clipped) 10.01m (32ft 10in), Height: 3.02m (9ft 10in)
Powerplant: one 1181kW (1585hp) Rolls-Royce Merlin 50M liquid cooled V-12 piston engine
Maximum Speed: 564km/h (351mph)
Range: 756km (470 miles)
Ceiling: 10,881m (35,700ft)
Crew: 1
Armament: Two 20mm (0.79in) Hispano cannon and four 7.7mm (0.303in) Browning machine guns in wings; up to 230kg (500lb) bomb load

LATE-WAR FIGHTERS

suggested that the P-39 would not have the performance necessary to operate at these heights, and the decision was taken to retain the Spitfires in service and arrange for adequate stocks of the British fighter to equip a second P-39 group, the 52nd Fighter Group, on its arrival in England. This course of action was controversial – many in the USAAF held that the P-39 was a superior aircraft to the Spitfire (which, arguably, it was at low level), and the idea that the 'Arsenal of the Free World' should be forced to utilize a foreign aircraft because its own was inadequate was politically awkward. Nonetheless, operational expediency won out, and the Spitfire would ultimately equip nine frontline squadrons of the Eighth Air Force.

First kill

Aircraft of the 31st Fighter Group engaged in the first major engagement by USAAF fighters when they contributed to the Allied 'air umbrella' covering the Dieppe raid of 19 August 1942, scoring their first confirmed kill, an Fw 190 – though they also lost Spitfires during the operation, largely due to combat inexperience.

Spitfires were not a totally unknown quantity to American pilots when the Eighth Air Force began operating them, however, as three 'Eagle' squadrons composed of US volunteer personnel

These Spitfire Vbs at Shaibah Airfield, Iraq, have had their RAF roundels crudely repainted into USAAF stars. The aircraft in the extreme foreground still has the RAF roundel on the starboard wing, implying the photo was taken while this work was ongoing.

69

LATE-WAR FIGHTERS

had been flying with the RAF since the first became operational in September 1940. These units were transferred to US control, complete with their Spitfires, on 29 September 1942, becoming the 4th Fighter Group.

In the same month, the two existing Spitfire-equipped fighter groups in the Eighth AF were transferred to Twelfth Air Force control for operations in North Africa. The 4th Fighter Group would retain their Spitfires until re-equipped in March 1943 with the P-47 Thunderbolt.

Twelfth Air Force service

Instead, it was with the Twelfth Air Force that the American Spitfires would see most of their operational usage. Initially based in Gibraltar, their Spitfires were fitted with large Vokes dust filters and painted in desert camouflage, going into action against Vichy French forces over Algeria. Three Dewoitine D.520s were destroyed for every one Spitfire lost in the US Spitfire group's first combat over Africa.

Subsequently committed to the fighting in North Africa, by the end of April, two US Spitfire pilots had achieved 'ace' status, and before the end of the Tunisian campaign, the US squadrons had begun to receive the Spitfire Mk IX, developed specifically in response to the Fw 190 and considerably faster than the Mk V it replaced.

Italian campaign

The Spitfire fighter groups followed the Allied armies across the Mediterranean, supporting the landings in Sicily, the 31st Fighter Group becoming the first USAAF fighter group to move onto the island before covering Operation Husky, the Allied landings on the Italian mainland at Anzio. By this time, the squadrons were operating a mix of Mk IX and Mk VIII Spitfires. Despite the numerical sequence, the Mk VIII was a more highly developed Spitfire variant than the Mk IX, though both possessed similar performance.

The Spitfire units supported the Allied drive up through Italy and saw their role shift ever more towards ground attack before being replaced by P-51s, though not without some protest. A mock combat was held between a Spitfire Mk IX and a P-51B

Supermarine Spitfire Mk VIII
Weight (maximum take-off): 3638kg (8020lb)
Dimensions: Length: 9.54m (31ft 4in), Wingspan: 11.23m (36ft 10in), Height: 3.86m (12ft 8in)
Powerplant: One 1275kW (1710hp) Rolls-Royce Merlin 63 liquid cooled V-12 piston engine
Maximum speed: 657km/h (408mph)
Range: 1062km (660 miles)
Ceiling: 13,106m (43,000ft)
Crew: 1
Armament: Two 20mm (0.79in) Hispano cannon and four 7.7mm (0.303in) Browning machine guns

Supermarine Spitfire Mk VIII
This Spitfire flew with 308th Fighter Squadron, 31st Fighter Group. It was fitted under the nose with a Vokes filter to prevent North African dust and grit being drawn into the engine.

LATE-WAR FIGHTERS

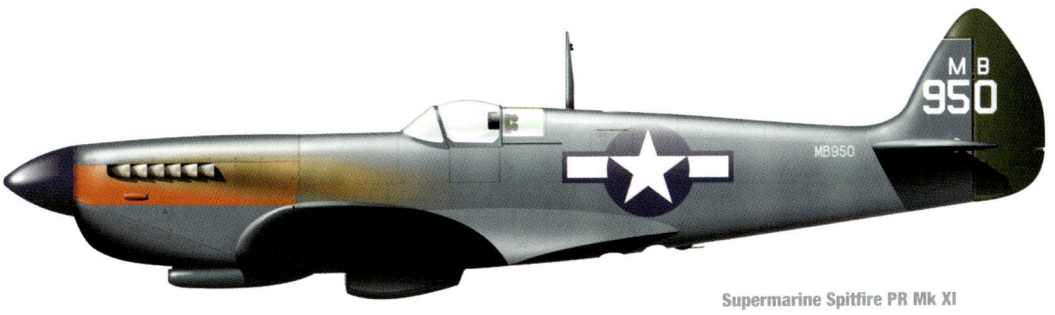

Supermarine Spitfire PR Mk XI
This PR Mk XI, based at RAF Mount Farm, UK, was part of the 14th Photographic Reconnaissance Squadron, 7th Photographic Reconnaissance Group, in 1944.

Supermarine Spitfire PR Mk XI
This aircraft served with the 7th Photographic Reconnaissance Group, based at Mount Farm, Oxfordshire, UK. It is estimated that the type took over three million intelligence photos during the course of 4,251 sorties over occupied Europe.

Supermarine Spitfire PR Mk XI
Weight (maximum take-off): 3597kg (7930lb)
Dimensions: Length: 9.47m (31ft 1in), Wingspan: 11.23m (36ft 10in), Height: 3.86m (12ft 8in)
Powerplant: One 1275kW (1710hp) Rolls-Royce Merlin 63 liquid cooled V-12 piston engine
Maximum speed: 671km/h (417mph)
Range: 909km (565 miles) with 90 imperial gallon external fuel tank
Ceiling: 13,410m (44,000ft)
Crew: 1
Armament: N/A

on 14 March 1944: the Mustang was completely outmanoeuvred, but the P-51 possessed a far better range and was therefore of greater usefulness at this stage of the war. The final US Spitfire operations took place in April, marking the end of around two years of intense Spitfire action.

Ace status

Despite the aircraft's widespread use, more Spitfires were employed in the USAAF than either the P-36 or early P-40 models, the aircraft never received a P for 'Pursuit' number and its American career remains obscure today. Thirteen US pilots achieved 'ace' status with the Spitfire, and although it made up the equipment of only two fighter groups, Spitfires destroyed 364 enemy aircraft in the Mediterranean Theatre of Operations. This makes the Spitfire the fourth most successful US fighter in terms of total numbers shot down in that theatre.

Photo reconnaissance role

In addition to its role as a combat aircraft, the Spitfire was also employed by the USAAF as a long-range strategic reconnaissance platform after the Lockheed Lightning proved vulnerable to interception.

Spitfire PR Mk XIs, known as 'Bluebirds' due to their all-over PRU blue colour scheme, were operated by the 8th Air Force's 14th Squadron of the 7th Photographic Group from 6 March 1944 until the end of the war in Europe.

LATE-WAR FIGHTERS

Bell P-63 Kingcobra

Although bearing a close resemblance to the P-39 and sharing the same unconventional layout, the Kingcobra was in fact a completely new design. Over two-thirds of all P-63s produced were supplied to the Soviet Union.

First flown exactly a year after the attack on Pearl Harbor, the P-63 retained the unusual fuselage layout of the P-39 with the engine positioned behind the pilot and the propeller being driven via a long shaft. Fitted with a new laminar flow wing, the Kingcobra persisted with the idiosyncratic 'car door' cockpit access of the earlier aircraft and featured the same armament of two 12.7mm (0.5in) Browning machine guns and one 37mm (1.5in) Oldsmobile cannon firing through the propeller spinner, augmented by two further 12.7mm (0.5in) machine guns in underwing fairings.

Unlike the P-39, the P-63 featured a second supercharger for high-altitude work, and performance was excellent at all altitudes. Unfortunately for the Bell fighter, the first prototype was damaged and the second lost soon afterwards, delaying flight testing until a third prototype was completed in April 1943. Production deliveries of the P-63A began in October 1943; had the P-51 Mustang not been so expeditiously re-engined with the V-1650 Merlin, it is highly likely that the P-63 would have been heavily used as an escort fighter with the USAAF.

However, with enough P-51s and P-47s in service, few units were formed on the P-63, and those that were remained at advanced training status in the United States, with the aircraft seeing no US service overseas. The absence of a clear role for the Kingcobra saw the aircraft modified into the intriguing RP-63A, a manned target aircraft featuring a reinforced skin designed to be shot at by 'frangible' bullets that would shatter on impact. Painted red, the RP-63 had a system that flashed the landing lights every time a hit was recorded, leading to the aircraft being nicknamed 'Pinball'. Following a successful test with five modified P-63As, 332 RP-63 target aircraft were constructed.

Eastern Front success

Despite the general indifference of its country of origin, the remarkable success of the P-39 over the Eastern Front saw further development go ahead with Soviet use in mind. The P-63C, of which 1227 were produced, featured a more powerful V-1710 engine and a long shallow ventral fin, while the P-63B was to have been fitted with a Packard V-1650 Merlin but was never built.

Later developments were the single P-63D, with a more powerful engine and a sliding hood replacing the cockpit door, and the P-63E, 13 of which were assembled and were identical save for a return to the car door-style cockpit access. The final P-63F featured a taller fin and rudder, but only two were constructed. In total, 3303 Kingcobras would roll out of Bell's factory, and 2421 of these were flown via Canada and Alaska across the Bering Sea to the Soviet Union.

Bell P-63E Kingcobra
This P-63E (42-69654) was a manned target aircraft used for target practice by aerial gunnery students, hence the bright orange colour scheme.

LATE-WAR FIGHTERS

Bell P-63C Kingcobra
Probably on the strength of 16 GvIAP in 1945, this P-63 was finished in all-over olive drab. The ventral fin identifies this as a P-63C.

Officially, an agreement with the US restricted Soviet use of the Kingcobra to the Pacific area of operations, and the type scored its first confirmed victory on 15 August 1945, when Lieutenant I. F. Miroshnichenko shot down a Ki-43 Hayabusa. There is some evidence, however, that P-63s were secretly used against Germany in the closing days of the war in Europe. Retained in frontline V-VS service until 1951, the Kingcobra eventually received the NATO reporting name of FRED. France's Armée de l'Air also received 300 P-63Cs in 1945. However, these were too late to engage in combat use over Europe, although they did see action in France's later conflict in Indochina.

Bell P-63C Kingcobra
Weight (Maximum take-off): 4853kg (10,700lbs)
Dimensions: Length: 9.96m (32ft 8in), Wingspan: 11.68m (38ft 4in), Height: 3.84m (12ft 7in)
Powerplant: One 1300kW (1800hp) Allison V-1710-117 V-12 liquid-cooled piston engine
Maximum Speed: 660km/h (410mph)
Range: 720km (450 miles)
Ceiling: 13,000m (43,000ft)
Crew: 1
Armament: One 37mm (1.45in) M10 cannon, four 12.7mm (0.5in) Browning M2 machine guns; up to 680kg (1500lbs) bomb load

US Air Force mechanics check over a P-63 Kingcobra in Fairbanks, Alaska, February 1949.

HEAVY FIGHTERS

Many air forces worldwide experimented with the concept of the 'heavy' fighter in the late 1930s, and the US was no exception. These twin-engined designs were intended to make up for any shortfall in manoeuvrability, due to their size, speed, range and heavy armament – and the P-38 Lightning was probably the best of the lot, though it did endure a painful introduction to operations. Larger fighters were also required to carry radar and deliver good endurance, essential for night fighting, though not all USAAF night-fighters were American in origin, as the British Beaufighter and Mosquito also saw service with US units.

- Bell YFM-1 Airacuda
- Bristol Beaufighter
- de Havilland Mosquito
- Douglas P-70 Havoc
- Lockheed P-38 Lightning
- Northrop P-61 Black Widow

Depicted is an aircraft from the first batch of Northrop P-61As. The Black Widow had the makings of a superb night-fighter, but suffered from an overcomplicated design.

HEAVY FIGHTERS

Bell YFM-1 Airacuda

Despite bristling with advanced features, the YFM-1 was an underwhelming aircraft. Although only 12 production aircraft were built, the Airacuda remained in squadron service when the US entered the war.

Bell YFM-1 Airacuda
This Bell YFM-1 is from the 10th Air Base Squadron of the Air Corps Technical School at Chanute Field in 1941.

The first design to emerge from the Bell Aircraft Corporation was the Airacuda, an aircraft that clearly demonstrated Bell's willingness to pursue unorthodox design features, something the company would gain a reputation for over the following decade. Intended as a 'bomber destroyer', the YFM-1 was the size of a typical medium bomber and was extremely heavily armed, featuring two 37mm (1.46in) Browning M4 cannon mounted one either side in each engine nacelle.

With the engines arranged to drive pusher propellers, the nose of each nacelle included a gunner's position, and though the gunner was able to aim the weapon if necessary, his role was primarily to reload the cannon when required. In the cockpit, tandem seating was provided for the pilot and co-pilot, who also doubled as both navigator and fire control officer and were provided with a Sperry 'Thermionic' fire control system (originally developed for anti-aircraft guns). The rear fuselage housed the radio operator, who was provided with two machine gun positions in waist blisters to defend against attack from the rear.

Flawed design

Despite its futuristic looks and impressive features, the Airacuda was a disaster. It wasn't as fast as the bombers it was intended to intercept, possessed only poor manoeuvrability and was riddled with design flaws. Its Allison engines were prone to overheat due to their pusher configuration. In service, the aircraft were towed to the end of the runway, and the engine started only when take-off was imminent. Although intended to be turbo-supercharged, the first aircraft flew without this feature and were deficient in power. Even when turbo superchargers were fitted, the regulating units were unreliable, and the engines were prone to constant backfiring. In a radical departure from the norm, the YFM-1 featured an Auxiliary Power Unit (APU) to power all the electrical systems on board. If this failed, and it frequently did, the aircraft was left with non-functional fuel pumps, hydraulics undercarriage and flaps.

Bell YFM-1 Airacuda
Weight (maximum take-off): 9809kg (21,625lb)
Dimensions: Length: 13.67m (44ft 10in), Wingspan: 21.29m (69ft 10in), Height: 4.14m (13ft 7in)
Powerplant: Two 810kW (1090hp) Allison V-1710-9 V-12 liquid-cooled piston engines
Maximum Speed: 446km/h (277mph)
Range: 4184km (2600 miles)
Ceiling: 9300m (30,500ft)
Crew: 5
Armament: Two 37mm (1.46in) M4 cannons flexibly mounted in engine nacelles, two 7.62mm (0.3in) M1919 Browning machine guns fixed forward firing in nacelles, two 12.7mm (0.5in) M2 Browning machine guns flexibly mounted in side blisters, up to 20 14kg (30lb) bombs in wing bays

Even the impressive armament was problematic: the guns tended to fill the gunners' cabins with smoke, and, with the propeller mounted directly behind, the ability of the gunners to escape in an emergency was questionable. As a result, the aircraft was generally flown with the nacelle gun positions unmanned. Despite these flaws, the service test YFM-1s were formed into an operational squadron in 1938 and were still in service in December 1941. By March 1942, however, all had been scrapped.

Bristol Beaufighter

In the absence of an effective domestically produced night fighter, the USAAF utilized the British Bristol Beaufighter until this role could be filled by an American design.

Derived from the Beaufort torpedo bomber, the Bristol Beaufighter heavy fighter entered RAF service in 1940 and proved extremely successful in a number of challenging roles. The start of its career as a night fighter coincided with the launch of the night 'Blitz' against London and other British cities. As the first night fighter able to carry airborne radar without suffering a significant drop in performance, the Beaufighter proved highly successful, achieving more victories over German aircraft than any other Allied night fighter. The culmination of the Beaufighter's career defending the British Isles occurred on the night of 19/20 May 1941, shooting down 24 Luftwaffe bombers. From mid-1942, the higher-performance de Havilland Mosquito began to replace the Beaufighter in night fighter units, although the Bristol aircraft would enjoy a highly successful secondary service as an anti-shipping aircraft.

The Beaufighter was one of the most heavily armed fighters of the entire war, with four 20mm (0.79in) cannon and six 7.7mm (0.303in) machine guns fitted as standard (all firing forward). The aircraft was also famed for its immense strength, although it was also noted to be heavy on the controls and not an easy aircraft to fly – especially for inexperienced pilots.

Adopted by the US

When the US entered the war, the USAAF had no dedicated night fighting aircraft or units, and though the excellent P-61 Black Widow flew in May 1942, this highly advanced aircraft was experiencing developmental delays. Meanwhile, though it did see limited operational use, the Douglas P-70 Havoc, which had been adapted for nocturnal use, was essentially a stopgap. A more effective solution

Bristol Beaufighter NF Mk VI
This aircraft is from the US 12th Air Force, based at Gerbini in Sicily, September 1943. It is thought to be from the 415th Night Fighter Squadron and has the not uncommon feature of an olive drab rear fuselage over its standard RAF night-fighter finish of medium sea grey overall with disruptive dark green pattern on its top sides.

Bristol Beaufighter NF Mk VI

Weight (maximum take-off): 9798kg (21,600lb)
Dimensions: Length: 12.7m (41ft 8in), Wingspan: 17.64m (57ft 10in), Height: 4.82m (15ft 10in)
Powerplant: Two 1245kW (1670hp) Bristol Hercules VI 14-cylinder air-cooled radial piston engines
Maximum Speed: 536km/h (333mph)
Range: 2478km (1540 miles)
Ceiling: 8077m (26,500ft)
Crew: 2
Armament: Four 20mm (0.79in) Hispano cannon fixed forward firing in lower forward fuselage, six 7.7mm (0.303in) Browning machine guns fixed forward firing in wings (two in port wing, four in starboard), optional underwing bomb racks for a maximum 227kg (500lb) bomb load

was required for US night fighter units, the first of which was formed in January 1943. Luckily, the increased availability of the Mosquito meant that the RAF was able to offer the US 100 examples of the highly capable Beaufighter Mk VIF through a 'reverse lend-lease' arrangement. This variant was equipped with AI Mk VIII radar housed in a thimble fairing in the nose. This was the first operational airborne interception radar to function in microwave frequencies.

Mediterranean service

Four USAAF squadrons would operate the type in the Mediterranean theatre, all four arriving in the summer of 1943 following training with the P-70 in the US. Operating initially from North Africa, the first US Beaufighter victory was scored on 24 July, and despite logistical problems arising from the non-US origins of the aircraft, spare parts, for example, were always in short supply. The Beaufighter would remain frontline equipment with US night fighter squadrons until the closing days of the war, seeing combat over Italy and France.

In addition to their nocturnal duties, Beaufighters were also kept busy during the day with convoy escort and ground attack missions. The Beaufighters were eventually replaced by P-61 Black Widows in two units, the other two American night fighter squadrons receiving the P-38M and de Havilland Mosquito shortly before the end of hostilities.

A US Army Air Force Beaufighter with the 414th Night Fighter Squadron undergoes repairs.

de Havilland Mosquito

The de Havilland Mosquito was the finest World War II night fighter developed in Britain, and although the USAAF had been keen to adopt it for US night fighting squadrons, only a few were obtained before the end of the war in Europe.

The Mosquito had been developed as a radical departure from the prevailing orthodoxy regarding bomber design; designed primarily for high speed, it carried no defensive armament. It was also built using a birch ply and balsa wood sandwich, conferring great strength and light weight whilst minimizing the aircraft's impact on light alloy and steel supplies, which were likely to become scarce in wartime. Despite considerable scepticism at the Air Ministry, the prototype flew in November 1940, and its capability was immediately obvious. The Mosquito entered service as a bomber and reconnaissance aircraft in mid-1942 and was more or less immune from fighter interception, proving highly successful and enjoying the lowest loss rate of any RAF bomber despite its lack of defensive armament.

Versatile warrior

By contrast, offensive armament had been schemed early in the design process, and the Mosquito was utilized as a fighter-bomber, anti-shipping aircraft and night fighter. Indeed, it was likely the most versatile World War II combat aircraft utilized by any nation. By June 1944, the NF Mk 30 had entered service, which boasted a 655km/h (407mph) top speed and could be fitted with either British or US radar in a 'bullnose' radome as well as electronic countermeasures equipment. This was the variant that was made available to the USAAF and would form the equipment of the 416th NFS, operating in the Mediterranean, replacing that unit's Beaufighters.

Earlier night fighter Mosquito variants had been requested by the USAAF, but the demands of the RAF meant that none could be spared until early 1945. By this late stage of the war, nocturnal targets in this theatre were few and far between, and only one victory claim was made by an American-crewed Mosquito. With the end of hostilities, the British aircraft was swiftly discarded and replaced with the P-61 Black Widow.

---

de Havilland Mosquito NF Mk 30
Weight (maximum take-off): 9798kg (21,600lb)
Dimensions: Length: 12.65m (41ft 6in), Wingspan: 16.51m (54ft 2in), Height: 4.65m (15ft 3in)
Powerplant: Two 1230kW (1650hp) Rolls-Royce Merlin 72 V-12 liquid-cooled piston engines
Maximum Speed: 655km/h (407mph)
Range: 2848km (1770 miles)
Ceiling: 11,887m (39,000ft)
Crew: 2
Armament: Four 20mm (0.79in) Hispano cannon fixed forward firing in the lower front fuselage

---

de Havilland Mosquito PR.XVI
This unarmed reconnaissance variant Mosquito (MM345) flew with the 653th (WR) Squadron, USAAF, based in Watton, Norfolk, UK.

HEAVY FIGHTERS

Douglas P-70 Havoc

Development of a night fighter version of the Douglas DB-7 attack bomber took place separately in Britain and America, and both nations would fly their own version of the Douglas night fighter in combat, though the RAF made much more operational use of the Havoc.

The concept of the night fighter had been largely neglected between the wars, but the requirement for an aircraft capable of intercepting enemy bombers by night became clearly apparent in the initial stages of World War II. Endurance was of primary importance to the night fighter in order to maintain standing patrols, requiring a large fuel load that necessitated the use of a larger aircraft than the standard day fighter.

The appearance of the revolutionary technology of airborne radar, which initially was large, heavy and required a second crew member to operate, hastened the development of the large twin-engine night fighter, most examples of which were initially derived from light bombers.

British service

In the late summer of 1940, the British started to receive the Douglas DB-7 attack bomber, which had been ordered by France. Of the 150 or so ex-French aircraft, named 'Boston' by the RAF, 100 were modified into night fighters, adopting the name 'Havoc'.

Night fighter features

The DB-7 possessed several features that rendered it ideal for this role: it had the ability to carry radar, offered a good performance and was fitted with a tricycle undercarriage, which made for easier operation at night.

Painted matt black overall, the Havoc I featured a 'solid' nose in place of the Boston's glazing mounting a total of eight 7.7mm (0.303in) machine guns and AI Mk IV or V radar was carried. Confusingly, some Havocs retained the glazed bombardier nose and were fitted with four machine guns in the lower fuselage and a bomb bay capable of carrying a 1090kg (2400lb) bomb load.

Douglas P-70A
Weight (maximum take-off): 8960kg (19,753lb)
Dimensions: Length: 14.5m (ft in), Wingspan: 18.7m (61ft 4in), Height: 5.5m (18ft)
Powerplant: Two 1193kW (1600hp) Wright R-2600-11 Twin Cyclone air-cooled radial piston engines
Maximum Speed: 545km/h (339mph)
Range: 1770km (1100 miles)
Ceiling: 8600m (28,215ft)
Crew: 2
Armament: Four 20mm (0.79in) Hispano AN/M2 cannon or six 12.7mm (0.5in) Browning machine guns in ventral tray, up to 907kg (2000lb) bomb load

Douglas P-70A
This P-70A from the 6th Night Fighter Squadron's Detachment B was assigned to the 15th Fighter Group, serving at Guadalcanal in spring 1943. It is a converted A-20C, serial number 39-774, and carries British AI Mk IV radar, with its arrowhead transmitter aerials and receiving antennas on the wings and below the cockpit. The plane was lost in a landing accident at Munda, Solomon Islands, in November 1943.

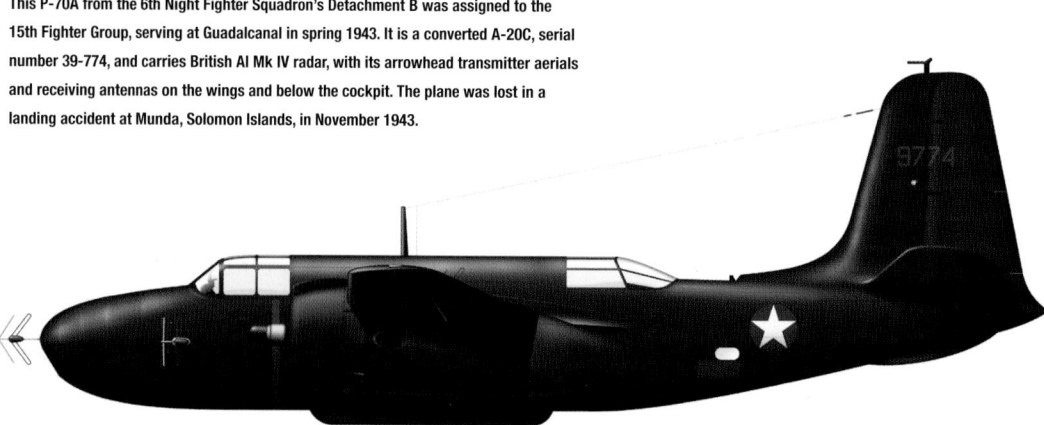

HEAVY FIGHTERS

Douglas TP-70B

This TP-70B, with its replacement rudder still in olive drab/medium green camouflage, is fitted with American centimetric radar in the nose and is based on an A-20G airframe. it is believed that this aircraft was from the 481st Operational Training Group, based in Orlando in 1944. The type was soon replaced by the Northrop P-61 Black Widow.

These aircraft were designated Havoc IV – later Havoc I (Intruder) – and were used for night intruder missions over occupied Europe from early 1941.

Somewhat later, two squadrons used Bostons for night intruding work, these being modified with four 20mm (0.79in) cannon in a ventral pack and designated Boston III (Intruder).

Havoc II

The Havoc I was followed by the Havoc II, which came equipped with a 12-gun nose developed by Martin-Baker. However, this was only operated by one squadron. Many British Havocs were fitted with the Helmore/GEC 'Turbinlite', a 2700 million candlepower airborne searchlight, in the nose. These Havocs were operated in concert with a single-engine fighter, the intention being that the Havoc would illuminate the target and the fighter would destroy it. In practice, the system proved disappointing, although a few successes were achieved.

P-70 conversion

In the US, the progress of the war in the Pacific and knowledge of the RAF's nocturnal use of the DB-7 saw the USAAF order 59 P-70s following the satisfactory conversion of a single A-20 to an XP-70.

The P-70 featured a solid nose containing the British AI Mk IV radar and was armed with four 20mm (0.79in) cannon in a tray under the fuselage. In 1943, these were followed by 39 P-70As with an armament of six 12.7mm (0.5in) machine guns in the ventral tray and updated radar.

Most of the P-70s' US service was in the training role, preparing crews who were to fly the P-61, Beaufighter or Mosquito – although the aircraft did provide the initial equipment for nearly all USAAF night fighter units.

Some of these aircraft saw brief operational service in the Pacific, and the P-70 is believed to have scored just two victories in US service.

Douglas TP-70B

Weight (maximum take-off): 8960kg (19,753lb)
Dimensions: Length 14.5m (ft in), Wingspan 18.7m (61ft 4in), Height 5.5m (18ft)
Powerplant: Two 1193kW (1600hp) Wright R-2600-23 Twin Cyclone air-cooled radial piston engines
Maximum speed: 545km/h (339mph)
Range: 1770km (1100 miles)
Ceiling: 8600m (28215ft)
Crew: Two
Armament: Six or eight 12.7mm (0.5in) Browning machine guns in ventral tray

HEAVY FIGHTERS

Lockheed P-38 Lightning

Extremely unorthodox when it first appeared, the versatile Lockheed P-38 was officially termed an interceptor but would also serve as an escort fighter, reconnaissance aircraft, bomber and night fighter.

It is difficult today to realize just how radical the P-38 looked when it first appeared in 1939. Unusually for a military aircraft, its striking looks directly influenced design in the civilian world: famed industrial designer Raymond Loewy cited it as a major influence, and, in 1941, a group from General Motors led by Styling Vice President Harley Earl visited Selfridge Field specifically to study it. The P-38's twin fins and overall aesthetic directly inspired those of the 1948 Cadillac and thus the huge swathe of tail-finned American cars that followed it. By the time the P-38's influence on automotive design was realized, however, the Lightning was on the brink of retirement from the USAF, but in 1941 it represented the state of the art in American fighter design.

Twin-engined 'interceptor'

Under designers Hal Hibberd and Clarence 'Kelly' Johnson, Lockheed had been exploring potential layouts for a twin-engine fighter aircraft for around a year before Specification X-608 was issued by the Army Air Corps, calling for a twin-engined interceptor. This was not just happenstance; Lockheed had been verbally briefed about the nature of the aircraft the Air Corps were seeking. The specification itself was in direct opposition to the then-prevalent thinking on what was required from an American fighter aircraft, which was profoundly conservative, with range requirements derived from the size of the continental United States. This represented an adherence to the belief that single-engine 'pursuit' aircraft was of most use at low and medium altitude, and a fixation on the armament of just one 12.7mm (0.5mm) and one 7.62mm (0.3in) machine gun; an armament that was manifestly inadequate by the mid-1930s. A small group of Air Corps officers felt that a much better aircraft could be acquired if these assumptions could be ignored and drew up the specification for two heavily armed, high-altitude fighters: one fighter and one twin. Calling the aircraft an 'interceptor' helped them to sidestep the prevailing assumptions about standard pursuit aircraft. The single-engine interceptor specification would result in the Bell P-39 Airacobra, but Lockheed was selected to produce the twin as the XP-38 'Lightning'.

Lockheed had schemed several potential two-engine layouts but settled on a twin-boom and central fuselage pod design as offering the best performance while delivering great range performance, as well as allowing for the fitment of a very heavy armament in the nose. This consisted

---

Lockheed P-38F

Weight (maximum take-off): 9798kg (21,600lb)
Dimensions: Length: 11.53m (37ft 10in), Wingspan: 15.85m (52ft), Height: 3.91m (12ft 10in)
Powerplant: Two 913kW (1225hp) Allison V-1710 -49 left hand rotation and -53 right hand rotation V-12 liquid-cooled piston engines
Maximum Speed: 628km/h (390mph)
Range: 1126km (700 miles)
Ceiling: 11,582m (38,000ft)
Crew: 1
Armament: One 20mm (0.79in) Hispano cannon and four 12.7mm (0.5in) Browning M2 machine guns fixed forward firing in nose

---

Lockheed P-38F-1
P-38F-1 was an ex-1st Fighter Group aircraft impounded by Portugal in 1942 while on route from England to North Africa. Repainted in Portuguese markings, it served alongside a whole squadron of P-39 Airacobras that suffered the same fate.

HEAVY FIGHTERS

Lockheed P-38G
This P-38G, 'Pat II', was flown by Colonel Oliver Taylor, commanding officer of the 14 Fighter Group, based in Foggia, Italy, April 1944.

Lockheed P-38H-1
P-38H-1 'Skidoo' (42-66504) was the aircraft of Lightning ace Lt. Perry Dahl, of the 432nd Fighter Squadron, 475th Fighter Group, from Dobodura airfield, Papua New Guinea, circa 1944.

Lockheed P-38H

Weight (maximum take-off): 9208kg (20,300lb)
Dimensions: Length 11.53m (37ft 10in), Wingspan 15.85m (52ft), Height 3.91m (12ft 10in)
Powerplant: Two 1062kW (1425hp) Allison V-1710-89 left hand rotation and -91 right hand rotation V-12 liquid cooled piston engines
Maximum speed: 647km/h (402mph)
Range (with drop tanks): 3862km (2400 miles)
Ceiling: 12,192m (40,000ft)
Crew: One
Armament: One 20mm (0.79in) Hispano AN/M2 cannon and four 12.7mm (0.5in) Browning M2 machine guns fixed forward firing in nose; up to 1452kg (3200lb) of bombs on underwing racks

of a 37mm (1.5in) cannon and four 12.7mm (0.5in) machine guns when the aircraft appeared, with space for the turbo-superchargers in the booms behind the engines. A retractable tricycle undercarriage was chosen, the XP-38 being the first fighter in the world to fly with such a feature.

Contracted to build a prototype on 23 June 1937, Lockheed subsequently made a few changes to the design, the most significant of which was the adoption of 'handed' engines that turned the two propellers in opposite directions, thus eliminating torque.

Test flight

Completed by the end of 1938, the XP-38 made its first flight on 27 January 1939, though this was marred by severe vibration of the wing flaps, which nearly led to the test pilot Benjamin S.

Kelsey abandoning the aircraft after three of the four flap brackets failed. Fortunately, Kelsey was able to land the XP-38 by maintaining an unusually nose-high attitude, scraping the bottom of the tail fins in the process. The problem was traced to poor gap sealing and insufficient strength of the flap brackets. After modification, further test flights were much more successful.

Overall performance was very good, and on 11 February, Kelsey set a new transcontinental speed record when he flew the XP-38 from March Field, California to Mitchel Field, New York at an average speed of 563km/h (350mph) – although the aircraft ended up wrecked when a power loss was experienced on approach to landing and the XP-38 overshot the field, though Kelsey escaped unharmed. Despite this unfortunate loss, the

HEAVY FIGHTERS

P-38H Lightning

CUTAWAY K

1 Starboard navigation light
2 Wingtip trailing edge strake
3 Landing light (underwing)
4 Starboard aileron
5 Aileron control rod/quadrant
6 Wing outer spar
7 Aileron tab drum
8 Aileron tab control pulleys
9 Aileron tab control rod
10 Aileron trim tab
11 Fixed tab
12 Tab cable access
13 Flap extension/retraction cables
14 Control pulleys
15 Flap outer carriage
16 Fowler-type flap (extended)
17 Control access panel
18 Wing spar transition
19 Outer section leading-edge fuel tanks (P-38J-5 and subsequent) capacity 208 litres (46 Imp gal) each
20 Engine bearer/bulkhead upper attachment
21 Firewall
22 Triangulated tubular engine bearer supports
23 Polished mirror surface panel (undercarriage visual check)
24 Cantilever engine bearer
25 Intake fairing
26 Accessories cooling intake
27 Oil radiator (outer sections) and intercooler (centre section) tripleintake
28 Spinner
29 Curtiss-Electric three blade (left) handed propeller
30 Four machine gun barrels
31 Cannon barrel
32 Camera-gun aperture
33 Nose panel
34 Bulkhead
35 Machine gun blast tubes
36 Four 0.5-in (12.7-mm) machine guns
37 Cannon flexible hose hydraulic charger
38 Chatellerault-feed cannon magazine (150 rounds)
39 Machine gun firing solenoid
40 Cannon ammunition feed chute
41 Nose armament cowling clips
42 Case ejection chute (port lower machine gun)
43 Ammunition box and feed chute (port lower machine gun)
44 Case ejection chute (port upper machine gun)
45 Ammunition box and feed chute (port upper machine gun)
46 Radio antenna
47 Ejection chute exit (stroudded when item 52 attached)
48 Nosewheel door
49 Nosewheel shimmy damper assembly and reservoir
50 Torque links
51 Towing eye
52 Type M10 tripletube rocket-launcher
53 Rearwardretracting nosewheel
54 Alloy spokes cover plate
55 Fork
56 Rocket-launcher forward attachment (to 63)
57 Nosewheel lower drag struts
58 Nosewheel oleo leg
59 Nosewheel pin access
60 Side struts and fulcrum
61 Actuating cylinder
62 Upper drag strut
63 Rocket-launcher forward attachment bracket
64 Rudder pedal assembly
65 Engine controls quadrant
66 Instrument panel
67 Spectacle grip sight mounting
68 Non-reflective stroud
69 Lynn-3 reflector sight mounting
70 Optically-flat bullet-proof windscreen
71 External rear-view mirror
72 Armoured headrest
73 Rearward-hinged canopy
74 Pilot's armoured seat back
75 Canopy hinge
76 Downwardwinding side windows
77 Wing root fillets
78 Nosewheel well
79 Port reserve fuel tank, capacity 50 Imp gal (227 litres)
80 Fuel filler cap
81 Main (double beam) spar
82 Fuel filler cap
83 Flap inner carriage
84 Port main fuel tank, capacity 75 Imp gal (341 litres)
85 Flap control access
86 Flap structure
87 Entry ladder release
88 Flap drive motor
89 Fuel surge tank and main hydraulic reservoir in aft nacelle
90 Radio equipment compartment
91 Turnover support
92 Flap control access
93 Aerial attachment
94 Starboard inner flap
95 Wing push-pull rod
96 Starboard main fuel tank, capacity as 79
97 Main spar
98 Engine control runs
99 Starboard reserve fuel tank, capacity as 79
100 Starboard oil tank
101 Cooling louvres
102 Cabin heater intake
103 Turbosupercharger cooling intakes
104 Turbine cooling duct
105 Exhaust turbine
106 Supercharger housing
107 Wingroot/boom fillet
108 Coolant/radiator return pipe (left and right)
109 Exhaust waste gate outlet
110 Access panel
111 Boom Joint (Station 265)
112 Radiator/coolant supply pipe
113 Mainwheel well
114 Mainwheel doors
115 Radiator intake
116 Starboard outer radiator fairing
117 Radiator grille
118 Engine coolant radiator assembly
119 Exit flap
120 Tool and baggage compartment
121 Boom structure
122 D/R master compass housing
123 Boom/tail attachment joint
124 Starboard lower attachment flanges (quatrefoil bulkhead)
125 Tail bumper skid shoe
126 Elevator control pulley
127 Rudder stop
128 Elevator control horn
129 Fixed tip
130 Radio aerials
131 Tail surface control pulleys
132 Aerodynamic mass balance attachments
133 Aerial attachments
134 Starboard rudder
135 Tab control rod and drum
136 Rudder trim tab
137 Elevator abbreviated torque tube
138 Tailplane stressed skin
139 Elevator pin hinges (eight off)
140 Elevato
141 Upper and lower mass balances
142 Elevator trim tab
143 Tailplane structure
144 Stiffeners
145 Port fin structure
146 Elevator pulley access
147 Rudder tab drum access
148 Tail running light (port)
149 Aerodynamic mass balance
150 Rudder framework
151 Rudder trim tab
152 Fixed tip
153 Tail surfaces/boom (quatrefoil bulkhead) attachment flanges
154 Rudder lower section
155 Tail bumper skid shoe
156 Elevator pulley access
157 Port tower fin
158 Elevator, rudder, and table cables
159 Battery compartment
160 Radiator exit flap
161 Engine coolant radiator assembly
162 Radiator housing
163 Radiator/coolant supply pipe
164 Radiator intake
165 Coolant/radiator return pipe
166 Oxygen cylinder
167 Port inner radiator fairing
168 Flare tube (port and starboard booms)
169 Mainwheel doors
170 Mainwheel well
171 Exhaust waste gate outlet
172 Turbine cooling duct
173 Exhaust turbine
174 Supercharger assembly
175 Supercharger/intercooler duct
176 Carburettor intake duct
177 Carburettor air intake
178 Abbreviated rear spar
179 Flap outer section
180 Tab cable access
181 Fixed tab
182 Aileron trim tab
183 Aileron full-span piano-wire hinge
184 Underwing pilot attachment
185 Raked web stiffener (outboard of rear spar)
186 Aileron structure
187 Outer wing pressed sheet ribs
188 Aileron counterweight
189 Junction box
190 Port navigatio lights
191 Port wingtip structure
192 Leading-edge ribs
193 Pitot head
194 Wing leadingedge skin (fabricovered
195 Wing root section I-beam box spar
196 Leading-edge stringers
197 Wing inner surface corrugation
198 Spar single/double I-beam box spar transition
199 Mainwheel leg doors
200 Rearwardretracting mainwheel
201 Mainwheel oleo leg
202 Alloy spokeld hub
203 Cantilever axle
204 Torque links
205 Hydraulic brake cable
206 Drag strut
207 Side strut
208 Drag links
209 Fulcrum
210 Actuating cylinder
211 Multi-bolt outer wing fixings
212 Turbosupercharger cooling intakes
213 Cabin heater intake
214 Cooling louvres
215 Carburettor duct
216 Outer section wing fillet
217 Insulated exhaust stroud duct
218 intercooler/ carburettor duct
219 Supercharger/intercooler duct
220 Outlet
221 Oil radiator shutter
222 Intercooler
223 Exhausts
224 Allison V-1710-89/91 twelve-cylinder Vee engine
225 Magnetos/distributors
226 Intake fairing
227 Header feed pipes
228 Port outer oil radiator
229 Spark-plug and magneto cooling intake
230 Coolant header tank
231 Propeller hub
232 Oil radiator (outer sections) and intercooler (centre section triple intake
233 Curtiss-Electric three-blade (right) handed propeller
234 Inner section underwing stores including
235 Jettisonable auxiliary fuel tank, or
236 Smoke generator

HEAVY FIGHTERS

P-38L LIGHTNING

In total, 3923 of the P-38L Lightning were built, making it the most widely-produced type.

Weight (maximum take-off): 9798kg (21,600lb)
Dimensions: Length: 11.53m (37ft 10in), Wingspan: 15.85m (52ft), Height: 3.91m (12ft 10in)
Range: 2100km (1300 miles)
Ceiling: 13,411m (44,000ft)
Crew: 1
Armament: One 20mm (0.79in) Hispano cannon and four 12.7mm (0.5in) Browning M2 machine guns fixed forward

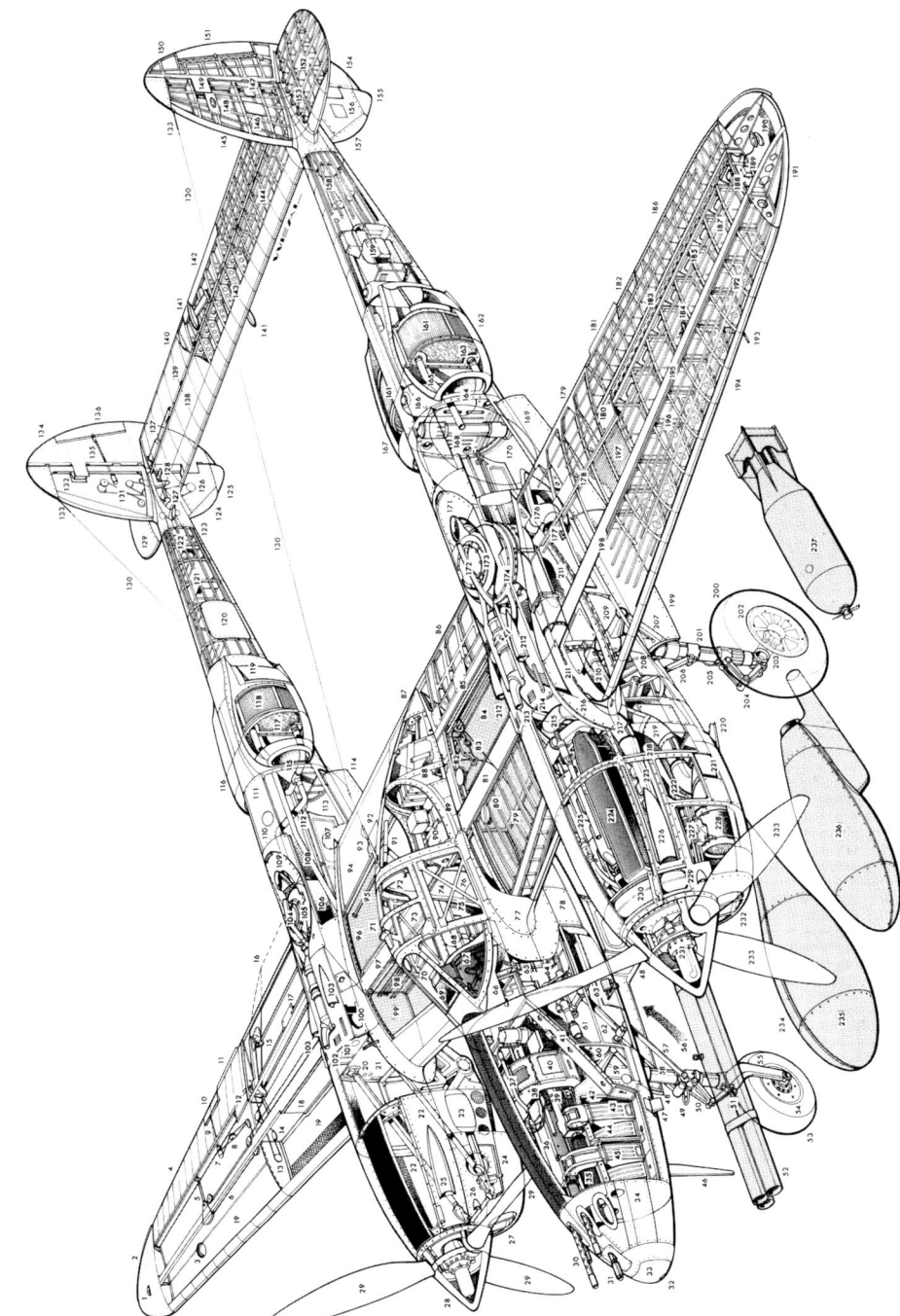

HEAVY FIGHTERS

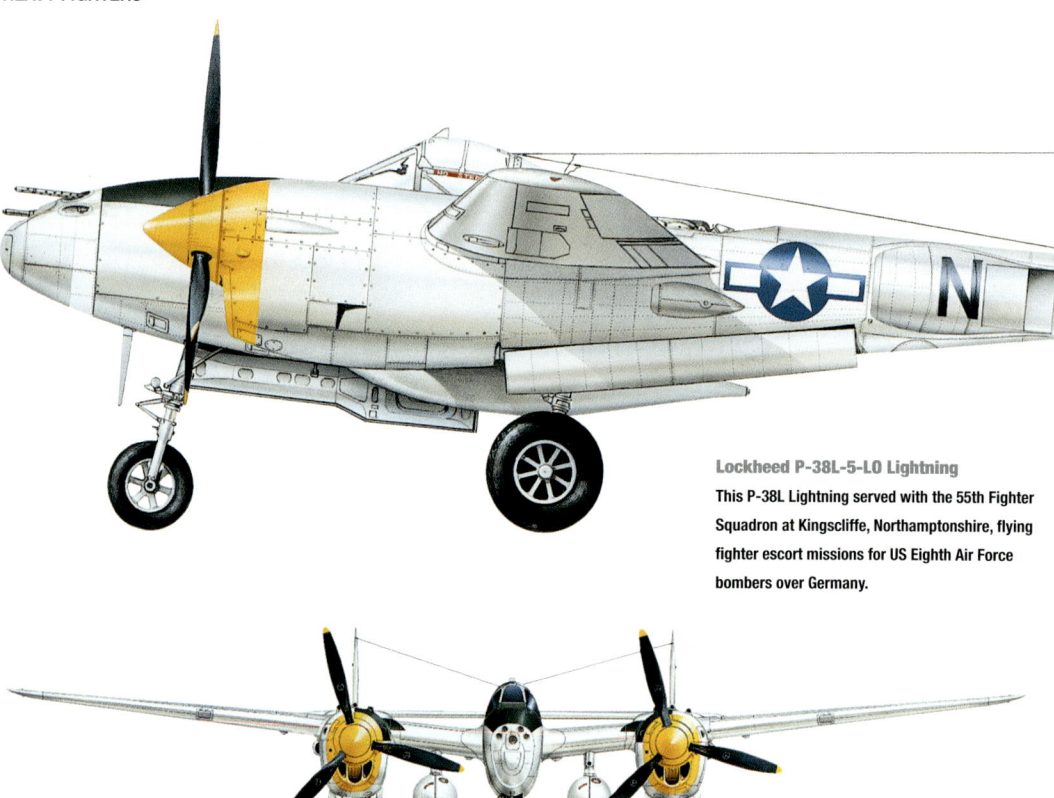

Lockheed P-38L-5-LO Lightning
This P-38L Lightning served with the 55th Fighter Squadron at Kingscliffe, Northamptonshire, flying fighter escort missions for US Eighth Air Force bombers over Germany.

obvious potential of the Lightning saw the Air Corps order 13 YP-38 service test aircraft in April 1939. At around the same time, Lockheed had decided that Air Corps expansion was imminent and would inevitably feature the P-38 and that European orders could be expected.

Consequently, Lockheed began the construction of 80 P-38s (including the 13 YP-38s) and sought to obtain greater factory space. The company's faith in the P-38's capability was vindicated in May 1940, when the French and British ordered 417 and 250 Lightnings respectively, although French capitulation in the following month saw the entire order taken over by Britain.

Initial YP-38 usage

The first YP-38 appeared in September 1940, but Lockheed's commitment to a wide variety of projects delayed the delivery of the rest until early 1941. During testing of the YP-38s, problems were revealed during high-speed dives, with tail buffeting and compressibility (localized airflow exceeding the speed of sound) occurring in the Mach 0.7–0.75 range (the maximum the P-38 could achieve). This could result in the aircraft 'tucking' into an ever-steeper

Lockheed P-38L-5-LO

Weight (maximum take-off): 9798kg (21,600lb)
Dimensions: Length: 11.53m (37ft 10in), Wingspan: 15.85m (52ft), Height: 3.91m (12ft 10in)
Powerplant: Two 1200kW (1600hp) Allison V-1710 -111 left hand rotation and -113 right hand rotation V-12 liquid-cooled piston engines
Maximum Speed: 666km/h (414mph)
Range: 2100km (1300 miles)
Ceiling: 13,411m (44,000ft)
Crew: 1
Armament: One 20mm (0.79in) Hispano cannon and four 12.7mm (0.5in) Browning M2 machine guns fixed forward firing in nose; up to 907kg (2000lb) of bombs on inner underwing racks, up to ten 127mm (5in) rockets or 454kg (1000lb) of bombs on outer underwing racks

HEAVY FIGHTERS

P-38L LIGHTNING

In total, 3923 of the P-38L Lightning were built, making it the most widely-produced type.

Weight (maximum take-off): 9798kg (21,600lb)
Dimensions: Length: 11.53m (37ft 10in), Wingspan: 15.85m (52ft), Height: 3.91m (12ft 10in)
Range: 2100km (1300 miles)
Ceiling: 13,411m (44,000ft)
Crew: 1
Armament: One 20mm (0.79in) Hispano cannon and four 12.7mm (0.5in) Browning M2 machine guns fixed forward

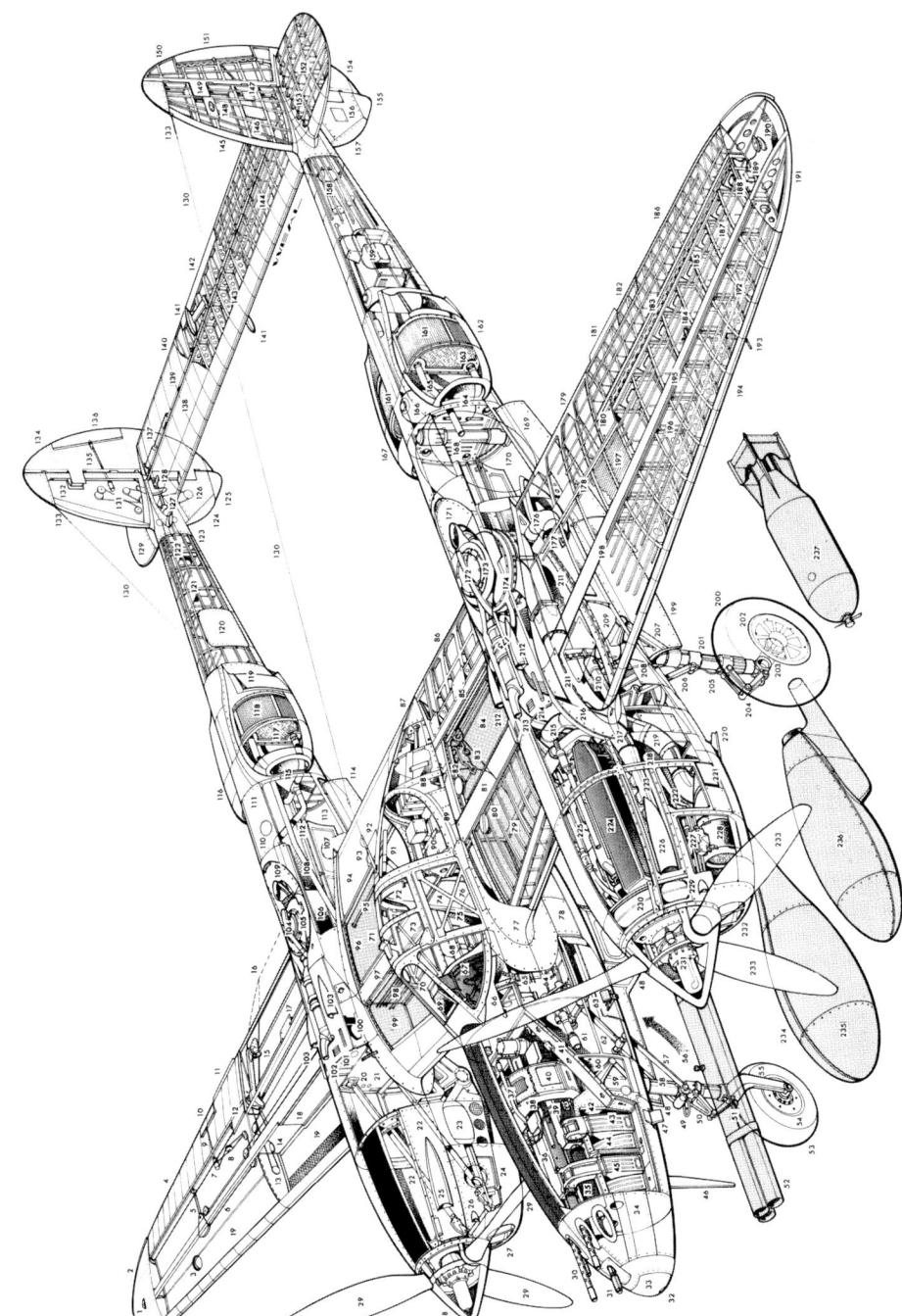

HEAVY FIGHTERS

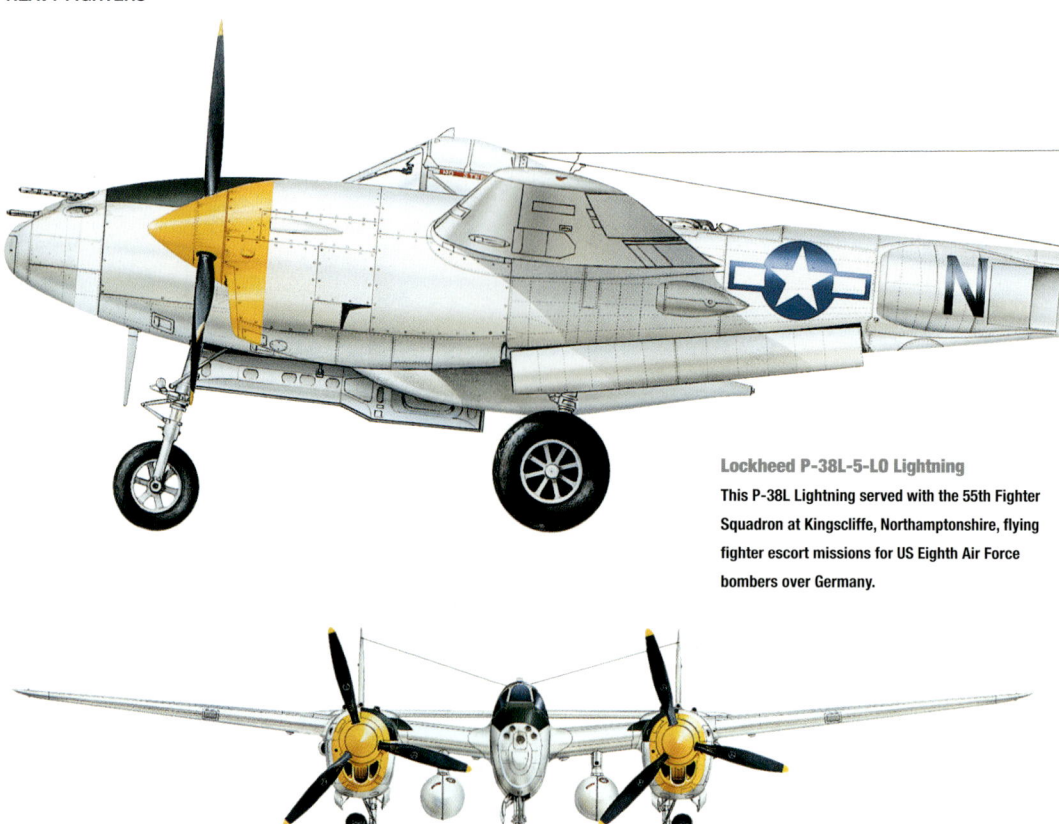

Lockheed P-38L-5-LO Lightning
This P-38L Lightning served with the 55th Fighter Squadron at Kingscliffe, Northamptonshire, flying fighter escort missions for US Eighth Air Force bombers over Germany.

obvious potential of the Lightning saw the Air Corps order 13 YP-38 service test aircraft in April 1939. At around the same time, Lockheed had decided that Air Corps expansion was imminent and would inevitably feature the P-38 and that European orders could be expected.

Consequently, Lockheed began the construction of 80 P-38s (including the 13 YP-38s) and sought to obtain greater factory space. The company's faith in the P-38's capability was vindicated in May 1940, when the French and British ordered 417 and 250 Lightnings respectively, although French capitulation in the following month saw the entire order taken over by Britain.

Initial YP-38 usage

The first YP-38 appeared in September 1940, but Lockheed's commitment to a wide variety of projects delayed the delivery of the rest until early 1941. During testing of the YP-38s, problems were revealed during high-speed dives, with tail buffeting and compressibility (localized airflow exceeding the speed of sound) occurring in the Mach 0.7–0.75 range (the maximum the P-38 could achieve). This could result in the aircraft 'tucking' into an ever-steeper

Lockheed P-38L-5-LO
Weight (maximum take-off): 9798kg (21,600lb)
Dimensions: Length: 11.53m (37ft 10in), Wingspan: 15.85m (52ft), Height: 3.91m (12ft 10in)
Powerplant: Two 1200kW (1600hp) Allison V-1710-111 left hand rotation and -113 right hand rotation V-12 liquid-cooled piston engines
Maximum Speed: 666km/h (414mph)
Range: 2100km (1300 miles)
Ceiling: 13,411m (44,000ft)
Crew: 1
Armament: One 20mm (0.79in) Hispano cannon and four 12.7mm (0.5in) Browning M2 machine guns fixed forward firing in nose; up to 907kg (2000lb) of bombs on inner underwing racks, up to ten 127mm (5in) rockets or 454kg (1000lb) of bombs on outer underwing racks

HEAVY FIGHTERS

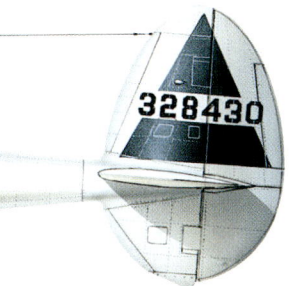

dive as compressibility caused high-speed staling of the centre section. These issues would not be satisfactorily solved until 1944, and in the meantime, pilots were instructed in recovery techniques and performance limitations for the P-38, which, by this time, was in full production for domestic and export use.

Early production models

Only 30 P-38s were built before switching to the P-38D. The P-38A was one example and was fitted with a pressurized cockpit. The P-38B and C did not exist due to a brief and inexplicable attempt on the part of the USAAC to standardize the 'D' suffix for all combat-worthy types. The P-38D featured self-sealing fuel tanks and improved armour. Only 36 P-38Ds were built before the P-38E began to be constructed alongside the British Lockheed Model 322-B, for which the name 'Atlanta' was considered before settling on the original American name. Unfortunately for the British, the export Lightning model was compromised by its lack of turbo-superchargers due to General Electric's inability to produce enough units even for US requirements, and the RAF was informed it would either have to accept this impediment or face a lengthy delay before turbo-supercharged aircraft could be delivered. In the event, the RAF went for a third option: cancellation, and of the 667 Lightnings on order, only three

P-38Hs were the first to have the bar added to the national insignia (illustrated). This factory-fresh example is seen on a test flight from Lockheed's Burbank facility in California, prior to delivery to the USAAF.

HEAVY FIGHTERS

Lockheed P-38J
A P-38J of the 432nd Fighter Squadron, 475th Fighter Group, based in New Guinea, late 1943.

Lockheed P-38J
This P-38J flew with the 338th Fighter Squadron, 55th Fighter Group, based at Nuthampstead, England, in spring 1944.

Lockheed P-38J
Weight (maximum take-off): 9806kg (21,600lb)
Dimensions: Length 11.53m (37ft 10in), Wingspan 15.85m (52ft), Height 3.91m (12ft 10in)
Powerplant: Two 1200kW (1600hp) Allison V-1710-89 left hand rotation and -91 right hand rotation V-12 liquid cooled piston engines
Maximum speed: 666km/h (414mph)
Range (with drop tanks): 3637km (2260 miles)
Ceiling: 13,411m (44,000ft)
Crew: One
Armament: One 20mm (0.79in) Hispano AN/M2 cannon and four 12.7mm (0.5in) Browning M2 machine guns fixed forward firing in nose; up to 1452kg (3200lb) of bombs underwing racks

---

were ever delivered for test purposes. Production of the first batch of RAF aircraft did, however, go ahead, and 140 of these aircraft were accepted by the USAAC as the P-322, with most serving as fighter trainers in the US.

Deployment to Europe and Africa
Three-hundred-and-ten P-38Es were constructed, and this variant could be considered the first that was truly combat capable. The 37mm (1.46in) cannon was discarded in favour of a 20mm (0.79in) weapon. Various other changes were implemented, including an improved radio. The P-38E was also responsible for the first Lightning air-to-air victory when, on 4 August 1942, two P-38s flying out of Adak, Alaska intercepted two Kawanishi H6K flying boats and shot down both. This event occurred a few weeks before the deployment of the P-38 to Europe. This was also the basis for the first Lightnings to be used for the reconnaissance role, two P-38Es initially being converted with four cameras replacing the guns in the nose and redesignated the F-4.

The F-4 was the first of many such photo-reconnaissance Lightnings, and a total of 99 P-38Es were ultimately converted to F-4s. Later, the F-5 would be converted from P-38H, J and L models, and more than 1200 were built. By the summer of 1942, production of the P-38F was in full swing, differing primarily from the P-38E in its use of uprated V-1710 engines and its ability to carry two (454kg) 1000lb bombs under the centre section.

In total, 547 P-38Fs would be built and would form the equipment of most of the first Lightning units to deploy to Europe and Africa. Ferried by air across the Atlantic in Operation 'Bolero' via Greenland and Iceland, three fighter groups had arrived in the UK by the late summer of 1942. One P-38 unit was held in Iceland for operations against Fw 200 Condor maritime patrol aircraft over the North Atlantic, and an Iceland-based P-38F shared in the destruction of an Fw 200 with a P-40 on 15 August

1942, the first USAAF victory against the Luftwaffe. Of these initial P-38s, none would see operational service from Britain, as all were transferred to Africa to support the Operation Torch landings. It was there that the P-38s would see their first major actions.

Engaged primarily in escort work, the P-38s fought frequently and brutally with German and Italian aircraft and suffered very heavy losses. Like all the crop of heavy fighters produced around the world in the late 1930s, such as the Westland Whirlwind, Messerschmitt Bf 110 and Kawasaki Ki-45 Toryu – of which the Lightning was likely the finest example – the P-38 struggled against more manoeuvrable single-seat fighters. The 48th Fighter Group, for example, lost 20 P-38s and 13 pilots in North Africa from mid-November 1942 to late January 1943, with five of these pilots being lost in a single mission on 23 January.

The situation improved when the P-38s switched to interdicting Luftwaffe transport aircraft, and the Lightnings proved highly effective. For example, the 82nd FG shot down 28 transports in a single day on 9 April 1943. The fighting efficacy of the P-38 improved after Lockheed introduced a combat flap modification, allowing the flaps to be lowered eight degrees at combat speeds and increasing manoeuvrability. Further engine upgrades resulted in the P-38G, of which 1462 were built, and the 601 examples of the P-38H, which introduced the ability to carry an increased bomb load of up to two 762kg (1600lb) bombs. These two variants would serve in large numbers against the Japanese. The P-38G was responsible for the P-38's greatest single mission when, on 18 April 1943, aircraft of the 339th FS flew a mission to intercept the aircraft carrying Admiral Ioroku Yamamoto, Commander in Chief of the Combined Fleet and architect of the Pearl Harbor attack. The interception was successfully made after an overwater flight of 700km (435 miles), resulting in three Mitsubishi G4M bombers and three A6M Zeros being shot down, and was the longest-distance interception mission of the entire war.

Fast-paced production

Limitations to the size of the intercoolers that could be fitted in the fuselage booms saw these moved to a chin position utilizing a cowling derived largely from that fitted to the Curtiss P-40F. This made up the only obvious external change to the single-seat Lightning when the P-38J began to appear during the aircraft's production life. This was followed by the almost identical P-38L, which featured engines of similar power to the P-38J albeit with the potential for greater development. 2970 and 3923 were built of the P-38J and L respectively, Lockheed having overcome initial Lightning production difficulties to the extent that some 432 P-38s per month were rolling off the line in January 1945. Although a few P-38Hs initiated escort missions with the Eighth Air Force in Europe, most of the P-38s committed to such missions were P-38Js – though by mid-1944, the appearance of the superior P-51 Mustang saw the P-38s shift increasingly to the ground attack mission, utilizing bombs and rockets.

'Droop Snoot'

As a result, around 25 P-38Js were modified as 'Droop Snoot' navigation and bomb-aiming lead ship with a Plexiglas nose, Norden bombsight, and seat and navigation equipment for a navigator/bombardier. In action, an entire P-38 squadron would bomb at the command of the Droop Snoot lead aircraft. Later, a small number of Droop Snoots were converted from P-38Ls with an AN/APS-15 radar bombsight and operator, allowing bombing through cloud cover. A further two-seat Lightning development was the P-38M night fighter carrying a radar operator in a second cockpit behind the pilot, the AN/APS-4 radar being mounted in an under-nose pod. Faster than the P-61 Black Widow, 75 examples of the P-38M were converted from P-38Ls and were just about to enter service as the war came to an end.

Other users

In addition to the widespread US use of the P-38, the only other relatively major wartime users were France and Italy. Two Free French squadrons converted to the F-5 in Tunisia from November 1943, subsequently following the Allied advance to Italy, Sardinia, Corsica and into Southern France. Similarly, two units of the Italian Co-Belligerent Air Force flew the F-5, though Italy received around 100 P-38Ls in the immediate post-war period. Three F-4s were used by the RAAF for long-range reconnaissance in the Pacific, and China received 15 P-38J and Ls, as well as F-5s following VJ-Day.

Post-war service

In general, however, the P-38 saw little service with nations after the war, largely due to its relative complexity and expense when, by this time, other, cheaper aircraft – particularly the P-51 – could do the same job just as well. The exceptions were Honduras and the Dominican Republic, both of which utilized around a dozen P-38s.

The final combat use of the P-38 occurred in 1957, when five Honduran P-38s bombed and strafed a village occupied by Nicaraguan forces during a border dispute.

HEAVY FIGHTERS

Northrop P-61 Black Widow

The heaviest piston engine fighter ever used by the USAAF, the P-61 was the first aircraft in the world designed from the outset to be fitted with radar.

Like the P-51 Mustang, the Black Widow was originally designed to a British requirement, though ultimately it would never see service with the RAF. Despite Northrop Aircraft Inc being less than a year old, with John K. Northrop having sold his earlier company to Douglas, the British Purchasing Commission approached Northrop to develop a heavily armed aircraft. This aircraft would need to be able to carry the new airborne radar, a crew member to operate it and enough fuel to mount standing patrols from dusk to dawn if necessary, allowing for the interception of incoming bombers before they arrived at their targets. It was assumed that interception would be impossible if take-off occurred only once the bombers were detected by ground radar.

Northrop drew up designs over the summer of 1940, by which time the USAAC had also decided that it required a specialized night fighter, after Lt. Gen. Delos C. Emmons visited Britain in 1940 and witnessed both the Luftwaffe's night bombing offensive as well as the potential of airborne radar. By the end of January 1941, the Air Corps had contracted for two XP-61 prototypes and a few weeks later ordered a service trials batch of 15 YP-61s. British interest in the P-61 was maintained, with USAAC approval, and the RAF even had priority for deliveries, with the first 50 production airframes earmarked for supply to Britain before the Air Corps received theirs. In the event, however, by the time the P-61 was available, the RAF had sufficient numbers of Mosquitos and did not operate the Black Widow.

The first XP-61 was completed in the early spring of 1942, and the first flight was made with a mock-up of the remotely controlled dorsal turret, this item being delayed due to the greater priority given to the B-29, which utilized the same turret design. Although flying characteristics were satisfactory, various major changes had to be made before the aircraft could enter production, primarily to the lateral flying controls. The P-61 eventually adopted an unconventional system wherein lateral control was primarily achieved by spoilers above and below each wing, ahead of the flaps, with small ailerons at the wingtips. Viewed with suspicion at first, this system proved highly effective, and the Black Widow possessed outstanding manoeuvrability for its size.

Dorsal turret

As the SCR-720 radar was still secret, this equipment was only fitted to the first XP-61 after it was delivered to the USAAF in April 1943. However, problems arose with the dorsal turret, supplies of which had become sufficient to allow it to be fitted to the YP-61s. In flight tests, rotating or elevating the guns caused severe buffeting, and further wind tunnel work was undertaken to try and solve the issue. In the interim, strengthening the turret and removing the two inboard guns was found to mollify the buffeting somewhat, and all YP-61s were consequently modified. By this time, the first P-61A production aircraft were also leaving the production line, and though the first 37 were delivered with the turret, the balance of 200 P-61As went into service without it, operating with a crew reduced to two. Initial aircraft were painted in the standard USAAF olive drab over grey. Tests, however, revealed that a high-gloss finish proved less conspicuous if caught in a searchlight beam than matt black, resulting in a switch to the Black Widow's distinctive all-black finish.

First operations

Initial P-61 operations took place in May 1944, the first Black Widow unit to be deployed being the 422nd Night Fighter Squadron assigned to the 9th Air Force based in England. The first P-61s arrived in the Pacific the following month, and it was here that the type achieved its first victory, when a Mitsubishi G3M was shot down on 30 June, though the ongoing reduction in enemy air activity meant further victories against the Japanese would be few. One particularly unusual mission is worthy of note, however. On 30 January 1945, a solitary P-61 performed aerobatics for several minutes to distract the guards at Cabanatuan prison camp, allowing Allied troops to approach the camp undetected before successfully attacking and liberating the camp.

In Europe, teething troubles would rob the P-61 of its first victory. Vectored to intercept a V-1 flying bomb on 15 July, Lt Herman Ernst dived to match the high speed of the missile, causing the Perspex rear fuselage cone to implode. This problem affected several P-61s before it was solved. The following night, Lt Ernst was once again vectored to intercept a V-1, and this time the interception was successful, earning the P-61 its first European victory. The following month saw the P-61 encounter manned enemy aircraft for the first time, and on the night of 14/15 August, a Heinkel He 177 was shot down, with further victories following swiftly. By war's end, three pilots and two radar operators would achieve 'ace' status.

As German aerial opposition dwindled, however, P-61s were increasingly utilized in the ground attack role, their heavy armament of four 20mm (0.79in) cannon being found to be particularly effective at destroying locomotives. P-61s also undertook night intruder sorties, using napalm to illuminate targets that were then attacked with underwing rockets. Pacific-based P-61s also switched to the ground attack role, using a P-38 shackle to carry a 454kg (1000lb) bomb under the fuselage and rockets under the wing. Underwing 1173 litre (310 US gallon) fuel tanks were also introduced, allowing the aircraft to achieve an endurance of 11 hours.

Ongoing work had been progressing both at Northrop and in the field to improve the P-61's combat capability. The P-61B, with numerous minor improvements, began to be received by the USAAF in July 1944. A new feature introduced with this variant was night binoculars, which, combined with an optical gunsight, allowed the pilot to sight on targets at distances some five times greater than without their use. During 1944, the buffeting problems caused by the turret were cured, and this feature was reintroduced midway through the P-61B's production run, several earlier P-61s subsequently being retrofitted with the turret at unit level. The P-61B was followed by the P-61C, which featured turbo supercharged engines and wing air brakes – but only 41 had been built by VJ-Day.

Further development was effectively curtailed by the end of the war, but the XP-61E long-range escort fighter was developed into the F-15 Reporter reconnaissance aircraft, of which 36 examples were built. The F-15 Reporter went on to provide most of the aerial maps used at the start of the Korean War, though by then the last night fighter Black Widows had retired, having been replaced by the F-82 Twin Mustang in May 1950.

Northrop P-61B
Weight (maximum take-off): 16,420kg (36,200lb)
Dimensions: Length: 15.11m (49ft 7in), Wingspan: 20.12m (66ft), Height: 4.47m (14ft 8in)
Powerplant: Two 1680kW (2250hp) Pratt & Whitney R-2800-65W Double Wasp 18-cylinder air-cooled radial piston engines
Maximum Speed: 589km/h (366mph)
Range: 2170km (1350 miles)
Ceiling: 10,100m (33,100ft)
Crew: 3
Armament: Four 20mm (0.79in) Hispano AN/M2 cannon fixed forward firing in ventral fuselage, four 12.7mm (0.5in) M2 Browning machine guns in remotely operated upper turret, underwing racks for bombs up to 726kg (1600lb) each or six 127mm (5in) unguided rockets; some aircraft were modified to carry one 454kg (1000lb) bomb under the fuselage

Northrop P-61B
This aircraft was named 'Time's a' Wastin' and was one of the most famous Black Widows in the Pacific Theatre.

HEAVY FIGHTERS

Northrop P-61B Black Widow
The aircraft depicted here, 42-39404 'Midnight Madness II', was assigned to Captain James W. Bradford of the 548th Night Fighter Squadron. Flying out from Ie Shima on 24 June 1945, the fighter destroyed a Mitsubishi G4M 'Betty' – one of only five kills credited to the squadron.

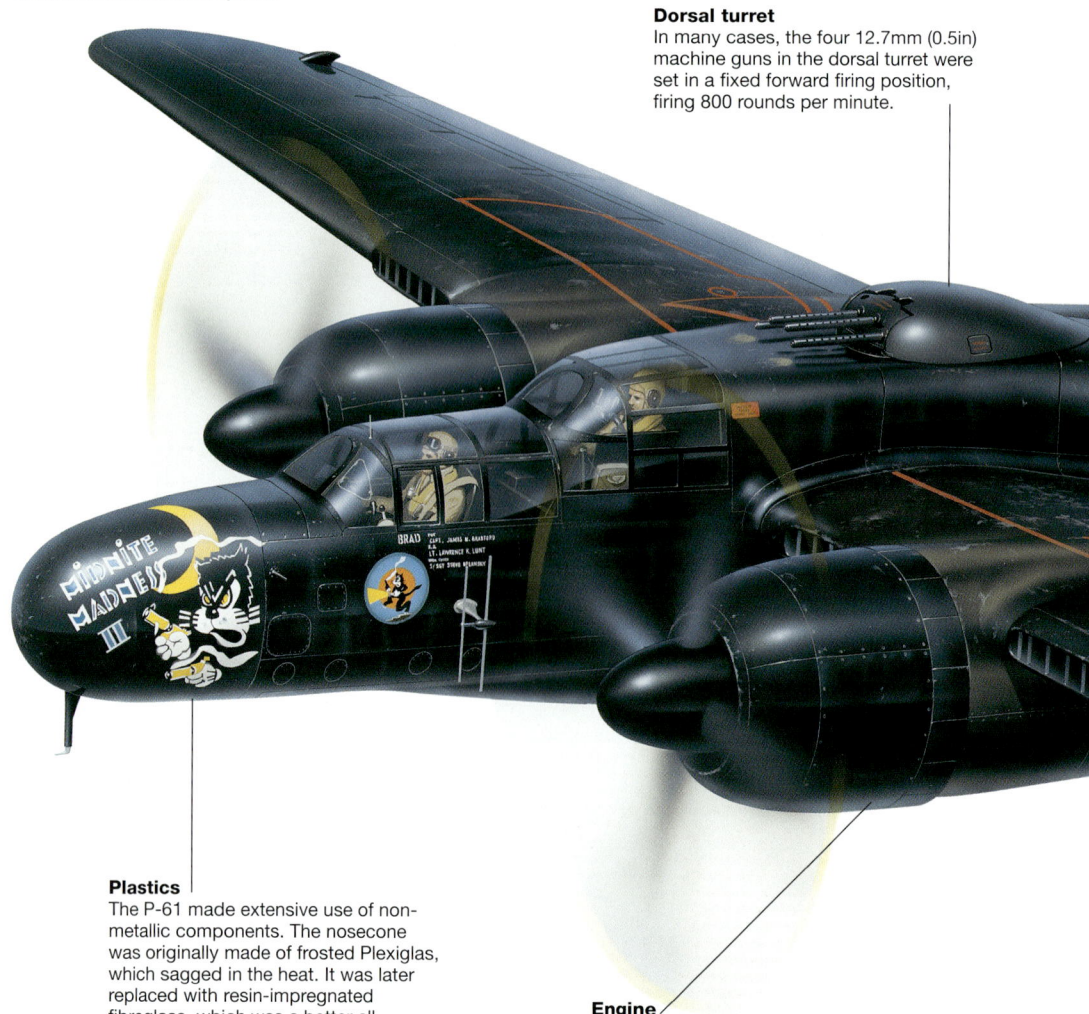

Dorsal turret
In many cases, the four 12.7mm (0.5in) machine guns in the dorsal turret were set in a fixed forward firing position, firing 800 rounds per minute.

Plastics
The P-61 made extensive use of non-metallic components. The nosecone was originally made of frosted Plexiglas, which sagged in the heat. It was later replaced with resin-impregnated fibreglass, which was a better all-weather compound.

Engine
The P-61B used two Pratt & Whitney R-2800-65 Double Wasp 18-cylinder radial engines rated at 1491kW (2000hp).

HEAVY FIGHTERS

Radio equipment
Early P-61Bs carried a SCR-729 VHF beacon locator; by sending out pulses and interrogating ground beacons, the SCR-729 could be used as a navigation aid.

Northrop P-61B
Weight (maximum take-off): 16,420kg (36,200lb)
Dimensions: Length: 15.11m (49ft 7in), Wingspan: 20.12m (66ft), Height: 4.47m (14ft 8in)
Powerplant: Two 1680kW (2250hp) Pratt & Whitney R-2800-65W Double Wasp 18-cylinder air-cooled radial piston engines
Maximum Speed: 589km/h (366mph)
Range: 2170km (1350 miles)
Ceiling: 10,100m (33,100ft)
Crew: 3
Armament: Four 20mm (0.79in) Hispano AN/M2 cannon fixed forward firing in ventral fuselage, four 12.7mm (0.5in) M2 Browning machine guns in remotely operated upper turret, underwing racks for bombs up to 726kg (1600lb) each or six 127mm (5in) unguided rockets; some aircraft were modified to carry one 454kg (1000lb) bomb under the fuselage

Cannon armament
The four 20mm (0.79in) Hispano M2 cannon were mounted in the belly in a staggered installation, with two outboard guns being positioned much further back.

NAVAL TYPES

NAVAL TYPES

Allied carrier aircraft were dominated by US designs during World War II. The F4F was by far the most successful Allied naval fighter of the early-war period, though it struggled against the Japanese A6M 'Zero'. The last two years of war at sea saw the total superiority of the F6F Hellcat and F4U Corsair, the latter of which would enjoy an unprecedented career long into the post-war era. This chapter also features the F2A Buffalo, which enjoyed mixed success with a variety of nations, and the impressive F7F Tigercat and F8F Bearcat, which were on the cusp of entering service at VJ Day.

- Brewster F2A Buffalo
- Grumman F4F Wildcat
- Grumman F6F Hellcat
- Grumman F7F Tigercat
- Grumman F8F Bearcat
- Vought F4U Corsair

Pilots sprint for their F4U Corsairs when word goes out that unidentified aircraft are approaching Roi-Namur, Marshall Islands, 20 June 1944.

NAVAL TYPES

Brewster F2A Buffalo

The rotund F2A beat the Grumman Wildcat to become the US Navy's first monoplane fighter. Unfortunately, the Brewster fighter proved wanting in combat with US forces, though it achieved greater success with other nations.

In the mid-1930s, the US Navy believed that the landing speed of the monoplane was too high for carrier operations, but as the biplane was clearly nearing the end of its development potential, it was felt that trials with a monoplane fighter should be carried out. Consequently, the prototype Brewster XF2A-1 was ordered along with Grumman's biplane XF4F-1 as a back-up. First flown on 2 December 1937, the XF2A-1 could hardly be called sleek, but it possessed a fully flush riveted stressed skin construction, split flaps and a hydraulically powered retractable undercarriage.

A-1s and A-2s

Accepted for production as the F2A-1, 54 were produced, and 11 F2A-1s were issued to VF-3 on USS *Saratoga* by the end of 1939, becoming the first operational monoplane carrier fighters in the US Navy. The F2A-1 was faster and handled better than early Grumman F4Fs, and initial carrier

Brewster F2A-2

The second unit to operate the F2A was VF-2, the 'Flying Chiefs', who took their F2A-2s aboard USS *Lexington* for a training cruise to Pearl Harbor in March 1941.

operations proved relatively trouble-free. The faster XF2A-2 followed, with a heavier armament of four 12.7mm (0.5in) machine guns, more fuel and other equipment. Forty-three were ordered. The decision was then taken to release the balance of F2A-1 production for export to Finland as the B-239. Belgium and the United Kingdom followed suit, ordering the F2A-2 (designated B-339 for export) in 1940, with the Netherlands East Indies ordering B-339s shortly after. The British bestowed the name 'Buffalo' on the fighter, and this swiftly became a universal nickname for the aircraft.

Limited manoeuvrability

Although the F2A-2 was faster than the F2A-1, weight growth resulted in a shortfall in other areas, particularly

Brewster F2A-2
Weight: (Maximum takeoff) 3125kg (6890lb)
Dimensions: Length 7.92m (26ft), Wingspan 10.67m (35ft), Height 3.56m (11ft 8in)
Powerplant: One 895kW (1200hp) Wright R-1820-40 Cyclone 9-cylinder air cooled radial piston engine
Maximum speed: 554km/h (344mph)
Range: 2688km (1670 miles)
Ceiling: 10,363m (34,000ft)
Crew: One
Armament: Four 12.7mm (0.50in) M2 Browning machine guns fixed forward-firing in wings; up to 91kg (200lb) bomb load

manoeuvrability, and the F2A-3, of which 108 were ordered by the US Navy, proved to be even worse. The F2A-3 was heavier, mostly due to increased fuel capacity, but possessed the same engine as the F2A-2, and performance was lowered on every count.

Withdrawn from carrier use

The higher weight also proved too much for the Buffalo's landing gear, and undercarriage failures were commonplace, resulting in the withdrawal of the F2A from US carriers. F2As were still aboard USS *Saratoga* at the time of Pearl Harbor. However, all had been transferred to shore-based roles within a month. The F2A's only major engagement in US service occurred during the Battle of Midway, when poor tactics saw Marine Corps unit VMF-221 lose 13 out of 20 F2As committed. Subsequently, all F2As were relegated to advanced fighter training, a role for which their easy flying characteristics and relatively high performance rendered them highly suitable.

In Finland, the B-239 formed the backbone of the fighter arm until the introduction of the Messerschmitt Bf 109G-2 in mid-1943. Against Soviet aircraft, the B-239 proved both highly successful and extremely popular with pilots, achieving a victory-to-loss ratio of 32 to 1.

In Britain, however, the Brewster was rejected for use in Europe, and most were sent to the Far East in the belief they were superior to any Japanese fighter. In reality, Japanese forces outnumbered the Allies and possessed better fighter aircraft, and virtually all the Brewsters were destroyed by March 1942, despite inflicting serious losses on the enemy. Four Allied pilots became 'aces' on the type.

Brewster F2A-3

Weight: (Maximum take-off) 3247kg (7159lb)
Dimensions: Length: 8.03m (26ft 4in), Wingspan: 10.67m (35ft), Height: 3.66m (12ft)
Powerplant: One 890kW (1200hp) Wright R-1820-40 Cyclone nine-cylinder air-cooled radial engine
Maximum Speed: 517km/h (321mph)
Range: 1553km (965 miles)
Ceiling: 10,100m (33,200ft)
Crew: 1
Armament: Two 12.7mm (0.5in) M2 Browning machine guns fixed forward firing in wings, two 12.7mm (0.5in) M2 Browning machine guns

Brewster F2A-3

VMF-221 took the F2A into action with American forces for the first and only time on 4 June 1942 at the Battle of Midway. Losses were catastrophic and only three of the 20 F2As that took off to intercept Japanese bombers were serviceable by 6 June.

NAVAL TYPES

Grumman F4F Wildcat

Although not particularly fast, the Grumman F4F was well-armed, manoeuvrable and exceptionally robust. Perhaps most important of all, it was easy to operate from a carrier, and would prove to be the most important Allied carrier fighter for the first half of the war.

Grumman had proposed a smaller and more powerful development of its successful F3F biplane fighter, designated the F4F-1, when the US Navy issued a specification for a new shipboard fighter in 1935. However, the startling appearance of the Brewster F2A monoplane, designed to the same specification as the biplane F4F – but offering a much greater predicted performance – prompted both Grumman and the Navy to reconsider the future of the F4F.

Grumman proposed a new monoplane design in place of the biplane F4F-1, and this was met with immediate acceptance by the Navy. As a result, the prototype XF4F-1 was never built, the contract being cancelled, and a new contract was placed with Grumman for the XF4F-2 monoplane in July 1936.

Closely matched rivals
Despite starting their design process somewhat later than Brewster, Grumman completed the XF4F-2 before the rival XF2A-1, reflecting their greater experience producing military aircraft. Test pilot Robert L Hall made its first flight on 2 September 1937. The two new monoplanes were very closely matched, and though the Grumman proved slightly faster than its Brewster rival, the XF2A was more manoeuvrable. Unfortunately for Grumman, the XF4F-2 was subject to a series of delays until eventually it suffered a forced landing due to engine failure in April 1938. This possibly led to the Navy's decision to select the Brewster F2A as its first monoplane fighter over the Grumman machine.

Nonetheless, Grumman remained convinced that the F4F possessed a

Grumman F4F-3
Weight: (Maximum take-off) 3367kg (7423lb)
Dimensions: Length: 8.76m (28ft 9in), Wingspan: 11.59m (38ft), Height: 3.61m (11ft 10in)
Powerplant: One 895kW (1200hp) Pratt & Whitney R-1830-86 Twin Wasp 14-cylinder air-cooled radial piston engine
Maximum Speed: 515km/h (320mph)
Range: 1360km (845 miles)
Ceiling: 12,000m (39,500ft)
Crew: 1
Armament: Six 12.7mm (0.5in) AN/M2 Browning machine guns fixed forward firing in wings; up to 90kg (200lb) bombload under wings

Grumman F4F-3
An F4F-3 of VF-7 aboard USS *Wasp*, December 1940. Note the basic non-camouflage scheme of gloss light grey with gloss chrome yellow upper wing surface, first introduced in October 1940. The national insignia is on the forward fuselage, in accordance with the March 1940 directive for types participating in the Neutrality Patrol.

NAVAL TYPES

Grumman F4F-3
This Grumman F4F-3 MF-1 was part of VMF-224, based at Guadacanal, summer 1942.

Grumman F4F-3
This F4F-3 No. F-15 was flown by Lt. Edward H. (Butch) O'Hare of VF-3 aboard USS *Lexington*.

great deal of potential and proposed fitting a more powerful version of the Pratt & Whitney Twin Wasp, incorporating a two-speed, two-stage supercharger, allowing the engine to maintain a high-power output to a much greater height than was previously possible. This proposition was met with enthusiasm by the Navy, and work on the updated aircraft proceeded rapidly. The new engine was considerably heavier than the earlier version, which required the substitution of the original wings with a new design of greater span and area. This redesign also resulted in the elegantly curved surfaces of both wing and tail being discarded in favour of a straight-edged angular planform that was to feature on most Grumman designs for the rest of the war and beyond.

On 12 February 1939, the rebuilt prototype flew for the first time as the XF4F-3 and immediately demonstrated a performance superior to both its progenitor and the Brewster F2A. Test flying continued into 1940 and resulted in numerous changes, the most significant being the repositioning of the horizontal tail surfaces from the rear fuselage to the tail fin and an increase to the dihedral of the wings.

In August 1939, a production contract was issued to Grumman for the first batch of F4F-3s, the first production machine making its maiden

NAVAL TYPES

Grumman F4F-4
This F4F-4 Wildcat, No. 28 of VC-39, was stationed on USS *Liscome Bay* in November 1943.

flight in February 1940, though it would be July before the second example followed it into the air. Both these aircraft were subsequently used for development flying. In October, the US Navy adopted the name 'Wildcat' for the F4F, beginning an unbroken line of US Navy Grumman 'cats' that would come to an end only when the F-14 Tomcat was retired in 2006.

By this time, the aircraft had already attracted considerable foreign interest, and orders were placed by Belgium, France and the UK in 1940. The French Aéronavale aircraft were to be powered by the Wright R-1820 Cyclone, fitted with French Darne 7.5mm (0.3in) machine guns and French radios and gunsights. However, both Belgium and France fell before the aircraft could be delivered, and the order was transferred to the UK, which named it the Martlet I. These became the first F4Fs to enter operational service anywhere in the world when deliveries began in July 1940. Two of these aircraft then achieved another first when they shot down a Junkers Ju 88 over the Orkney Islands on Christmas day 1940 – the first instance of a US-built aircraft in British service claiming a combat victory.

Later aircraft built for subsequent British contracts were powered by the 895kW (1200hp) Pratt & Whitney S3C4-G with a two-speed supercharger and folding wings. These aircraft were named the Martlet II. To expedite deliveries, however, the Royal Navy agreed to take the first ten of the order for 100 without the folding wing capability.

US usage

Meanwhile, deliveries of production aircraft to the US Navy began in December 1940, and during the following month, the first examples began to equip VF-7 and VF-4 aboard USS *Wasp* and USS *Ranger* respectively. Though generally enjoying a smooth entry into service, early aircraft suffered from a propensity for the wing-mounted flotation bags to inflate of their own accord, throwing the aircraft into an uncontrollable dive. The US Navy quickly discarded the bags, but not before at least one fatal accident occurred because of such a failure, and they remained

Grumman F4F-4

Weight: (Maximum take-off) 3978kg (8762lb)
Dimensions: Length: 8.85m (29ft), Wingspan: 11.59m (38ft), Height: 3.44m (11ft 4in)
Powerplant: One 895kW (1200hp) Pratt & Whitney R-1830-86 Twin Wasp 14-cylinder air-cooled radial piston engine
Maximum Speed: 515km/h (320mph)
Range: 2051km (1275 miles) with external tanks
Ceiling: 10,370m (34,000ft)
Crew: 1
Armament: Six 12.7mm (0.5in) AN/M2 Browning machine guns fixed forward firing in wings; up to 90kg (200lb) bombload under wings

NAVAL TYPES

Grumman F4F
A Grumman F4F, No. 42-F-1 of VF-42, serving aboard USS *Ranger*.

fitted to export F4Fs. Another feature disliked by pilots, though not actually dangerous, was the manually retracted undercarriage, which required approximately 30 turns of a handle to raise and lower. Although this was a fairly common feature at the time, most of its contemporaries switched fairly rapidly to a powered retraction system, though no such feature was ever fitted to the Wildcat.

Successful service use saw further contracts placed with Grumman for the F4F-3 and F4F-3A, which featured the same (more powerful) engine as fitted to British Martlet IIs. Slightly confusingly, 30 examples of a version of the F4F-3A were to be delivered to Greece. However, when that nation surrendered, the aircraft had only got as far as Gibraltar. The Greek F4Fs were then taken on by the UK and designated the Martlet III(B). Without folding wing capability, these aircraft were used at shore bases in the Western Desert.

Pacific War

When the US entered World War II in December 1941, Navy and Marine

Grumman F4F Wildcats fly in tactical formation of four-plane divisions, comprised of two-plane sections, circa mid-1943.

NAVAL TYPES

squadrons possessed 245 Wildcats, and the F4F was plunged into intense action almost immediately in the desperate and ultimately unsuccessful defence of Wake Island later the same month, achieving its first combat victories in US service in the process. During this action, Captain Henry Elrod managed to sink the Japanese destroyer *Kisaragi* with the Wildcat's distinctly modest bomb load.

Against its primary opponent, the A6M Zero, the Wildcat was at a speed disadvantage, and the sprightly Zero was considerably more manoeuvrable, especially at lower speeds. The F4F could only hold its own due to its remarkable resilience to gunfire and the superior tactics of the American pilots. Wildcat ace James 'Jimmy' Thach stated that 'the F4F airplane is pitifully inferior in climb, manoeuvrability and speed' to the Zero in his report following the Battle of Midway.

A reconnaissance modification of the F4F-3 was also developed, known as the F4F-3P, with its two reserve fuel tanks replaced with Fairchild F-56 cameras. With a reduced fuel load, it could only be used for short-range tactical reconnaissance missions, but it retained the standard armament so was able to defend itself if necessary. Eighteen F4F-3Ps were produced and were used in action at Espiritu Santo and during the invasion of Attu Island.

F4F-4

Grumman had by this time developed the F4F-4, which featured two extra 12.7mm (0.5in) guns and introduced folding wings for the first time, utilizing Grumman's patented 'sto-wing' system, which allowed the wings to swing through 90 degrees to be stored pointing backwards alongside the fuselage. This feature immediately doubled the number of Wildcats that could be stored on any given carrier and effectively ended any chance of the Brewster F2A continuing to serve aboard a carrier, as it was never modified to feature a folding wing. The F4F-4 entered service in December 1941 and rapidly became the most numerous variant; by the time of the decisive Battle of Midway in June 1942, all the USN fighter units committed were equipped, at least in part, with F4F-4s. Unfortunately, the added weight of the extra armament and the folding wing had a detrimental effect on the overall performance of the aircraft, and the F4F-4 was less popular with pilots than its predecessor.

By the time the Guadalcanal campaign began during the summer of 1942, a long-range photo-reconnaissance Wildcat had entered service, replacing the earlier F4F-3P, the F4F-7, of which only 21 were built. The F4F-7 was unarmed, carried a single camera, and featured an enormous 2594L (685 US gallon) internal fuel capacity sufficient to give it a theoretical endurance of 24 hours, though a flight of this duration was never actually undertaken as it was clearly beyond the capability of a human pilot.

F4F-5

During 1942, the F4F-5, a version equipped with a Cyclone engine, was flown for comparative flight tests with the standard Twin Wasp-powered F4F-4. Although a US contract was

Eastern Aircraft FM-2
This FM-2, No.8 of VC-93, was stationed aboard USS *Steamer Bay*, June 1945.

NAVAL TYPES

Eastern Aircraft FM-2
This FM-2 Wildcat, Black 20, served with VC-36 aboard USS *Core*, April 1944.

Eastern Aircraft FM-2

Weight: (Maximum takeoff) 3751kg (8270lb)
Dimensions: Length: 8.85m (29ft), Wingspan: 8.53m (28ft), Height: 3.44m (11ft 4in)
Powerplant: One 1006kW (1350hp) Wright R-1820-65 air-cooled radial piston engine
Maximum Speed: 534km/h (332mph)
Range: 2051km (1275 miles) with external tanks
Ceiling: 10,570m (34,700ft)
Crew: 1
Armament: Four 12.7mm (0.5in) AN/M2 Browning machine guns fixed forward firing in wings; two 250 lb. bombs or six 5-in. rockets

not forthcoming, this variant did see service with the Royal Navy as the Martlet IV, 220 examples of which were acquired by Britain. Arguably the most unusual variant appeared during 1942: the F4F-3S, a floatplane fighter intended to operate where airfields were unavailable. A hundred sets of floats were produced to convert F4F-3s for maritime operations. However, apart from the prototype, nicknamed the 'Wild Catfish', none were ever used. During the same year, General Motors began production of the F4F-4, fitted with just four wing guns, as the FM-1 (or Martlet V in the UK), eventually producing 1600 examples.

FM-2

During 1943, with Grumman concentrating on Hellcat development and production, General Motors undertook total responsibility for Wildcat assembly, eventually delivering over 4400 examples (over half of the 7860 Wildcats produced in total) of the F4F-8 variant, designated FM-2 when built at General Motors. This was the final version, instantly recognizable due to its taller vertical tail, and was primarily used on escort carriers, known as 'jeep carriers' in US service, which were too small to handle larger, more modern fighters. The impeccable deck manners of the FM-1 and FM-2, combined with their ability to fly off a small carrier without catapult assistance (no such equipment being fitted to escort carriers), saw the Wildcat widely employed on these vessels by both the US and UK, where the FM-2 was designated the Wildcat VI, the Martlet name having been dropped in March 1944. US escort carriers were exclusively equipped with the FM-2 and Grumman TBF Avenger to operate in the anti-submarine role and against shore targets.

Somewhat unexpectedly, despite the Wildcat's increasing obsolescence by this late stage of the war, the FM-2 achieved the best kill-to-loss ratio of any subtype of a US fighter, destroying 422 Japanese aircraft for the loss of just 13 FM-2s in air-to-air combat, a ratio of 32 to 1. This final Wildcat variant was also responsible for the last Royal Navy victories in Europe when, on 26 March 1945, eight Messerschmitt Bf 109Gs attacked a squadron of Avengers and Wildcats from HMS *Searcher* off the Norwegian coast. The Wildcats shot down three Bf 109s and seriously damaged a fourth for no loss. Post-war, there was no place for the aged Wildcat with either the US or Royal Navy, and the type was disposed of extremely quickly, with hundreds of examples being unceremoniously dumped into the sea – a sad end for a decisive aircraft.

NAVAL TYPES

Grumman F6F Hellcat

The US Navy's premier carrier fighter of World War II, the F6F Hellcat was ultimately credited with more combat victories than any other naval fighter in history. It achieved this by combining decent performance with excellent deck landing characteristics and an immensely strong airframe to devastating effect.

Aware of the threat posed by high-performance aircraft then being developed in Japan, at the end of the 1930s, the US Navy sought to procure a better fighter than the F4F Wildcat, which was then still under development. The Vought F4U Corsair offered world-beating performance, but early testing was progressing slowly, and it was considered prudent to develop an alternative fighter as a back-up to the Vought aircraft.

In June 1941, the Navy ordered two prototypes of an 'improved F4F', which was originally planned to consist of an F4F airframe fitted with the Wright R-2600 Cyclone. However, the Grumman design team, led by Leroy Grumman himself, felt that an entirely new design would be far superior.

Although the development of an entirely new aircraft carried the risk of significant delay, Grumman managed to get this brand-new aircraft into combat a mere 14 months after the prototype's first flight.

The F6F was considerably larger than the Wildcat it was intended to replace and possessed a loaded weight around 60 per cent greater than that of the earlier aircraft. The weight growth called for the use of a larger wing, and the wing area of the F6F was the largest of any single-engine fighter of World War II. Typical of Grumman products, the aircraft boasted remarkable structural strength and would earn an enviable reputation in service for its ability to absorb punishment and remain airborne.

A great deal of attention was paid to pilot protection, and a full 96kg (212lb) of the F6F's empty weight consisted of armour. This was the opposite approach to the design philosophy of the F6F's principal foe, the Mitsubishi A6M 'Zero', which sacrificed protection to achieve the

Grumman F6F-3
Weight: (Maximum take-off) 6000kg (13,217lbs)
Dimensions: Length: 10.17m (33ft 4in), Wingspan: 13.08m (42ft 10in), Height: 4.4m (14ft 5in)
Powerplant: One 1492kW (2000hp) Pratt & Whitney R-2800-10 Double Wasp two row 18-cylinder air-cooled radial piston engine
Maximum Speed: 600km/h (373mph)
Range: 1755km (1090 miles)
Ceiling: 11,438m (37,500ft)
Crew: 1
Armament: Six 12.7mm (0.5in) Browning AN/M2 machine guns fixed forward firing in wings; up to 907kg (2000lb) bomb load or six 127mm (5in) rockets

Grumman F6F-3
This F6F-3 No. 33 served with VF-16 aboard USS *Lexington*, April 1944.

NAVAL TYPES

Grumman F6F-3
F6F-3 (42179) No.15 of VF-44, flying from USS *Langley*, 24 October 1944.

best possible performance from its relatively low-powered engine. During the early design period, consideration was given at Grumman to pursuing a similar approach to that adopted by Mitsubishi, but it was concluded that the loss of versatility and increased vulnerability that would result from this design philosophy was not acceptable. Further concern was raised by the initial combat reports coming back from Naval aviators who had clashed with Zeros in action.

Such reports suggested that the F6F would require the best speed and climb rate possible to effectively combat the Japanese aircraft, and doubts were raised at Grumman as to whether relying solely on the R-2600 Cyclone intended for the XF6F-1 as development of the engine was a sensible course of action, not least because the R-2600's development was beginning to lag behind that of Pratt & Whitney's impressive R-2800 Double Wasp, which offered a 1491kW (2000hp) potential against the Cyclone's 1267kW (1700hp). Grumman obtained Navy approval to fit the R-2800 to the second prototype F6F, designated XF6F-3, the designation XF6F-2 being reserved for a variant powered by a turbo-supercharged R-2800, which was briefly tested in January 1944 but that progressed no further.

Urgent production

Flying for the first time on 26 June 1942, the Cyclone-powered prototype XF6F-1 was followed into the air by the Double Wasp-powered XF6F-3 barely more than a month later on 30 July. By this time, the R-2800 had become the powerplant of choice, and such was the urgency attached to the programme that large-scale production was ordered by the Navy as the F6F-3 Hellcat on 23 May 1942, before either prototype had even flown.

Thankfully, flight trials were highly satisfactory, with what few shortcomings that appeared being eradicated in the production-standard machines. These differed externally from the prototype solely in the elimination of the propeller spinner and a change in the design of the undercarriage wheel fairings. Somewhat less immediately successful were the carrier acceptance trials, which saw the arrestor hook torn completely out of an early production F6F and a second landing incident result in the failure of the entire rear fuselage. Localized structural strengthening was applied, and no further trouble of this kind was encountered. Compared to its great rival, the F4U Corsair, the flight and carrier trials of the F6F were remarkably trouble-free. The first squadron to fly the F6F-3 was VF-9, with initial deliveries beginning in January 1943, the unit embarking on USS *Essex* during the spring of that year. On 31 August, VF-5, operating from USS *Yorktown*, took the F6F-3 into combat for the first time as part of a force attacking Japanese positions on Marcus Island.

British Hellcats

At much the same time, the British Royal Navy began to receive F6F-3s, designated Hellcat I, as part of lend-lease arrangements, the uninspiring name 'Tarpon' having been initially chosen but discarded in favour of the American name before the service entry of the aircraft. Replacing the Sea Hurricane, the first Hellcats were supplied to 800 Squadron on 1 July 1943. They began their Royal Navy service with anti-shipping missions

NAVAL TYPES

Grumman F6F-5
This F6F-5 Hellcat (94267) was part of the New York Navy Reserve.

along the Norwegian coast before escorting Fairey Barracudas attacking the battleship Tirpitz, an operation that resulted in three Hellcats shooting down a German fighter each. Like their US counterparts, however, most British Hellcat operations would take place in the Pacific.

Formidable fighter

Production built up very rapidly, with 2555 F6Fs constructed by Grumman during 1943. The conversion of F4F units to the new fighter proceeded quickly as a direct result. In combat against the Japanese, the F6F proved more formidable than its forebear, and its excellent deck landing qualities and huge strength endeared it to pilots. Against the A6M Zero, the fighter which the Hellcat had been so urgently required to fight, the F6F, proved highly successful. The Hellcat could follow the Zero through most manoeuvres and enjoyed a useful margin of performance over its Japanese foe. With an inexorable reduction in Japanese fighter pilot quality due to the loss of experienced aircrew and a gradual reduction in effective training, the Hellcat proved awesomely successful in air-to-air combat. The high point of its career was undoubtedly the Battle of the Philippine Sea in June 1944. During this battle, F6Fs shot down 243 Japanese aircraft in what would become known as the 'Marianas Turkey Shoot'. With many more aircraft lost when two Japanese carriers were sunk, this battle effectively destroyed the ability of the Imperial Japanese Navy to conduct carrier operations as they had lost 90 per cent of their operational aircraft and aircrew. It was a blow from which the Japanese Navy would not recover.

By the end of the war, US F6F pilots had made 5168 air-to-air victory claims, with all but eight scored in the Pacific. This was an inflated figure, but it was clear that the Hellcat shot down more enemy aircraft than any other carrier fighter during World War II, or indeed ever. The most successful US Navy fighter pilot, Captain Donald McCampbell, scored all 34 of his credited victories in the Hellcat, including nine shot down during a single mission on 24 October 1944, the most in a single mission by any American pilot.

Grumman F6F-5

Weight: (Maximum take-off) 6002kg (13,221lb)
Dimensions: Length: 10.17m (33ft 4in), Wingspan: 13.08m (42ft 10in), Height: 4.4m (14ft 5in)
Powerplant: One 1492kW (2000hp) Pratt & Whitney R-2800-10 Double Wasp two row 18-cylinder air-cooled radial piston engine
Maximum Speed: 600km/h (373mph)
Range: 2606km (1620 miles) with external fuel tank
Ceiling: 11,438m (37,500ft)
Crew: 1
Armament: Six 12.7mm (0.5in) Browning AN/M2 machine guns fixed forward firing in wings; up to 1814kg (4000lb) bombload or six 127mm (5in) rockets or two 298mm (11.75in) Tiny Tim rockets

NAVAL TYPES

During 1943, work had been undertaken to increase the aircraft's usefulness by adapting the Hellcat to both the reconnaissance and night fighting roles. The former resulted in the F6F-3P high-altitude photo reconnaissance version, with cameras fitted in the fuselage directly behind the pilot. The night fighter required a rather more extensive modification, mounting a fairly large pod on the starboard wing containing the AN/APS-6 radar unit. The cockpit featured red lighting to reduce glare, and a radar altimeter was fitted. The outer Plexiglas windscreen was removed to cut down on reflections, and landing lights were installed. Designated F6F-3N, 149 of this night fighter variant were produced, entering service during February 1944 with VF(N)-76 aboard USS *Yorktown* and achieving their first victory during the same month.

External improvements

Few changes were made to the basic Hellcat over its production life, but the desire to maximize the speed performance of the aircraft, which was relatively modest compared to its contemporaries, saw the development of an aerodynamically improved version of the F6F-3 in January 1944. This variant achieved a speed of 660km/h (410mph) at 6405m (21,000ft). Although this version would not enter production, a new variant incorporating some of the improvements of this aircraft went into production during April 1944 as the F6F-5 and was in widespread service by the late summer of that year. The

Grumman F6F-5
F6F-5 No. 7 of VF-29 flew from USS *Cabot*, April 1945.

Grumman F6F-5P
F6F-5P No.132 was piloted by Lt. John J. Sargent of VF-84, aboard USS *Bunker Hill*, February 1945.

major external differences were a new, closer-fitting engine cowling, the deletion of the windows behind the cockpit canopy and the removal of the curved front windscreen as fitted to the F6F-3. Provision was made for the first time for the aircraft to carry underwing stores, and in some later-production F6F-5s, two 20mm (0.79in) cannon replaced two of the standard 12.7mm (0.5in) machine guns. In total, 7870 F6F-5s were built, including a few F6F-5P reconnaissance versions and 1434 of the F6F-5N, which featured the same wing-mounted AN/APS-6 radar pod as the F6F-3N.

Also, 935 F6F-5s were also supplied to the Royal Navy, entering service as the Hellcat II. By August 1945, 10 British squadrons were operating the Hellcat, including examples of both the reconnaissance and night fighting versions. The latter formed the equipment of the final two Royal Navy Hellcat squadrons, which disbanded in August 1946.

F6F-6

An F6F-6 version with a more powerful Double Wasp (and the fastest of all the Hellcats) was the last to be developed during the war. However, all production was terminated at VJ-Day, and only two prototype XF6F-6s were built. After the war, the Hellcat quickly disappeared from US carrier decks, replaced in the air-to-air role by the F8F Bearcat.

Additionally, the fighter-bomber duties of the Hellcat were better served by its old rival, the F4U Corsair, which was faster and could carry more ordnance.

Korean War combat

The F6F served on in reserve squadrons for a few years, but the last US combat usage of the Hellcat was as a guided missile. Explosive-laden F6F-5K remote-controlled flying bombs were used against targets in North Korea in the summer of 1952. Post-war, the F6F was supplied to the French Aéronavale and saw further combat during the early 1950s with French forces in Indochina, but the final user was the Uruguayan Navy, which withdrew its surviving Hellcats as late as 1960. A total of 12,275 Hellcats were built, despite the entire production life of this incredibly successful aircraft lasting only three years and one month.

The motion of its props causes an 'aura' to form around this F6F aboard USS *Yorktown*, 1943.

Grumman F7F Tigercat

The impressive Tigercat showcased exceptional performance and was a potentially devastating heavy fighter. Later, it would see action in the Korean War. However, in Wolrd War II, the Tigercat saw the briefest of service.

Grumman F7F-2N Tigercat
The Tigercat was utilized quite extensively in Korea. This F7F-3N was on the strength of HEDRON-1 (1st Marine Aircraft Wing Headquarters Squadron) at Pohang, Korea, in 1952.

Grumman flew the promising XF5F Skyrocket twin-engine fighter during 1940, but once the US entered the war, it was cancelled to allow the company to concentrate on development of the Hellcat. Nonetheless, both the US Navy and Grumman maintained an interest in the twin-engine fighter concept, and the large new Midway class carriers promised to be of sufficient size to allow the operation of a larger aircraft than had hitherto been possible. As a result, development of a more powerful version of the same basic concept was undertaken, resulting in the F7F Tigercat.

Unrealized potential

Making its maiden flight in December 1943, the F7F was the first US Navy carrier aircraft to possess a nose wheel undercarriage. The fuselage was intended to present as small a frontal area as possible to minimize drag and was notably slender. Armament was heavy, with four 12.7mm (0.5in) machine guns and four 20mm (0.79in) cannon. Fitted with two R-2800 engines slung under its shoulder-mounted wing, the aircraft's performance proved outstanding, but trials revealed that operating the large Tigercat from existing carrier decks, though possible, was difficult. As a result, the decision was taken to equip 12 land-based Marine Corps squadrons with the F7F. Only 35 of the initial F7F-1 single-seaters were built before production switched to the F7F-2N, a two-seat night-fighter featuring a position for the radar operator behind the pilot and an AN/APS-6 radar, which replaced the nose machine guns. VMF(N)-533 was the first Marine Corps unit to convert to the F7F-2N, arriving in Okinawa on 14 August 1945.

The wartime service of the F7F, however, would prove vanishingly brief, due to the surrender of Japan occurring the very next day. The unit subsequently flew operational patrols in the area, before moving to China.

Post-war production amounted to 250 of the improved single seat F7F-3 variant, 60 of which were converted to F7F-3N night fighters. After the aircraft failed its carrier qualification trials following a wing failure during a heavy landing, both variants were only used by shore-based units. Marine Corps Tigercats would see combat in Korea, with night fighter F7F-3Ns shooting down two Polikarpov Po-2 biplanes – the only victories attained by the Tigercat. A final variant, the strengthened F7F-4N, did pass its carrier qualification, but only 12 were built. All F7Fs were withdrawn in 1952.

Grumman F7F-1 Tigercat
Weight: (maximum take-off) 10,730kg (23,636lb)
Dimensions: Length: 13.85m (45ft 5in), Wingspan: 15.7m (51ft 6in), Height: 5.06m (16ft 7in)
Powerplant: Two 1600kW (2100hp) Pratt & Whitney R-2800-22W Double Wasp 18-cylinder air-cooled radial engines
Maximum Speed: 687km/h (427mph)
Range: 1882km (1170 miles), 2880km (1790 miles) with 1136 (300 gallon) litre external tank
Ceiling: 11,040m (36,200ft)
Crew: 1
Armament: Four AN/M3 20mm (0.79in) cannon in wing roots, four 12.7mm (0.5in) M2 Browning machine guns in fuselage nose; up to two 454kg (1000lb) bombs or eight 12.7mm (0.5in) rockets under wings, one 1136 litre (300 US gallon) fuel tank or one 568 litre (150 US gallon) napalm tank under fuselage

NAVAL TYPES

Grumman F8F Bearcat

Grumman's ultimate piston-engine fighter, the Bearcat delivered an outstanding performance and was the most numerous US Navy fighter for several years.

In 1943, Grumman initiated the development of a higher-performance aircraft to replace the F6F Hellcat, which was then just beginning operational service. During the previous year, Jake Swirbul, the vice president of Grumman, had met with F4F pilots who had seen combat at the Battle of Midway to see what they wanted from a future carrier fighter, and rate of climb was rated as potentially the most important attribute a new fighter could possess. No readily available US engine at the time could deliver greater power than the R-2800 as fitted to the Hellcat, and thus the only way to achieve a usefully improved climb performance was to design the smallest and lightest airframe around the existing engine.

As a result, the F8F, as first flown in August 1944, was 1.5m (4.9ft) shorter than the Hellcat, 2.1m (6.9ft) shorter in span, and around 500kg (1100lb) lighter. As a result, it proved to be 80km/h (50mph) faster and demonstrated a spectacular rate of climb. So much so that at the Cleveland Air Races in 1946, a stock F8F-2 Bearcat would set an unofficial time-to-height record, climbing

Grumman F8F-1B

This Bearcat served in the South Vietnamese Air Force in the 1950s, after being donated by French forces following their withdrawal.

from a standing start to 10,000ft in 94 seconds – a record that would stand for 10 years.

Two thousand F8Fs were ordered, with deliveries beginning in February 1945. The first unit, VF-19, received its aircraft in May. This unit was en route to the Pacific theatre aboard USS *Langley* when the conflict ended. As a result, it saw no combat service. Grumman had built just over 200 F8Fs by VJ-Day, and 765 examples would be built in total. Although it formed the equipment of 28 squadrons by mid-1949, making it the most numerically important fighter in the US Navy inventory at the end of the 1940s, the F8F was rapidly withdrawn from service as the new crop of jet fighters appeared.

Rare Bear

By 1951, all Bearcats had been replaced by jets in frontline units, though the F8F would see action

Grumman F8F-1 Bearcat
Weight: (Maximum take-off) 5878kg (12,947lb)
Dimensions: Length: 8.62m (28ft 3in), Wingspan: 10.94m (35ft 10in), Height: 4.23m (13ft 10in)
Powerplant: One 1600kW (2,100hp) Pratt & Whitney R-2800-34W Double Wasp 18-cylinder air-cooled radial engine
Maximum Speed: 677km/h (421mph)
Range: 1778km (1105 miles), 3162km (1965 miles) with external tanks
Ceiling: 11,804m (38,700ft)
Crew: 1
Armament: Four 12.7mm (0.5in) M2 Browning machine guns in wings; up to two 454kg (1000lb) bombs or four 12.7mm (0.5in) rockets under wings

with French forces in the Indochina War during the same year. In 1989, a considerably modified F8F named 'Rare Bear' set the 3km (1.86 miles) World Speed Record for piston-engine aircraft at 850.26km/h (528.33mph). This record stands to the present day.

NAVAL TYPES

An F8F Bearcat warms up its engine at a Pacific base, circa mid-1945. Note the ground crewman on the wing and the fire extinguisher below.

NAVAL TYPES

Vought F4U Corsair

The Corsair weathered a problematic service entry due to its unforgiving deck landing characteristics to become one of the most successful fighters of World War II. It remained in frontline service for decades after the end of the conflict.

One of the greatest combat aircraft in history, the F4U had the longest production run of any US piston-engine-powered fighter and would achieve the last known air-to-air 'kill' by a piston-engined aircraft thirty years after it first flew. Rolled out in May 1939, the impressive prototype XF4U-1 possessed the largest and most powerful engine, the largest propeller and the largest wing of any Naval fighter yet built. Its most striking design feature though was its distinctive inverted gull wing design, adopted to allow clearance for the huge propeller without requiring prohibitively long undercarriage legs.

Designed by Rex Beisel, it flew for the first time on 29 May 1939, though testing was delayed after the aircraft overturned as the result of an emergency landing on a golf course. Returned to flight test by the late summer of 1940, the XF4U-1 gained early fame by becoming the first US fighter to exceed 650km/h (400mph) in level flight. It also delivered an excellent rate of climb and an impressive ceiling of 10,736m (35,200ft). Unfortunately, the aircraft exhibited some less-than-desirable handling characteristics, not least a disconcerting tendency to drop a wing when it approached touchdown speed.

Nonetheless, the excellent performance of the aircraft saw an initial order for 584 F4U-1s placed on 3 March 1941, even as the XF4U-1 was being put through the standard Navy tests. This was an immense order by the standards of the day and reflected the increasing expectation that the US would be involved in imminent war. The size of the order was beyond the ability of Vought to produce on its own, and associate contractors for Corsair production were sought. Both Brewster Aeronautical Corporation and the Goodyear Aircraft Corporation committed to Corsair production during November 1941, and both these companies would produce substantial numbers of Corsairs as the F3A-1 and FG-1 respectively.

Vought lead the charge

Vought's new Dallas factory delivered the first production F4U-1s during June 1942. By the time these appeared, combat reports of air-to-air combat over Europe had filtered back to the

Vought F4U-1A

Weight: (Maximum take-off) 6350kg (14,000lb)
Dimensions: Length: 10.16m (33ft 4in), Wingspan: 12.5m (41ft), Height: 5.13m (16ft 10in)
Powerplant: One 1492kW (2000hp) Pratt & Whitney R-2800-8 Double Wasp 14-cylinder air-cooled radial piston engine
Maximum Speed: 671km/h (417mph)
Range: 1633km (1015 miles)
Ceiling: 11,247m (36,900ft)
Crew: 1
Armament: Six 12.7mm (0.50in) M2 Browning machine guns fixed forward firing in wings

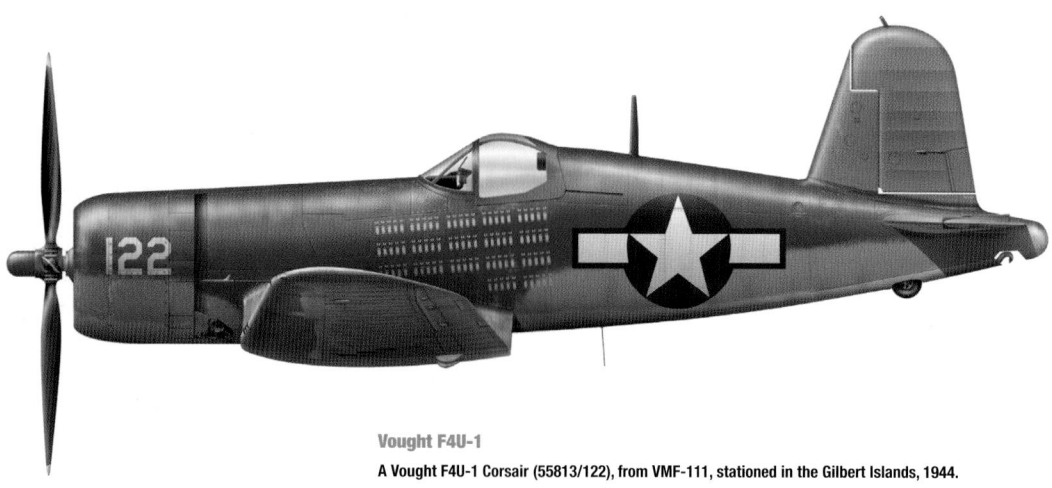

Vought F4U-1
A Vought F4U-1 Corsair (55813/122), from VMF-111, stationed in the Gilbert Islands, 1944.

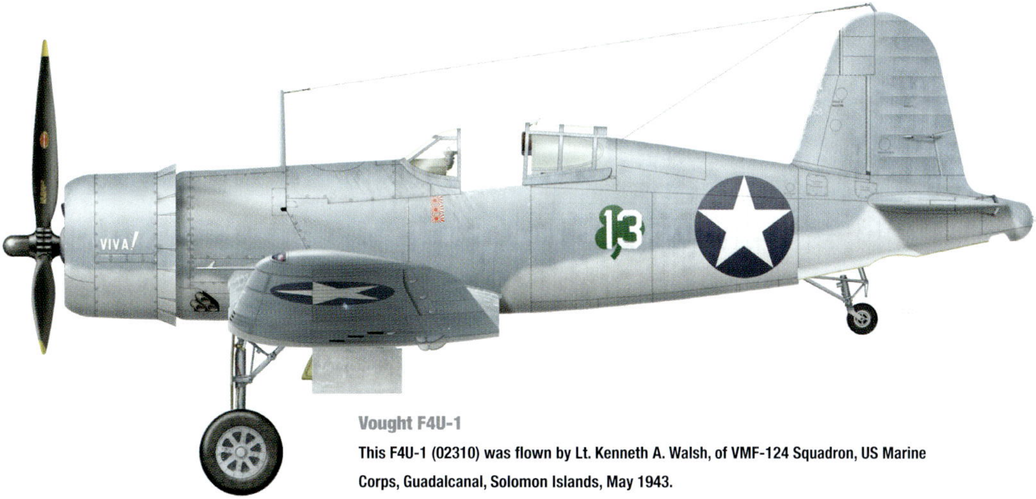

NAVAL TYPES

Vought F4U-1
This F4U-1 (02310) was flown by Lt. Kenneth A. Walsh, of VMF-124 Squadron, US Marine Corps, Guadalcanal, Solomon Islands, May 1943.

Vought F4U-1A
Flown by 1st Lt. Stout, VMF-422, US Marine Corps, this F4U-1A (serial number 17965) was based at Engibi, Marshall Islands, May 1944.

Vought F4U-1A
This F4U-1A (serial number 55995) was piloted by Lt. Ira C. Kepford, flying with VF-17, USS *Bougainville*, Solomon Islands, February 1944.

NAVAL TYPES

Vought FG-1D
This FG-1D (76660/660) flew with US Marine Corps fighter squadron VMF-312.

US, and the design had been altered as a result. The most significant change arose from the need to fit a heavier armament than what was fitted to the prototype: two 7.62mm (0.3in) machine guns in the nose and two 12.7mm (0.5in) in the wings. The wings were therefore redesigned to accept three 12.7mm (0.5in) machine guns each, and the nose guns and associated synchronizing gear were discarded. This change required space in the wings that contained fuel tanks, and these had to be moved to the fuselage.

For reasons related to the aircraft's centre of gravity, the fuel tank could only be placed above the aircraft's wing, requiring the cockpit to be moved 92cm (3ft) rearwards. This change, when combined with the nose-high attitude necessary when making a carrier approach, made for an extremely poor forward view, a criticism that would dog the Corsair for its entire operational life, although the issue was ameliorated somewhat over the course of its service career, culminating in the raised cockpit and downward-angled cowling of the late model F4U-5 and AU-1. However, this was not yet a problem when service deliveries of the Corsair began to be received in July 1942, as the aircraft had not yet undertaken carrier trials. Urgently requiring a higher-performance fighter than the F4F Wildcat to combat Japanese forces in the Pacific, the decision was taken to give land-based Marine Corps squadrons priority for F4U-1 deliveries, the outcome of carrier trials being irrelevant for these units. As a result, the first operational unit to receive Corsairs was VMF-124 of the Marine Corps in September 1942, subsequently taking the F4U into combat for the first time when they were dispatched to support beleaguered US forces on Guadalcanal in February 1943. Despite manifest inexperience – the aircrew possessed an average of 20 hours experience on type – the Marine pilots rapidly established air superiority over the islands. The formidable combat capability of the Corsair was firmly established, and within six months, all Marine Corps fighter units based in the South Pacific would be equipped with the F4U.

While the Corsair's enviable reputation as a fighter was being staked over the Solomons, the beginnings of its unenviable reputation as a difficult deck landing aircraft was

Vought FG-1D
Weight: (Maximum takeoff) 5951kg (13,120lbs)
Dimensions Length: 10.16m (33ft 4in), Wingspan: 12.5m (41ft), Height: 5.13m (16ft 10in)
Powerplant: One kW (2250hp) Pratt & Whitney R-2800-8W Double Wasp 14-cylinder air-cooled radial piston engine
Speed: 684km/h (425mph)
Range: 1633km (1015 miles)
Ceiling: 10,333m (33,900ft)
Crew: One
Armament: Six 12.7mm (0.50in) M2 Browning machine guns fixed forward-firing in wings; up to 907kg (2000lb) bomb load

quickly emerging during carrier trials aboard USS *Core*. These confirmed the difficulties of operating the F4U-1 at sea with poor visibility, and the tendency for a wing to abruptly drop when near the stall was found to be compounded by unfortunately stiff shock absorbers in the undercarriage, which resulted in the aircraft bouncing back up after the wheels touched the carrier deck, regularly leading to the hook missing all the arrestor wires and an inevitable crash. Even if this were not to occur and an arrestor wire was successfully engaged by the tail hook, the tendency to bounce combined with the low-profile canopy of the early Corsair could result in the pilot's head

NAVAL TYPES

Vought F4U-1C

Weight: (Maximum takeoff) 6350kg (13,999lb)
Dimensions: Length 10.16m (33ft 4in), Wingspan: 12.5m (41ft), Height: 5.13m (16ft 10in)
Powerplant: One kW (2000hp) Pratt & Whitney R-2800-8 Double Wasp 14-cylinder air-cooled radial piston engine
Maximum speed: 671km/h (417mph)
Range: 1633km (1015 miles)
Ceiling: 11,246m (36,895ft)
Crew: One
Armament: Four 20mm (0.79in) Hispano AN/M2 cannon fixed forward-firing in wings

being smashed against the inside of the canopy.

Nevertheless, despite the widespread belief that the Corsair failed its US carrier qualification tests and the British Fleet Air Arm instead developed landing techniques for it, three USN F4U units had in fact successfully carrier-qualified before the Royal Navy even started to receive Corsairs. The fact that the F4U was acknowledged to be an admittedly difficult aircraft for the average pilot to deck land, particularly when compared to its great rival, the comparatively docile F6F Hellcat, undoubtedly contributed to the decision to equip land-based Marine Corps units with Corsairs and operate Hellcats from carriers. This course of action was chosen primarily for logistical reasons, primarily to simplify spare parts supply, but undeniably tarred the F4U's reputation. On the other hand, it placed Marine Corps units, typically the last in line to receive the latest combat types, in the unusual position of receiving an

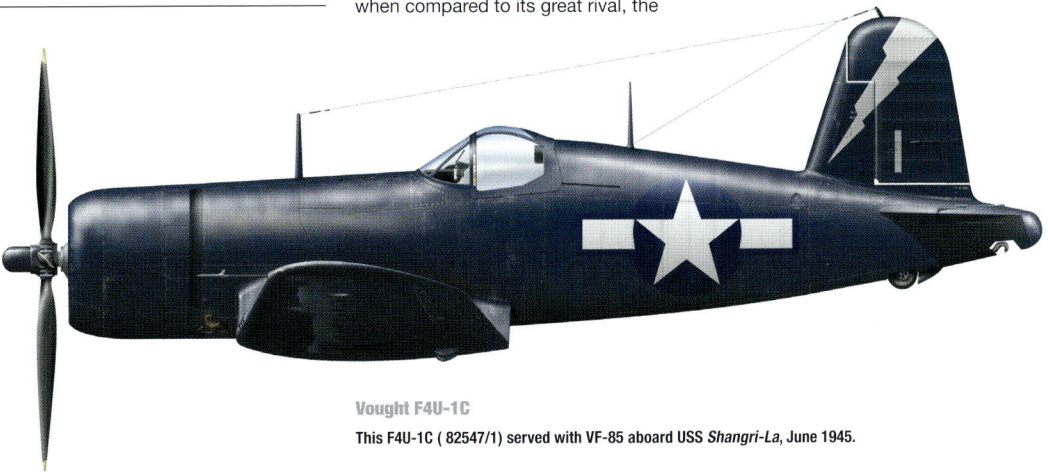

Vought F4U-1C
This F4U-1C (82547/1) served with VF-85 aboard USS *Shangri-La*, June 1945.

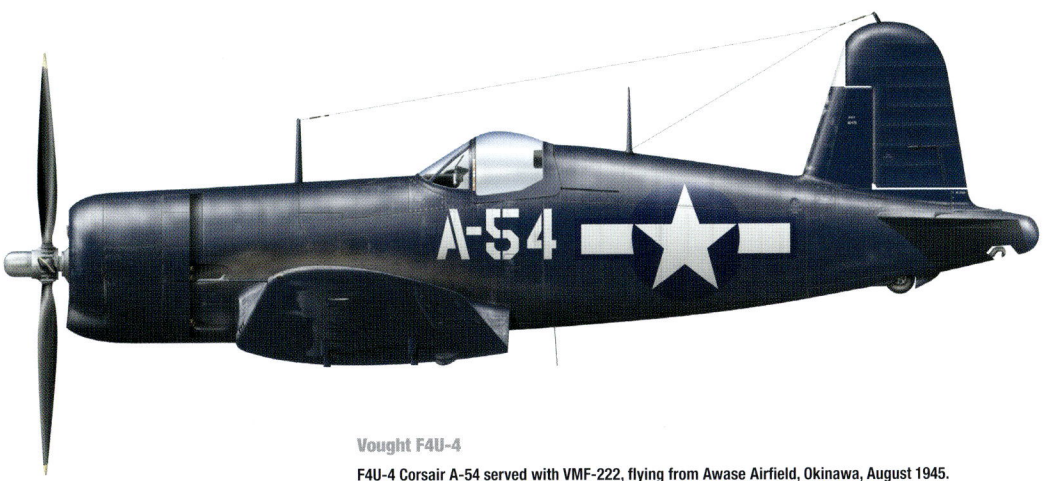

Vought F4U-4
F4U-4 Corsair A-54 served with VMF-222, flying from Awase Airfield, Okinawa, August 1945.

NAVAL TYPES

aircraft that many considered a superior fighting machine to the F6F before their US Navy equivalents.

Distinctive profile

With the US Navy dropping the F4U from its carrier inventory in favour of the Hellcat, urgent and ultimately successful measures were taken by Vought to improve the F4U's deck manners. From the 759th aircraft onwards, a raised cockpit canopy was fitted, improving pilot view aircraft and endowing the Corsair with its distinctive profile – one that would remain largely unchanged until the end of production nearly a decade later.

This change also reduced the unfortunate tendency for pilots to strike their head on the inside of the canopy when landing and aircraft so-equipped were retrospectively designated F4U-1A. A small spoiler was fitted to the starboard wing to prevent wing drop near the stall and the tail wheel leg was lengthened to lower the nose angle on the ground, improving pilot view when on the ground.

The shock absorbers were altered to make them less stiff and fitted with a slow-release valve that restricted their rebound after the initial compression on landing, thus greatly reducing the tendency to bounce.

Carrier trials with these improvements took place aboard USS *Gambier Bay* in March 1944 and proved entirely satisfactory. Modifications were then made to all Corsairs currently in service, paving the way for the resumption of full shipboard operations by the US.

Vought F4U-1D
Weight: (Maximum takeoff) 5951kg (13,120lbs)
Dimensions Length: 10.16m (33ft 4in), Wingspan: 12.5m (41ft), Height: 5.13m (16ft 10in)
Powerplant: One kW (2250hp) Pratt & Whitney R-2800-8W Double Wasp 14-cylinder air-cooled radial piston engine
Speed: 684km/h (425mph)
Range: 1633km (1015 miles)
Ceiling: 10,333m (33,900ft)
Crew: One
Armament: Six 12.7mm (0.50in) M2 Browning machine guns fixed forward-firing in wings; up to 907kg (2000lb) bomb load

British service

By the time this was taking place, however, the British Royal Navy had been regularly operating the Corsair from carriers since mid-1943 and had encountered no major insuperable difficulty in doing so. British Corsairs were easily distinguished as they had 22cm (8in) clipped from each wingtip to allow the aircraft to fit in the hangar decks of Royal Navy carriers, this modification also resulting in the side effect of improving the stall characteristics of the fighter. The operational debut of the Corsair in British hands occurred in April 1944 in both Europe and the Pacific, with 1834 Squadron supplying fighter cover for Fairey Barracudas dive-bombing the *Tirpitz* in Norway, while aircraft from HMS *Illustrious* escorted Barracudas and Grumman Avengers attacking the oil refineries on Sabang, Sumatra. The first Corsairs received by the Royal Navy were designated Corsair I, with raised cockpit versions becoming the Corsair II. F3As from Brewster, of which the Royal Navy would receive over half of all produced, and Goodyear FG-1s were referred to as the Corsair III and IV respectively. The only other wartime user was New Zealand, with early delivery of Corsairs to the RNZAF being authorized by the US following the impressive showing of New Zealand squadrons flying the P-40 in the South Pacific, particularly in air-to-air combat. Eventually, 424 Corsairs equipped 13 RNZAF squadrons, with the first 30 being delivered in March 1944.

Subsequent variants

Further development by Vought concentrated on improving the Corsair's versatility and performance. The F4U-2 was a night fighter variant which appeared in January 1943 and featured an AN/APS-6 radar in a pod near the starboard wingtip. Only 32 were converted from standard F4U-1s by the Naval Aircraft Factory (Vought at the time being swamped with other work), although a further two aircraft were converted to F4U-2 standard by frontline units. Despite the tiny number produced, the F4U-2 did see combat, with the first going into action with VF(N)-101 aboard USS *Enterprise* and USS *Intrepid* in early 1944. The F4U-3 was a turbo-supercharged version that did not see production, but the F4U-4 featuring the R2800-18W water-boosted engine with a four-bladed propeller began to enter service in early 1945. It was the most formidable wartime Corsair to actually enter service, capable as it was of 721km/h (448mph) and with a spectacular rate of climb while still being able to carry all the same external stores (e.g. rockets, bombs, drop tanks) as the F4U-1.

Super Corsair

By the time the F4U-4 was entering active service, the Corsair was seeing more use as a ground attack asset than an air superiority fighter and was demonstrating that a single-seat fighter bomber was a superior close aircraft than the larger, slower aircraft traditionally employed by the USN for this role, such as the Grumman TBF Avenger and Curtiss SB2C Helldiver. Despite this role shift, Goodyear developed a variant with the 2237kW (3000hp) Pratt & Whitney R-4360 Wasp Major and a teardrop canopy specifically for intercepting low-level kamikaze attackers: the F2G Super Corsair. Although capable of spectacular speed, the end of the war saw the project's cancellation, though several examples of the few built were to prove successful in air-racing. For example, F2Gs won the Thompson trophy races both in 1947 and 1949.

Post-war production consisted of the F4U-5 with a more powerful engine, the AU-1, a dedicated attack variant for the Marine Corps, and the F4U-7, which was developed for the French Navy. French Corsairs were particularly busy, with both AU-1s and F4U-7s conducting strikes in Indochina between 1954 and 1956, during the Suez crisis of 1956, and then in Algeria during the same year, continuing operations there until 1962. A Honduran F4U-5 achieved the last confirmed 'kill' by a piston-engine fighter when it shot down an El Salvadorean Mustang and two FG-1 Corsairs in July 1969. Honduras finally retired the last Corsairs in frontline service anywhere in the world in 1981.

Vought F4U-1D

Involved in the assault on Okinawa in May 1945, this F4U-1D (57530) was flown by 1st Lt. Merritt O. Chance of VMF-312, US Marine Corps.

JET AIRCRAFT

Lockheed were the first American manufacturer to consider a jet-propelled fighter, their L-133 'Starjet' was an advanced canard design with blended wing and fuselage, but the aircraft was rejected in 1942 as too complex. The L-1000 axial flow turbojet that was intended to power the L-133 was originally designed by Nathan C. Price at the Doble steam car company. Though this engine was being test run from 1943 onwards, it was decided that acquiring existing British jet engine designs was a simpler course of action and the first USAAF jet fighters flew with licence-built British engines. In the event, no American jet fighter would see combat before the end of hostilities. The following aircraft are featured in this chapter:

- Bell P-59 Airacomet
- Lockheed P-80 Shooting Star
- Ryan FR-1 Fireball

The first production Lockheed P-80As were painted smooth to create a more aerodynamic finish. Later P-80s had a natural metal finish.

JET AIRCRAFT

Bell P-59 Airacomet

Historically significant as the first American jet aircraft to fly, the Airacomet proved to have an underwhelming performance, and few were built. It did, however, give the USAAF invaluable experience in operating and flying jet-powered aircraft.

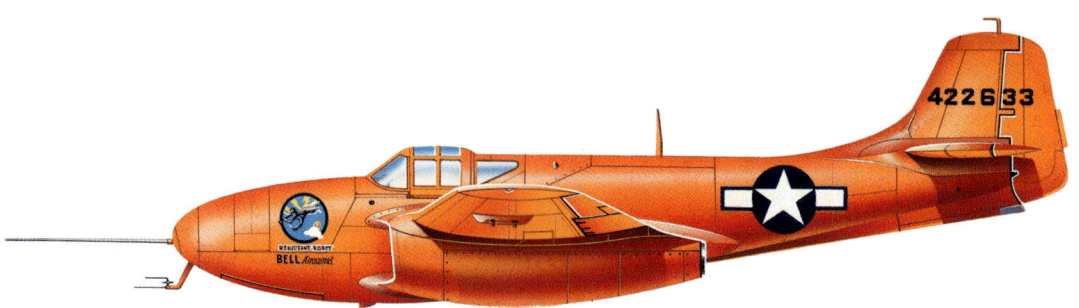

Development of the P-59 began after General Henry H. 'Hap' Arnold, Chief of the Army Air Force, was shown Frank Whittle-designed turbojets being tested in England in April 1941, along with the experimental jet-powered Gloster E28/39 just before its first flight. Manufacturing rights to the Whittle turbojet were acquired for General Electric, and Bell was chosen to design the aircraft to be powered by it.

Not fit for service

Constructed in great secrecy, the first P-59 was disguised with a dummy propeller when on the ground, and the designation P-59 was taken from an earlier (cancelled) fighter project. The aircraft's first flight took place on 1 October 1942, but flight testing was slow due to numerous problems encountered with the new power plants, and only 15 hours of flying time had been achieved by April 1943. The appearance of the second and third prototypes hastened the testing process, and Bell constructed a service test batch of 13 YP-59As. However, it became rapidly apparent that the Airacomet did not possess sufficient performance to enter operational service. In mock combat with a P-47D and P-38J, the YP-59A was outclassed in performance and manoeuvrability, and its poor directional stability at high speed made the Airacomet an inadequate gun platform.

Noting its twin-engine configuration and low wing loading, the Army Air Forces Board concluded, however, that the aircraft would make an excellent research platform and advanced trainer, and 100 P-59As were ordered in March 1944 – enough for the formation of the three-squadron 412th Fighter Group, but in the event, the last 50 were cancelled. The final 30 Airacomets to be built were constructed to P-59B standard with an additional fuel tank in each wing.

The 412th FG operated the P-59A for a little over a year as the USAAF's first jet fighter unit before it re-equipped on the Lockheed P-80 Shooting Star. The Airacomet never saw frontline service. Nonetheless, the P-59 had served to prove the viability of the jet engine as a fighter powerplant. The Airacomet also

Bell P-59 Airacomet
This Bell P-59B Airacomet (44-22633) was with the 445th Fighter Squadron in 1945 and operated from both Muroc and March Field, California, before deactivation in January 1946.

Bell P-59 Airacomet
Weight (maximum take-off): 5902kg (13,000lb)
Dimensions: Length: 11.62m (38ft 2in), Wingspan: 13.87m (45ft 6in), Height: 3.65m (12ft)
Powerplant: Two General Electric I-16 turbojets
Maximum Speed: 658km/h (409mph)
Range: 837km (520 miles)
Ceiling: 14,090m (46,200ft)
Crew: 1
Armament: One 37mm (1.5in) M4 cannon and three 12.7mm (0.5in) machine guns fixed, forward firing in nose

offered personnel the first experience of jet fighter operation. These personnel would soon be tasked with flying and maintaining jet aircraft of much greater performance.

Lockheed P-80 Shooting Star

The P-80 was developed with great speed and entered service just as the war in Europe was drawing to a close. As the first successful American jet fighter, it would subsequently see extensive post-war service.

Following the disappointing performance of the Bell P-59 Airacomet, it was decided to pursue a second jet design featuring a version of the British Halford (later de Havilland) H-1 'Goblin' engine licence-built by Allis-Chalmers. Production of this engine ran into delays, and instead, the P-80 would be fitted with the General Electric I-40 (later designated J33 when it entered production at Allison), an American development of the British Power Jets W.2B.

New design

Meanwhile, development of the airframe was passed to Lockheed, seeing as Bell, at that time, was overburdened with other programmes. With Britain and Germany clearly demonstrating a considerable lead in jet aircraft development, the need to produce an American jet fighter as quickly as possible was emphasized.

As a result, a design was proposed by Kelly Johnson and a prototype promised within 150 days. The prototype P-80 was duly completed at Lockheed's 'Skunk Works' 143 days

Lockheed P-80A-1-LO

P-80A-1-LO (44-85226) of the 412th Fighter Group, the first unit to equip with P-80 Shooting Stars in 1946.

after construction began and was delivered to Muroc airfield for testing on 16 November 1943.

Treacherous tests

With delays afflicting American engine production, the first XP-80A (named Lulu-Belle), powered by an imported and British-built de Havilland Goblin, was flown on 8 January 1944 by Lockheed test pilot Milo Burcham. On 13 September, this was followed by the first of 12 service test YP-80As, by which time the engine had been changed to the J33. This switch was not regarded favourably – Milo Burcham claimed that the J-33-powered XP-80A was 'a dog'.

The Shooting Star test programme proved dangerous: Burcham would lose his life in October 1944 while flying the third YP-80A, and his successor Tony LeVier suffered a broken back after bailing out of a stricken YP-80A

Lockheed P-80A

Weight (maximum take-off): 6356kg (14,000lb)
Dimensions: Length: 10.51m (34ft 6in), Wingspan: 11.85m (38ft 10in), Height: 3.45m (11ft 4in)
Powerplant: One 1746kg (3850lb) static thrust General Electric J33-GE-9 centrifugal flow turbojet engine
Maximum Speed: 898km/h (558mph)
Range (with two drop tanks): 1770km (1100 miles)
Ceiling: 13,716m (45,000ft)
Crew: 1
Armament: Six 12.7mm (0.5in) Colt Browning M2 machine guns fixed forward firing in nose; up to 908kg (2000lb) bomb load or 10 12.7cm (5in) rockets under wings

JET AIRCRAFT

Lockheed P-80A-1
P-80A-1 (44-85044) of Flight Test Division, Wright Field, Ohio, United States, with an overall white finish, circa 1948.

the following March, though he later recovered.

Less fortunate was the most successful American fighter pilot of all time, Major Richard Bong, who was killed performing a production P-80A acceptance flight in August 1945.

Operational testing

Despite the problems, four YP-80As were sent to Europe for operational testing. Although one crashed in a fatal accident in England, two of the pre-production Shooting Stars were used for reconnaissance missions in Italy in February and March 1945.

Subsequently, 1715 P-80s were built and saw intense service in the Korean War, where a Shooting Star was shot down by a MiG-15 in the world's first jet versus jet aerial combat. In two-seat trainer form as the T-33 Shooting Star, the aircraft would prove spectacularly successful: 6557 were built, and the last only retired from service (with Bolivia) in July 2017.

Ryan FR-1 Fireball

The particular requirements of carrier aircraft resulted in the development of the mixed-power Ryan Fireball, the only fighter to enter service equipped with both a piston and a jet engine.

The potential of the jet engine came at the cost of long take-off runs, high landing speeds and high fuel consumption, all elements that were less than ideal for a carrier aircraft. Therefore, the US Navy proposed to utilize a turbojet in the tail of a conventional piston-engined aircraft to act as a supplementary power unit. Good take-off and landing characteristics would be supplied by the piston engine, which also delivered an acceptable range, whilst the jet could be utilized to significantly boost speed and climb performance when the need arose.

New powerplant

A requirement for such an aircraft was issued in December 1942, and Ryan responded with the XFR-1. Fitted with a Wright Cyclone in the nose and a General Electric I-16 jet engine buried in the rear fuselage, the only clue to its unusual powerplant were the large wing root air intakes and the tricycle undercarriage, which was adopted to avoid the jet engine scorching the deck, as at the time, US carriers featured wooden decks.

Flying for the first time on 25 June 1944, development proceeded quickly, and an order for 100 FR-1s was placed on 2 December 1943, later increased to 700 aircraft. VF-66 was created specifically to bring the Fireball into service following the appearance of the first production FR-1s in March 1945, but two accidents in early 1945,

JET AIRCRAFT

Ryan FR-1 Fireball
Piloted by Lt. Commander John Gray, this Ryan Fireball FR1 was part of Fighter Squadron 66 (VF-66), based at NAS North Island, California, May 1944. The same aircraft is shown in the photograph below.

one fatal, saw the loss of both the third prototype and an early production machine. This was followed by an in-depth investigation, which delayed service entry. As a result, the airframe structure was strengthened and a maximum load factor of 5g, rather than 7.5g as originally designed, was imposed.

After the completion of carrier qualification trials during May 1945, VF-66 was preparing for deployment in the Pacific when the atomic bomb attacks on Hiroshima and Nagasaki brought the war to an abrupt conclusion. As a result, production of the FR-1 was cancelled after 66 aircraft had been built. Ryan later produced a prototype of a developed version with a General Electric XT31-GE-2 turboprop in the nose and a J31 jet engine in the rear fuselage. Nicknamed the 'Dark Shark', this aircraft flew in 1946, but with the development of adequately carrier-capable aircraft powered solely by jet engines, no production followed. The unique FR-1 continued in service until mid-1947.

Ryan FR-1 Fireball
Weight: (Maximum takeoff) 4810kg (10,595lb)
Dimensions: Length: 9.86m (32ft 4in), Wingspan: 12.2m (40ft), Height: 3.97m (13ft)
Powerplant: One 1063kW (1425hp) Wright R-1820-72W Cyclone nine-cylinder air-cooled radial engine
Maximum Speed: 685km/h (426mph)
Range: 1657km (1030 miles)
Ceiling: 13,145m (43100ft)
Crew: 1
Armament: Four 12.7mm (0.5in) Browning MG 53-2 machine guns; up to eight 12.7mm (0.5in) rockets underwing and one 454kg (1000lb) bombs

Index

Note: page numbers in **bold** refer to information contained in captions.

Adak, Alaska 88
Aéronavale 100, 108
Africa 24, 88–9
  North 16, 20, 21, 42, 70
Air Ministry 79
Aircraft and Armament Experimental Establishment (A&AEE) 39
Alaska 72, 88
Albanian front 21
Algeria 64, 70, 117
Allis-Chalmers 121
Allison 11, 19, 22, 27–9, 39, 42, 45, 53, 76, 121
American Volunteer Group (AVG) ('Flying Tigers') 11, 15, 24, **26**, 27
Antwerp 57
Anzio 70
Archer, Lt. Col. Lee **43**
Armée de l'Air 73
Arnold, Gen Henry H 'Hap' 120
Atlantic Ocean 88
atomic bombs 123
Attu Islans 102
Australia 18, 20, 49

Balikpapan oil refineries 63
Beisel, Rex 112
Belgium 46, 96, 100
Bell Aircraft Corporation 76
Bell Airacobra Mk I 20, **20**
Bell P-39 Airacobra 6, 9, 19–21, 68–9, 72, 82
  Bell P-39C Airacobra 30
  Bell P-39D Airacobra **19**, 20, 21
  Bell P-39E Airacobra 21
  Bell P-39F Airacobra 21
  Bell P-39L Airacobra 21
  Bell P-39M Airacobra 21
  Bell P-39N Airacobra 21, **21**
  Bell P-39Q Airacobra **9**, 21
  Bell P-39Q-20 Airacobra **9**
Bell P-59 Airacomet 120, **120**, 121
  Bell P-59A Airacomet 120
  Bell P-59B Airacomet 120
Bell P-63 Kingcobra 72–3
  Bell P-63A Kingcobra 72
  Bell P-63B Kingcobra 72
  Bell P-63C Kingcobra 72, 73, **73**
  Bell P-63D Kingcobra 72
  Bell P-63E Kingcobra 72, **72**
  Bell P-63F Kingcobra 72
Bell RP-63A 72
Bell XP-39 Airacobra 22
Bell YFM-1 Airacuda 76, **76**
Bell YP-59A 120
Berlin 46, 48
Berlin, Donovan R 14, 22
Blitz, the 77

Bloch MB-150 16
Boeing B-17 Flying Fortress 48, 57
Boeing B-29 Superfortress 48–9, 65, 90
Boeing P-12 12
Boeing P-26 Peashooter 12, **12**, 14
Bolivia 122
Bong, Major Richard 122
Borneo 63
Bougainville (escort carrier) **113**
Bradford, Capt James W 92
Brazil 64, **65**
Brewster Aeronautical Corporation 98, 112
Brewster F2A Buffalo 95, 96–7, 99, 102
  Brewster F2A-1 (B-239 export) 96, 97
  Brewster F2A-2 (B-339 export) 96, **96**, 97
  Brewster F2A-3 97, **97**
Brewster F3A 117
Brewster F3A-1 112
Brewster FG-1 112
Brewster XF2A-1 96, 98
Brewster XF2A-2 96
Bristol Beaufighter 10, 75, 77–8, **78**, 79, 81
  Bristol Beaufighter Mk VIF 78
Bristol Beaufort 77
Britain 16, 20, 24, 57–8, 63–5, 77, 86, 90, 97, 105–6, 121
  battle of 68
British Halford H-1 'Goblin' engine 121
British Purchasing Commission 23, 27, 37, 90
Brown, Lt Harry Winston **14**
Bunker Hill (aircraft carrier) **107**
Burcham, Milo 121
Burma 16, **64**

Cabot (light aircraft carrier) **107**
Cadillac, 1948 82
Caldwell, Clive 24
Canada 29, 72
Chance, 1st Lt Merritt O 117
Chennault, Gen Clare 15
Chi-Kai, Capt Chow 36
Chiang Kai-Shek, Madame 15
China 10, 11, 12, 15, 18, 24, **26**, 27, 48, 49, 89, 109
China-Burma-India (CBI) theatre 63
Chinese Air Force 10, 36
Chinese Nationalist Air Force **10**
Chinese nationalist forces **10**, **17**
Chrysler 62
Cleveland Air Races 108
Clinger, 1st Lt Dallas A **26**, **27**
cockpit canopies
  'bubble' **50**, 59, **61**, 63
  teardrop 46–8
Commonwealth CA-17 Mustang Mk XX 49
Consolidated B-24 Liberator 42
Core (aircraft carrier) **103**, 114
Corsica 63, 89
Curtis, Lt Robert **44**
Curtiss BF2C-1 Goshawk 10

Curtiss F-11C Goshawk 10
Curtiss Hawk 81A 22, 23
  Curtiss Hawk 81A-1 23
  Curtiss Hawk 81A-2 24
Curtiss Hawk 87 (Kittyhawk) 27–8
Curtiss Hawk III 10, **10**
Curtiss Hawk Model 75 14–17, **14–15**, 22, 23
  Curtiss H75-C1 (Hawk 75A-4) 16
  Curtiss H75A 16
  Curtiss H75A-1 16
  Curtiss H75A-2 16
  Curtiss H75A-3 16
  Curtiss Hawk 75-H 15
  Curtiss Hawk 75-M 15
  Curtiss Hawk 75-N 15
  Curtiss Hawk 75-O 15
  Curtiss Hawk 75-P 22
  Curtiss Hawk 75A-5 15, **17**
  Curtiss Hawk 75A-7 17
  Curtiss Hawk Model 75A 16, **16**
Curtiss Hawk Model H81-A2 **24**
Curtiss Model 75-I 22
Curtiss Model 75-P 22
Curtiss Mohawk 16
Curtiss P-36 (& Hawk Model 75) 14–17, **14–15**, 71
  Curtiss P-36A Hawk **14**, 15, **15**
  Curtiss P-36C **17**
Curtiss P-40 Warhawk 6, 9, 22–9, **22**, 37, 71, 88–9, 117
  Curtiss P-40B Warhawk 23, 25, 27
  Curtiss P-40C Warhawk 11, 23, **23**, 25, **25**
  Curtiss P-40D **26**, 27, 28
  Curtiss P-40E Warhawk **25**, **26**, 27, 28, 29, **30–1**
  Curtiss P-40F 28, **28**, 89
  Curtiss P-40K 27, 28, 28–9, **29**
  Curtiss P-40L 28, 29
  Curtiss P-40M 28, 29
  Curtiss P-40N 28–9, **29**
  Curtiss P-40Q 29
  Curtiss P-40R-1 28
  Curtiss P-40R-2 28
Curtiss P-46 27
Curtiss P-47 29, 49, 57, 72
Curtiss P-51 29, 70
Curtiss SB2C Helldiver 117
Curtiss Sussu (Hawks) 16–17
Curtiss Tomahawk I 23–4
Curtiss Tomahawk IIA 24
Curtiss Tomahawk IIB 25
Curtiss XP-40 22
Curtiss XP-40 F 28
Curtiss XP-51F 49–52
Curtiss XP-51G 49
Curtiss Y1P-36 15, 16
Curtiss YP-37 22
Curtiss-Wright 22
Curtiss-Wright A-19R 11
Curtiss-Wright C-46 Commando 11

INDEX

Curtiss-Wright CW-19L 11
Curtiss-Wright CW-21 Demon 11, **11**
    Curtiss-Wright CW-21A Demon 11
    Curtiss-Wright CW-21B Demon 11, **11**

D-Day landings 42, 48, 49
Dahl, Lt Perry **83**
Dallas, Texas 42–6, 112
Davenport, Lt John E. **44**
de Havilland Goblin
    XP-80A 121
    YP-80A 121
de Havilland Mosquito **20**, 75, 77, 78, 79, 81, 90
    NF Mk 30 79, **79**
    PR.XVI **79**
Desert Air Force 28
Detroyat, Marcel 16
Dewoitine D.520 70
Dieppe 39, 69
Doble steam car company 119
Dominican Republic 52, 89
Dortmund-Ems Canal 39
Douglas 90
Douglas A-20 Havoc 81
    Douglas A-20C Havoc **80**
    Douglas A-20G Havoc **81**
Douglas DB-7 attack bomber 80, 81
Douglas P-70 Havoc 77, 78, 80–1
    Douglas P-70 Havoc I (Intruder) 80, 81
    Douglas P-70 Havoc II 81
    Douglas P-70 Havoc IV 81
    Douglas P-70A Havoc **80**
Douglas TP-70B **81**
'Droop Snoot' navigation 89
Dutch East Indies 17

Earl, Hartley 82
Eastern Front 20–1, 64, 72–3
Ecuador 13
Egypt 35
Eisenhower, Dwight D. 48
El Salvador 52, 117
Elrod, Capt. Henry 102
Emmons, Lt Gen Delos C 90
England **33**
Enterprise (carrier) 117
Ernst, Lt Herman 90–1
Espiritu Santo 102
Essex (aircraft carrier) 105

Fairey Barracudas 106, 117
Far East 97
Fausel, Robert 11
Fiat BR. 20 bomber 11
Finland 16–17, 96, 97
Focke-Wulf Fw 189 21
Focke-Wulf Fw 190 21, 39, 57, 68, 69, 70
Focke-Wulf Fw 200 Condor 88–9
Football War 52

France 15–16, 20, 21, 23, 29, 49, 57, 58, **58**, 64, 73, 78, 80, 86, 89, 100, 110
    Allied invasion of 46
    Southern 89
France, Victor **38**
Franco-Thai war 10, 15
Free French 89
Free French Air Force 21
French Air Force **16**
French Navy 117

Gambier Bay (escort carrier) 116
General Electric 19, 54, 87, 120, 121, 123
General Motors 37, 82, 103
Germany 16, 21, 23, 24, 25, 39, 46, 58, 68, 73, 89, 121
Gibraltar 70, 101
Gloster E28/39 120
Glover, Major Frederick **47**
Goodyear F2G Super Corsair 117
Goodyear FG-1 117
Gracie, Squadron Leader Edward John **20**
Gray, Lt Commander John **123**
Greece 101
Grumman, Leroy 104
Grumman F2A monoplane 98
Grumman F3F (F4F-1) 98
Grumman F4F Wildcat 7, 95, 96, 98–103, **101**, 104, 106, 114
    Grumman F4F-3 **98**, 99–100, **99**, 101, 102
    Grumman F4F-3 MF-1 **99**
    Grumman F4F-3A 101
    Grumman F4F-3P 102
    Grumman F4F-3S 103
    Grumman F4F-4 **100**, 102
    Grumman F4F-5 102–3
    Grumman F4F-7 102
    Grumman F4F-8 103
Grumman F6F Hellcat 7, 95, 103, 104–8, **108**, 109, 110, 115–16
    Grumman F6F-3 Hellcat **104**, **105**, 107–8
    Grumman F6F-3N 108
    Grumman F6F-3P 107
    Grumman F6F-5 Hellcat **106**, 107–8, **107**
    Grumman F6F-5K remote-controlled flying bombs 108
    Grumman F6F-5N 108
    Grumman F6F-5P 108
    Grumman F6F-6 Hellcat 108
Grumman F7F Tigercat 95, 109
    Grumman F7F-1 Tigercat 109, **109**
    Grumman F7F-2N Tigercat 109, **109**
    Grumman F7F-3 Tigercat 109
    Grumman F7F-3N Tigercat 109
    Grumman F7F-4N Tigercat 109
Grumman F8F Bearcat 95, 108, 110, **111**
    Grumman F8F-1 Bearcat **110**
Grumman F14 Tomcat 100
Grumman FM-1 103
Grumman FM-2 Wildcat **102**–3, 103

Grumman TBF Avenger 103, 117
Grumman XF4F-1 96, 98
Grumman XF4F-2 98
Grumman XF4F-3 99
Grumman XF6F-1 105
Grumman XF6F-2 105
Grumman XF6F-3 Hellcat 105
Grumman XF 5F Skyrocket 109
Guadalcanal **80**, **99**, 102, **113**, 114
Guchek, Petr **21**

Hall, Robert L 98
Harker, Ronnie 45
Hawaii 23, 25, 27
Hawker Hurricane 16, 20, 24, 25, 58
    Mk II 64
Hawker Sea Hurricane 105
Hawker Typhoon 59
'heavy' fighter concept 75–93
Heinkel He 177 91
Hibberd, Hal 82
Hill, Pilot Officer Hollis H 39
Hiroshima 123
Hitchcock, Lt Col Tommy 45
Holloway, Col Bruce K 29
Honduras 52, 89, 117

Iceland 88
Ie Shima 65
Illustrious (air craft carrier) 117
Imperial Japanese Navy 106
India 16
India-Burma border 42
Indochina 73, 108, 117
Indochina War 110
Intrepid (aircraft carrier) 117
Iran 21
Iraq **69**
Italian Co-Belligerent Air Force 21, 89
Italy 20–1, 46, 48, 70–1, 78, 89
Iwo Jima 48–9, **50**

Japan 10–13, 17–18, 20, 25, **26**, 27, 36, 42, 48–9, 65, 89–90, 95, 97, 102–6, 114
Java 11, 27
jet aircraft 119–23
Johnson, Clarence 'Kelly' 82, 121
Junkers Ju 52 28
Junkers Ju 88 100

kamikaze pilots 117
Karachi 36
Kartveli, Alexander 13, 18, 53, 54
Kawanishi H6K 88
Kawasaki Ki-45 Toryu 89
Kelsey, Benjamin S 83
Kepford, Lt Ira C **113**
Khlobystov, Aleksei 25
Kindelberger, James 'Dutch' 37
Kisaragi (destroyer) 102

125

INDEX

Korea 52, 65
Korean War 52, 91, 108–9, 109, **109**, 122
Kunming **17**

Lagares da Silva, Capt Newton **65**
Lancaster bomber 45
Langley (aircraft carrier) **105**, **110**
Legrand, Sergeant André-Armand 16
Lend-Lease programme 18, 19, **21**, **22**, 25, 63, 105
LeVier, Tony 121–2
Lexington (aircraft carrier) 104
Lockheed F-4 88, 89
Lockheed F-5 Lightning 18, 88, 89
 see also Lockheed P-38 Lightning
Lockheed L-133 'Starjet' 119
Lockheed Model 322-B 87
Lockheed P-38 Lightning 6, 7, 20, 46, 71, 75, 82–9
 Lockheed P-38A Lightning 89
 Lockheed P-38B Lightning 89
 Lockheed P-38C Lightning 89
 Lockheed P-38D Lightning 89
 Lockheed P-38E Lightning 87, 88
 Lockheed P-38F Lightning **82**, 88–9
 Lockheed P-38F-1 Lightning **82**
 Lockheed P-38G Lightning **83**, 89
 Lockheed P-38H Lightning **83**, **84–5**, **87**, 88, 89
 Lockheed P-38H-1 Lightning **83**
 Lockheed P-38J Lightning **86**, 88, **88**, 89
 Lockheed P-38L Lightning 88, 89
 Lockheed P-38L-5-LO Lightning **86**
 Lockheed P-38M Lightning 78, 89
Lockheed P-80 Shooting Star 7, 120, 121–2
 Lockheed P-80A Shooting Star **119**, **121**, 122
 Lockheed P-80A-1 Shooting Star **122**
Lockheed P-322 88
Lockheed 'Skunk Works' 121
Lockheed T-33 Shooting Star 122
Lockheed XP-38 Lightning 22, 82–3
Lockheed XP-80A 121
Lockheed YP-38 86–7
Loewy, Raymond 82
Loudon, Captain Charles P 58
Luftwaffe 46, 57, 58, 77, 89, 90

Macchi MC. 202 Folgore 24
'Marianas Turkey Shoot' 106
Marrett, 1st Lt Samuel H 13
Martin-Baker 81
McCampbell, Capt Donald 106
Mediterranean 20, 28–9, 42, 63, 70–1, 78–9
Messerschmitt Bf 109 21, 28, 68
 Messerschmitt Bf 109E 16, 24
 Messerschmitt Bf 109F 68
 Messerschmitt Bf 109G 103
 Messerschmitt Bf 109G-2 97
Messerschmitt Bf 110 28, 89
Mexico 64
Midway, battle of 97, **97**, 102, 110
Mikoyan-Gurevich MiG-3 64

Miroshnichenko, Lt I F 73
Mitchell, RJ 68
Mitsubishi A5M 10, 12
Mitsubishi A6M Zero 11, 12, 30, 89, 95, 102, 104–6
Mitsubishi G3M 12, 90
Mitsubishi G4M 'Betty' 89, 92
Morane-Saulnier MS 406 15, 16
Mullins, Lt Walter H 'Moon' **47**

Nagasaki 123
Nakajima B5N 17
Nakajima Ki-43 Hayabusa 73
Nanking 10, 12
New Guinea 29, 63
New York Navy Reserve **106**
New Zealand 29, 117
Nicaragua 89
night fighters 75, **75**, 77–82, **77**, 90, **92**, 107–9
North American A-36 42
 North American A-36A **37**
North American B-25 Mitchell 42
North American F-6A 42
North American F-6B 42
North American F-6D 46
North American F-6K 46
North American F-82 Twin Mustang 91
North American Mustang IA 39, 42
North American Mustang MK I 39, 42, 45
North American Mustang X 42
North American NA-73X 37–9
North American P-51 Mustang 7, 33, 37–52, **48**, 53, 62, 65, 72, 89, 90
 North American P-51A Mustang 42
 North American P-51B Mustang 33, **38–9**, **40–1**, 42, 46, 48, 49, 70–1
 North American P-51C Mustang **44–5**, 46, 48, 49
 North American P-51C-1ONT Mustang **43**, **44**
 North American P-51D Mustang 33, 46–9, **47–51**, 52, 65
 North American P-51D-25-NT Mustang **52**
 North American P-51H Mustang 52
 North American P-51K Mustang 46, 49, **52**
North American XP-51B 42
North Atlantic Treaty Organization (NATO) 73
Northrop, John K 90
Northrop F-15 Reporter 91
Northrop P-61 Black Widow 75, 77, 78, 79, 81, 89, 90–1
 Northrop P-61B Black Widow 91, **91**, **92–3**
 Northrop P-61C Black Widow 91
Northrop XP-61 90
 Northrop XP-61E 91
Northrop YP-61 90
Norway 16, 103, 106, 117

O'Hare, Lt Edward H (Butch) **99**
Okinawa 109
Operation Bolero 88
Operation Husky 70
Operation Torch 16, 20, 89

Pacific arena 17, 20, 29, **50**, 64, 65, 73, 81, 89–91, **91**, 101–3, 106, 110, **111**, 114, 117, 123
 Central Pacific 63
 South Pacific 114, 117
Pacific Operational Area 48
Packard 28, 45, 72
Page, George 11
'Palm Sunday Massacre' 28
Pearl Harbor 13, **14**, 17, 20, 24, 25, 27, 36, 42, 89, 97
Perdomo, Lt Oscar F 65
Philippine Sea, battle of 106
Philippines 13, 23, 25–7, 64
Philippines Army Air Corps 12
plastics **92**
Pratt & Whitney engines 14, 15, 53, **60**, **92**, 99, 100, 105, 117
Preddy, Major George 49
Price, Nathan C 119
'pursuit' aircraft 6

radar, airborne 77, 78, 80, **80**, 81, 90, 107
Ranger (aircraft carrier) 100, **101**
Rangoon 42
Rasmussen, Phillip 17
Rechkalov, Grigory 21
reconnaissance aircraft 18, 24, 39, 42, 46–8, 71, **71**, 79, 82, 88–9, 91, 102, 107–8
Republic Aviation 13
Republic Aviation EP-1 13
Republic P-43 Lancer 18, 53–4, **53**
 Republic P-43A Lancer 18, **18**
Republic P-44 'Rocket' 53
Republic P-47 Thunderbolt 6, 7, 18, 20, 33, 46, 53–65, **57**, **58**, 70
 Republic P-47A Thunderbolt 53
 Republic P-47B Thunderbolt **54**, 55–7
 Republic P-47C Thunderbolt 55–7, 59
 Republic P-47D Thunderbolt 57, 58–9, **59–61**, 62–4, **62**, **65**, **66–7**
 Republic P-47D-25 Thunderbolt **56**
 Republic P-47G Thunderbolt 57
 Republic P-47M Thunderbolt 65
 Republic P-47N Thunderbolt **7**, **63**, 65
Republic XP-47 Thunderbolt 18
Republic XP-47B 53–5
Republic XP-47E 59–62
Republic XP-47F 62
Republic XP-47H 62
Republic XP-47J 'Superbolt' 63, 64
Republic XP-47K 59
Republic XP-47L 59
Republic XP-72 63
Republic YP-43 18
reverse lend-lease agreement 78
Rolls-Royce 45
 Merlin engines 7, 28, **37**, 45, 46, 48, 49, 68, 72
 Mustang X 42
Royal Air Force (RAF) 10, 16, 37
 and the Bell P-39 Airacobra 20, **20**, 21, **21**
 Bomber Command 49

INDEX

Curtiss-Wright CW-19L 11
Curtiss-Wright CW-21 Demon 11, **11**
   Curtiss-Wright CW-21A Demon 11
   Curtiss-Wright CW-21B Demon 11, **11**

D-Day landings 42, 48, 49
Dahl, Lt Perry **83**
Dallas, Texas 42–6, 112
Davenport, Lt John E. **44**
de Havilland Goblin
   XP-80A 121
   YP-80A 121
de Havilland Mosquito **20**, 75, 77, 78, 79, 81, 90
   NF Mk 30 79, **79**
   PR.XVI **79**
Desert Air Force 28
Detroyat, Marcel 16
Dewoitine D.520 70
Dieppe 39, 69
Doble steam car company 119
Dominican Republic 52, 89
Dortmund-Ems Canal 39
Douglas 90
Douglas A-20 Havoc 81
   Douglas A-20C Havoc **80**
   Douglas A-20G Havoc **81**
Douglas DB-7 attack bomber 80, 81
Douglas P-70 Havoc 77, 78, 80–1
   Douglas P-70 Havoc I (Intruder) 80, 81
   Douglas P-70 Havoc II 81
   Douglas P-70 Havoc IV 81
   Douglas P-70A Havoc **80**
Douglas TP-70B **81**
'Droop Snoot' navigation 89
Dutch East Indies 17

Earl, Hartley 82
Eastern Front 20–1, 64, 72–3
Ecuador 13
Egypt 35
Eisenhower, Dwight D. 48
El Salvador 52, 117
Elrod, Capt. Henry 102
Emmons, Lt Gen Delos C 90
England **33**
Enterprise (carrier) 117
Ernst, Lt Herman 90–1
Espiritu Santo 102
Essex (aircraft carrier) 105

Fairey Barracudas 106, 117
Far East 97
Fausel, Robert 11
Fiat BR. 20 bomber 11
Finland 16–17, 96, 97
Focke-Wulf Fw 189 21
Focke-Wulf Fw 190 21, 39, 57, 68, 69, 70
Focke-Wulf Fw 200 Condor 88–9
Football War 52

France 15–16, 20, 21, 23, 29, 49, 57, 58, **58**, 64, 73, 78, 80, 86, 89, 100, 110
   Allied invasion of 46
   Southern 89
France, Victor **38**
Franco-Thai war 10, 15
Free French 89
Free French Air Force 21
French Air Force **16**
French Navy 117

Gambier Bay (escort carrier) 116
General Electric 19, 54, 87, 120, 121, 123
General Motors 37, 82, 103
Germany 16, 21, 23, 24, 25, 39, 46, 58, 68, 73, 89, 121
Gibraltar 70, 101
Gloster E28/39 120
Glover, Major Frederick **47**
Goodyear F2G Super Corsair 117
Goodyear FG-1 117
Gracie, Squadron Leader Edward John **20**
Gray, Lt Commander John **123**
Greece 101
Grumman, Leroy 104
Grumman F2A monoplane 98
Grumman F3F (F4F-1) 98
Grumman F4F Wildcat 7, 95, 96, 98–103, **101**, 104, 106, 114
   Grumman F4F-3 **98**, 99–100, **99**, 101, 102
   Grumman F4F-3 MF-1 **99**
   Grumman F4F-3A 101
   Grumman F4F-3P 102
   Grumman F4F-3S 103
   Grumman F4F-4 **100**, 102
   Grumman F4F-5 102–3
   Grumman F4F-7 102
   Grumman F4F-8 103
Grumman F6F Hellcat 7, 95, 103, 104–8, **108**, 109, 110, 115–16
   Grumman F6F-3 Hellcat **104**, **105**, 107–8
   Grumman F6F-3N 108
   Grumman F6F-3P 107
   Grumman F6F-5 Hellcat **106**, 107–8, **107**
   Grumman F6F-5K remote-controlled flying bombs 108
   Grumman F6F-5N 108
   Grumman F6F-5P 108
   Grumman F6F-6 Hellcat 108
Grumman F7F Tigercat 95, 109
   Grumman F7F-1 Tigercat 109, **109**
   Grumman F7F-2N Tigercat 109, **109**
   Grumman F7F-3 Tigercat 109
   Grumman F7F-3N Tigercat 109
   Grumman F7F-4N Tigercat 109
Grumman F8F Bearcat 95, 108, 110, **111**
   Grumman F8F-1 Bearcat **110**
Grumman F14 Tomcat 100
Grumman FM-1 103
Grumman FM-2 Wildcat **102**–3, 103

Grumman TBF Avenger 103, 117
Grumman XF4F-1 96, 98
Grumman XF4F-2 98
Grumman XF4F-3 99
Grumman XF6F-1 105
Grumman XF6F-2 105
Grumman XF6F-3 Hellcat 105
Grumman XF 5F Skyrocket 109
Guadalcanal **80**, **99**, 102, **113**, 114
Guchek, Petr **21**

Hall, Robert L 98
Harker, Ronnie 45
Hawaii 23, 25, 27
Hawker Hurricane 16, 20, 24, 25, 58
   Mk II 64
Hawker Sea Hurricane 105
Hawker Typhoon 59
'heavy' fighter concept 75–93
Heinkel He 177 91
Hibberd, Hal 82
Hill, Pilot Officer Hollis H 39
Hiroshima 123
Hitchcock, Lt Col Tommy 45
Holloway, Col Bruce K 29
Honduras 52, 89, 117

Iceland 88
Ie Shima 65
Illustrious (air craft carrier) 117
Imperial Japanese Navy 106
India 16
India-Burma border 42
Indochina 73, 108, 117
Indochina War 110
Intrepid (aircraft carrier) 117
Iran 21
Iraq **69**
Italian Co-Belligerent Air Force 21, 89
Italy 20–1, 46, 48, 70–1, 78, 89
Iwo Jima 48–9, **50**

Japan 10–13, 17–18, 20, 25, **26**, 27, 36, 42, 48–9, 65, 89–90, 95, 97, 102–6, 114
Java 11, 27
jet aircraft 119–23
Johnson, Clarence 'Kelly' 82, 121
Junkers Ju 52 28
Junkers Ju 88 100

kamikaze pilots 117
Karachi 36
Kartveli, Alexander 13, 18, 53, 54
Kawanishi H6K 88
Kawasaki Ki-45 Toryu 89
Kelsey, Benjamin S 83
Kepford, Lt Ira C **113**
Khlobystov, Aleksei 25
Kindelberger, James 'Dutch' 37
Kisaragi (destroyer) 102

INDEX

Korea 52, 65
Korean War 52, 91, 108–9, 109, **109**, 122
Kunming **17**

Lagares da Silva, Capt Newton **65**
Lancaster bomber 45
Langley (aircraft carrier) **105**, **110**
Legrand, Sergeant André-Armand 16
Lend-Lease programme 18, 19, **21**, **22**, 25, 63, 105
LeVier, Tony 121–2
Lexington (aircraft carrier) 104
Lockheed F-4 88, 89
Lockheed F-5 Lightning 18, 88, 89
 see also Lockheed P-38 Lightning
Lockheed L-133 'Starjet' 119
Lockheed Model 322-B 87
Lockheed P-38 Lightning 6, 7, 20, 46, 71, 75, 82–9
 Lockheed P-38A Lightning 89
 Lockheed P-38B Lightning 89
 Lockheed P-38C Lightning 89
 Lockheed P-38D Lightning 89
 Lockheed P-38E Lightning 87, 88
 Lockheed P-38F Lightning **82**, 88–9
 Lockheed P-38F-1 Lightning **82**
 Lockheed P-38G Lightning **83**, 89
 Lockheed P-38H Lightning **83**, 84–5, **87**, 88, 89
 Lockheed P-38H-1 Lightning **83**
 Lockheed P-38J Lightning **86**, 88, **88**, 89
 Lockheed P-38L Lightning 88, 89
 Lockheed P-38L-5-LO Lightning **86**
 Lockheed P-38M Lightning 78, 89
Lockheed P-80 Shooting Star 7, 120, 121–2
 Lockheed P-80A Shooting Star **119**, **121**, 122
 Lockheed P-80A-1 Shooting Star **122**
Lockheed P-322 88
Lockheed 'Skunk Works' 121
Lockheed T-33 Shooting Star 122
Lockheed XP-38 Lightning 22, 82–3
Lockheed XP-80A 121
Lockheed YP-38 86–7
Loewy, Raymond 82
Loudon, Captain Charles P 58
Luftwaffe 46, 57, 58, 77, 89, 90

Macchi MC. 202 Folgore 24
'Marianas Turkey Shoot' 106
Marrett, 1st Lt Samuel H 13
Martin-Baker 81
McCampbell, Capt Donald 106
Mediterranean 20, 28–9, 42, 63, 70–1, 78–9
Messerschmitt Bf 109 21, 28, 68
 Messerschmitt Bf 109E 16, 24
 Messerschmitt Bf 109F 68
 Messerschmitt Bf 109G 103
 Messerschmitt Bf 109G-2 97
Messerschmitt Bf 110 28, 89
Mexico 64
Midway, battle of 97, **97**, 102, 110
Mikoyan-Gurevich MiG-3 64

Miroshnichenko, Lt I F 73
Mitchell, RJ 68
Mitsubishi A5M 10, 12
Mitsubishi A6M Zero 11, 12, 30, 89, 95, 102, 104–6
Mitsubishi G3M 12, 90
Mitsubishi G4M 'Betty' 89, 92
Morane-Saulnier MS 406 15, 16
Mullins, Lt Walter H 'Moon' **47**

Nagasaki 123
Nakajima B5N 17
Nakajima Ki-43 Hayabusa 73
Nanking 10, 12
New Guinea 29, 63
New York Navy Reserve **106**
New Zealand 29, 117
Nicaragua 89
night fighters 75, **75**, 77–82, **77**, 90, **92**, 107–9
North American A-36 42
 North American A-36A **37**
North American B-25 Mitchell 42
North American F-6A 42
North American F-6B 42
North American F-6D 46
North American F-6K 46
North American F-82 Twin Mustang 91
North American Mustang IA 39, 42
North American Mustang MK I 39, 42, 45
North American Mustang X 42
North American NA-73X 37–9
North American P-51 Mustang 7, 33, 37–52, **48**, 53, 62, 65, 72, 89, 90
 North American P-51A Mustang 42
 North American P-51B Mustang 33, **38–9**, **40–1**, 42, 46, 48, 49, 70–1
 North American P-51C Mustang 44–5, 46, 48, 49
 North American P-51C-1ONT Mustang **43**, **44**
 North American P-51D Mustang 33, 46–9, **47–51**, 52, 65
 North American P-51D-25-NT Mustang **52**
 North American P-51H Mustang 52
 North American P-51K Mustang 46, 49, **52**
North American XP-51B 42
North Atlantic Treaty Organization (NATO) 73
Northporn, John K 90
Northrop F-15 Reporter 91
Northrop P-61 Black Widow 75, 77, 78, 79, 81, 89, 90–1
 Northrop P-61B Black Widow 91, **91**, **92–3**
 Northrop P-61C Black Widow 91
Northrop XP-61 90
 Northrop XP-61E 91
Northrop YP-61 90
Norway 16, 103, 106, 117

O'Hare, Lt Edward H (Butch) **99**
Okinawa 109
Operation Bolero 88
Operation Husky 70
Operation Torch 16, 20, 89

Pacific arena 17, 20, 29, **50**, 64, 65, 73, 81, 89–91, **91**, 101–3, 106, 110, **111**, 114, 117, 123
 Central Pacific 63
 South Pacific 114, 117
Pacific Operational Area 48
Packard 28, 45, 72
Page, George 11
'Palm Sunday Massacre' 28
Pearl Harbor 13, **14**, 17, 20, 24, 25, 27, 36, 42, 89, 97
Perdomo, Lt Oscar F 65
Philippine Sea, battle of 106
Philippines 13, 23, 25–7, 64
Philippines Army Air Corps 12
plastics **92**
Pratt & Whitney engines 14, 15, 53, **60**, **92**, 99, 100, 105, 117
Preddy, Major George 49
Price, Nathan C 119
'pursuit' aircraft 6

radar, airborne 77, 78, 80, **80**, 81, 90, 107
Ranger (aircraft carrier) 100, **101**
Rangoon 42
Rasmussen, Phillip 17
Rechkalov, Grigory 21
reconnaissance aircraft 18, 24, 39, 42, 46–8, 71, **71**, 79, 82, 88–9, 91, 102, 107–8
Republic Aviation 13
Republic Aviation EP-1 13
Republic P-43 Lancer 18, 53–4, **53**
 Republic P-43A Lancer 18, **18**
Republic P-44 'Rocket' 53
Republic P-47 Thunderbolt 6, 7, 18, 20, 33, 46, 53–65, **57**, **58**, 70
 Republic P-47A Thunderbolt 53
 Republic P-47B Thunderbolt **54**, 55–7
 Republic P-47C Thunderbolt 55–7, 59
 Republic P-47D Thunderbolt 57, 58–9, **59–61**, 62–4, **62**, **65**, **66–7**
 Republic P-47D-25 Thunderbolt **56**
 Republic P-47G Thunderbolt 57
 Republic P-47M Thunderbolt 65
 Republic P-47N Thunderbolt **7**, **63**, 65
Republic XP-47 Thunderbolt 18
Republic XP-47B 53–5
Republic XP-47E 59–62
Republic XP-47F 62
Republic XP-47H 62
Republic XP-47J 'Superbolt' 63, 64
Republic XP-47K 59
Republic XP-47L 59
Republic XP-72 63
Republic YP-43 18
reverse lend-lease agreement 78
Rolls-Royce 45
 Merlin engines 7, 28, **37**, 45, 46, 48, 49, 68, 72
 Mustang X 42
Royal Air Force (RAF) 10, 16, 37
 and the Bell P-39 Airacobra 20, **20**, 21, **21**
 Bomber Command 49

INDEX

Boston III (Intruder) (Douglas DB-7) 81
'Bostons' 80, 81
and the Bristol Beaufighter 77, **77**, 78
and the de Havilland Mosquito 79
and the Douglas DB-7 81
and the Douglas P-70 Havoc 80
Fighter Command 24
and the Kittyhawk 27–9
and the Kittyhawk II (P-40F) 28
and the Kittyhawk III (P-40M) 28
and the Kittyhawk IV (P-40N) 29
and the Lockheed P-38 Lightning 87–8
and the Mustang Mk II 42
and the Mustang Mk III 49
and the Mustang Mk IV 49
and Mustangs 39, 42, 49
and the Northrop P-61 Black Widow 90
and the Spitfire 68–70, **69**
and the Thunderbolt Mk I 63
and the Thunderbolt Mk II 63, **64**
and Thunderbolts 63–4, **64**
and Tomahawks 23–4, **26**
and the Vultee P-66 Vanguard 36, **36**
Royal Australian Air Force (RAAF) 18, 27–8, 29, 89
Royal Navy 100, 103
    and the Corsair I 117
    and the Corsair II 117
    and the Corsair III 117
    and the Corsair IV 117
    and Corsairs 115, 117
    Fleet Air Arm 115
    and the Hellcat I 105–6
    and the Hellcat II 108
    and the Martlet I 100
    and the Martlet II 100, 101
    and the Martlet III 101
    and the Martlet IV 103
    and the Martlet V 103
    and the Wildcat VI 103
Royal Netherlands East Indies Air Force 11, 17, 49, 96
Royal Netherlands East Indies Army **11**
Royal New Zealand Air Force (RNZAF) 117
Ryan FR-1 Fireball 123, **123**
Ryan XFR-1 123

Sabang, Sumatra 117
St Omer, France 58
Saipan 63
Salerno landings 42
Saratoga (ship) 96, 97
Sardinia 89
Sargent, Lt John J **107**
Schilling, David C **60**
Schmued, Edgar 37
Schwab, Lt Alfred 42
Searcher (escort carrier) 103
Seversky, Alexander de 53
Seversky Aviation 13
Seversky AP-4 18
Seversky P-35 13, 15, 18
    Seversky P-35A 13, **13**

Seversky SEV-1XP 15
Seversky XP-41 18
Shangri-La (aircraft carrier) **115**
Sicily 20, 28, 42, 70
Sino-Japanese War, Second 10, **10**
Sluder, Lt Col Chester L **45**
Smith, RT **24**
Solomon Islands 114
Soviet Air Force **21**
Soviet Navy 29, 64
Soviet Union **9**, 10, 16, 19–21, 25, 29, 48, 64, 72–3, 97
Steamer Bay (escort carrier) **102**
Sterling, Lt Gordon 17
'sto-wing' system 102
Stout, 1st Lt **113**
Suez crisis 117
Supermarine Spitfire 7, 16, 20, 24, 28, 29, 33, 46, 49, 68–71
    MK I 68
    MK II 68
    Mk IX 70–1
    MK V 68, 70
    MK VIII 70, **70**
    Mk XI ('Bluebirds') 71, **71**
    PR MK XI **71**
    Vb **68–9**
Sweden 13, 36
Swirbul, Jake 110

Taylor, Col Oliver **83**
Tervo, Altto Kalevi 16–17
Thach, James 'Jimmy' 102
Thailand 10, 15
Tirpitz (battleship) 106, 117
Tokyo 49
Tunisia 42, 70, 89
Turkey 25
'Tuskegee Airmen' 29

Ukrainian Front **21**
United Kingdom 36, 96, 100, 103
United States Air Corps 6, 13, 15
United States Air Force (USAF) 63, 82
United States Air National Guard 52
United States Army 6, 13, 22, 23
United States Army Air Corps (USAAC) 6–7, 12–15, 18–19, 22, 27, 42, 53–4, 86–8, 90
    Specification X-608 82
    see also US Army Air Forces
United States Army Air Force (USAAF) 6–7, 9, **9**, 12, 14, 20, 33, 36, 89, 120
    and the Bell P-63 Kingcobra 72, **73**
    and the Bristol Beaufighter 77, **77**, 78
    and the Curtiss P-40 Warhawk 24, 28, 29
    and the de Havilland Mosquito 79
    and the Douglas P-70 Havoc 81
    and jet engines 119
    and night-fighters 75
    and the North American P-51 Mustang 37, 42, 45
    and the Northrop P-61 Black Widow 90, 91

and the Republic P-47 Thunderbolt 57, 62, 63
and the Supermarine Spitfire 68–71, **69**
United States Marine Corps 97, 109, 114–17
United States Navy **6**, 7, 10, 96–102, 104–5, 109–10, 112, 116, 123
Uruguayan Navy 108

V-1 flying bombs 49, 64, 65, 90–1
V-VS service 73
Vichy France 16, 70
Vought AU-1 114, 117
Vought F4U Corsair 7, 29, 95, **95**, 104, 105, 108, 112–17
    Vought F4U-1 Corsair **6**, 112–13, **112–13**, 114, 117
    Vought F4U-1A Corsair **112–13**, 116
    Vought F4U-1C Corsair **115**
    Vought F4U-1D Corsair **116**, **117**
    Vought F4U-2 Corsair 117
    Vought F4U-3 Corsair 117
    Vought F4U-4 Corsair **115**, 117
    Vought F4U-5 Corsair 52, **114**, 117
    Vought F4U-7 Corsair 117
Vought FG-1 Corsair 117
Vought FG-1D **114**
Vought XF4U-1 112
Vultee BT-13 Valiant 36
Vultee J-10 36
Vultee P-66 Vanguard 33, 34, **36**

Wagner, Lt Col Boyd 27
Wake Island 102
Walsh, Lt Kenneth A **113**
Wangjing **64**
Wasp (aircraft carrier) **98**, 100
Western Desert 24, **26**, 27–8, 101
Westland Whirlwind 89
'wet wings' 18
Whittle, Frank 120
Wright engines 14, 15, 100, 104, 123
Wright Field 15, 42
Wyler, William 63

XP-70 81

Y1P-36 16
Yamamoto, Admiral Ioroku 89
Yangchow **10**
Yorktown (aircraft carrier) 105, 107, **108**

Picture Credits

Photos
AirSeaLandPhotos: 6, 7, 30, 34, 48, 54, 57, 58, 69, 78, 94
Amber Books: 8, 22, 53, 63, 87
Getty Images: 16 (Albert Harlingue), 73 (Keystone), 74 (Galerie Bilderwelt)
National Archives & Records Administration: 108
Naval History & Heritage Command: 101, 111
Public Domain: 118, 123

Artworks
Amber Books: 13, 15, 17 both, 23–27 all, 33, 37, 41, 43 all, 44 top, 48–51 all, 52 top, 54–56 all, 59 bottom, 60–62 all, 67, 70, 71 bottom, 72, 85–86 all, 88 both, 91–93 all, 96–98 all, 106, 109, 110, 120–122 all
Ronny Bar: 5, 38–39 all, 44 middle and bottom, 45, 47 all, 113 all, 116
Ed Jackson (artbyedo.com): 73
Teasel Studios: 10–12 all, 14, 18–21 all, 36, 52 bottom, 59 top, 64, 65, 68, 71 top, 76, 77, 79–81 all, 123
Rolando Ugolini: 28, 29, 31, 82–83 all, 99–105 all, 107 both, 112, 114–115 all